torn by the issues

TORN BY THE ISSUES

Edited by: Stephen B. Maguire and Bonnie Wren

Contributing researchers and writers: Jon DeBlase, Paul Fields, Fred Hoey, Francis Hoey, Jennifer Maguire, Bonnie Wren, John Wren.

Copy Editor: Sharon O'Conner

Special Thanks to: Philip Brandes, John and Susan Daniel, Edie Gallagher, Peter Fields, Eric Larson, Shelly Lowenkopf, Barrie and Karen Maguire, Paul Maguire, Virginia Maguire, Tim Thompson, Sam Traten.

torn by the issues

AN UNBIASED REVIEW
OF THE WATERSHED ISSUES
IN AMERICAN LIFE

(A COLLABORATION
OF UNLIKE MINDS)

EDITED BY STEPHEN MAGUIRE AND BONNIE WREN

Fithian Press, Santa Barbara, 1994

Published by FITHIAN PRESS
a division of Daniel and Daniel, Publishers, Inc.
P.O. Box 1525
Santa Barbara, CA 93102

Design by Jeannie Sprecher, Sprecher Design House

LIBRARY OF CONGRESS CATALOGING-IN-PUBLICATION DATA

Torn by the issues: an unbiased review of the watershed issues in American
    life—a collaboration of unlike minds / Stephen B. Maguire, Bonnie Wren,
    editors; contributing researchers and writers, Jennifer Maguire…[et. al.].
        p.   cm.
    Includes bibliographic references.
    ISBN 1-56474-093-5
    1. United States—Social conditions—1980-   2. United States—
Economic conditions—1981-   I. Maguire, Stephen.   II. Wren,
Bonnie.   III. Maguire, Jennifer.
HN59.2.T67   1994
306'.0973–dc20   94-4072
                                                                                  CIP

To our mother,
Dolly Diehl Maguire,
who always encouraged us
to express ourselves.

foreword

this book was conceived as a result of a series of conversations

between two concerned citizens, my brother and myself, who each

have, like everyone else, a unique and personal political response to

world events. We both think it's obvious that many systems in this

country and in the world are not working very well. We agree that

attempts to formulate solutions to these problems are hampered by a lack of knowledge about the facts and history of these issues, in spite of the media blizzard in this "Information Age." We feel that if concerned citizens of every political stripe could inform themselves, and adopt a respectful tone of voice in this dialogue, then maybe we as a culture could stop spinning our wheels and find solutions to these fairly dire problems that confront us on the eve of the twenty-first century.

Stephen is a registered Republican, with a preference for the conservative approach that includes a compassionate response to the suffering of the underclasses. I am registered as an Independent and my response to the issues is a complicated combination of bleeding-heart liberalism, conservatism and libertarianism. I find that many people want to give an equally complicated description of their particular political response. Everyone thinks they hold the correct point of view, and that other, differing points of view are uninformed and incorrect. A respectful, solution-oriented dialogue does not happen very readily.

The perceived disparity, and deeply felt hostility, between the political right and left make a respectful dialogue either painfully difficult or impossible. Those on the right can't understand how anyone of intelligence and integrity could remain on the left, after considering all the facts. Those on the left feel exactly the same way. Charges of stupidity or evil intentions are rampant.

This broad political spectrum from the right to the left has always appeared in the course of human affairs since the dawn of history. It takes various forms and goes by differing labels, but it is always there. Could it be that this polarity is natural, inevitable, and underlying all creativity in nature? Perhaps we should stop wishing it would go away, and try to relax and enjoy it. Perhaps it's what makes human life energetic and creative.

In any case, Stephen and I decided to create this book to provide a source of pertinent information on some of the major controversial issues confronting us, including a respectful summary of the opposing viewpoints, so the debate could unfold intelligently. We feel that solutions can be formulated to the satisfaction of all citizens if the American people inform themselves, admit and allow the huge diversity of opinion, and talk to each other respectfully.

Bonnie Wren

introduction

how frustrating it is to be a citizen in today's world! We watch events swirling around us, events that affect us personally but over which we simply have no control. We feel helpless. We feel insignificant. It seems pointless sometimes even to think we can make a difference.

Isn't that how we all feel when we watch the news, listen to politicians speak, or hear debaters debate? Our lives are affected by the decisions of people we don't know and who don't know us. We drift helplessly as the tide of events pushes us along its flood path.

If only those in power would do the right things for us. Why, in a democracy, don't we have control of our government?

The answer is simpler than we may think. In this democracy,

we do have control.

We elect the politicians that run our government. To remain in office, they must do whatever gets them votes. So they do exactly what we, the voters, want. However, while democracy seems perfect in theory, it is not always so perfect in practice.

One reason we have so many problems is that we, the citizens, don't have the answers. We don't have enough information to know the answers. Our president, our senators, our representatives may actually have some correct answers, but first they want to be re-elected. So they must vote according to our wishes, even if we, as a population of citizens, have no idea what is right.

That is democracy, and that is the problem with democracy.

The solution is equally obvious.

informed, educated citizens.

If we, as a nation of informed citizens, know the answers and want change, change will come. Our elected officials will follow our lead no matter what opinion they may have previously voiced on any subject. Democrats, Republicans, Independents, all fall in line when those who elect them want something to happen.

So . . . How do we do this?

Of course, all forms of media work towards this purpose. Books, television, magazines, and newspapers bombard us with data. Despite this avalanche of information, gathering all pertinent facts on a particular subject is extremely difficult for any individual citizen.

torn by the issues

If only we could turn to a single source, an unbiased source of

facts.

Why not a reference of facts, only facts, covering both sides of an argument? Such information could turn a political argument into a worthwhile exchange of information and a learning experience.

I believe that our nation's problems have solutions. I believe that we are smart enough to reach correct decisions about these problems if we are working with correct and complete information.

This book is a start. It attempts to collect, in one volume, the facts, history, and viewpoints on a number of subjects that are both current and controversial. We have tried to present facts and opinions on both sides of several important issues. Future editions will include additional information that is brought to our attention by our readers and other interested parties. Our goal is to provide a source of information—unbiased, factual information—to serve as a foundation for healthy, productive discussions of, and workable solutions to, the many issues affecting us today.

Citizens with broad-based knowledge and solid understanding of any single issue today hold more power than any special interest group can muster. As citizens in this democracy, we do have power. Unbelievable power. Untapped power. To tap its strength, to realize its effects, to see it bring about a change for the better, we must all be well-informed citizens.

We hope that in the years to come, this book will grow to become a trusted source of information on many issues that require our attention today.

We hope you find this first edition interesting, informative, and enlightening. We welcome your response.

Stephen Maguire
President, Maguire Products, Inc.

torn by the issues

abortion

abortion is the expulsion of a fetus from the uterus before it is mature enough to survive on its own. It can be either spontaneous or induced. Spontaneous abortion happens when the woman's body is unable to sustain the pregnancy due to a physical problem with the fetus or with her own reproductive system. The result is a natural expulsion called miscarriage.

Throughout history, women who are faced with an unwanted pregnancy have used various methods to self-induce an abortion. Herbal concoctions and even poisons have been used. Various instruments have been used, often with disastrous consequences.

The two medical methods most frequently used to induce abortion are vacuum aspiration and dilation and evacuation. Vacuum aspiration or suction curettage, which is performed between seven and thirteen weeks (first trimester) of the pregnancy is the most common method. It is usually performed on an outpatient basis in a doctor's office or clinic. The physician first dilates the woman's cervix, and then inserts a small tube attached to a suction device. The suction empties the contents of the uterus through the tube. A spoon-shaped instrument (curette) is then used to scrape the walls of the uterus to remove any remaining tissue.

Procedure time is about ten minutes and is usually followed by bleeding and cramping that may last for several days.

From thirteen to twenty-four weeks of pregnancy, the most common medical method of abortion is dilation and evacuation. With this method, the woman's cervix is anesthetized. The cervix is then dilated and, as in the first-trimester vacuum aspiration abortions, the physician uses suction to empty the uterus. Because the fetus is larger in more advanced pregnancies, forceps are also used to evacuate the uterus. Finally, the walls of the uterus are scraped with a curette. This process takes from ten to thirty minutes.

Abortion has become one of the safest of modern medical procedures. Having an abortion in the first three months of pregnancy is statistically safer than childbearing. However, the procedure is not without side effects and dangers. About 2% of the women who have early abortions experience some complications. Second trimester abortions are somewhat more risky.

Potential Complications

- Blood clots in the uterus that require further suctioning.
- Infections, excessive bleeding.
- Tears in the cervix which may require stitches.
- Perforation of the wall of the uterus and/or other organs.
- Incomplete abortions which may require a repeated procedure.

A *Brief History of Abortion in the U.S.*

Bloodletting, unsanitary surgery, and ingestion of poisons such as quicksilver were methods once commonly used to induce abortion.

1850

One in four pregnancies was terminated by abortion.

1950

One in four pregnancies was terminated by abortion.

1990

One in four pregnancies was terminated by abortion.

Abortion has been a troubling issue throughout history. In the U.S., until the mid-nineteenth century, abortion was considered legal if performed before fetal movement could be detected. This point, called quickening, usually occurs during the fourth or fifth month of pregnancy. Abortion practices during the eighteenth and nineteenth centuries were dangerous and often resulted in the death of the woman. Bloodletting, unsanitary surgery, and ingestion of poisons such as quicksilver were methods once commonly used to induce abortion.

Significant anti-abortion activity began in the mid-1800s as a result of the American Medical Association's concern about the increasing number of unsafe—and often fatal—abortions being performed by unqualified abortionists. In an attempt to solve this problem, the AMA called for an end to these dangerous practices. Within the next fifty years, many state laws were passed that outlawed abortion except to preserve the life or health of the woman. While the accessibility of abortions was reduced, demand was not. Performing illegal abortions became a lucrative business, and illegal abortions continued to be a major cause of maternal death well into the twentieth century.

The Roman Catholic Church was not significantly involved in the abortion debate in the U.S. until the late nineteenth century. In 1869, the Vatican proclaimed a new church law that abortion of "ensouled" fetuses was punishable by excommunication. The term "ensouled" could be defined as that moment when a human soul enters the body, and that being becomes truly a separate individual. According to

Catholic doctrine, a male fetus was ensouled at forty days, a female fetus at eighty days after conception. Prior to ensoulment, abortion was neither considered homicide nor did it carry the consequence of excommunication. The Church has since changed this doctrine and has insisted that ensoulment takes place at the moment of conception. Today, the Roman Catholic Church is one of the leading pro-life advocates in the U.S.

Abortion continues to be a fiery topic of debate and controversy in contemporary America. For the last three decades, the U.S. has been bombarded with a barrage of contradictory legislative and judicial decisions and a myriad of differing social, moral, and religious opinions concerning abortion. Some advocacy groups have even resorted to violence. Generally, the two opposing camps involved in the abortion debate are known as "pro-life" and "pro-choice."

The Pro-Life Position

One of the most disputed issues of the abortion debate is the question of when an individual life actually begins. Pro-life advocates generally believe that life begins at the moment of conception. The unborn entity is, therefore, possessed of basic human rights, and abortion is considered a violation of those rights. Pro-life supporters see abortion as the murder of the innocent, unborn human being. This, the most fundamental belief of pro-life supporters, is often supported by religious doctrine. Many religiously affiliated pro-life advocates see contraceptive use as a form of abortion as well. They believe married couples should not use contraceptives because the number of children a married couple has should be God's decision, and that children are "gifts of the Lord."

Many religiously affiliated groups also advocate chastity education in place of sex education in public schools. Through teaching chastity, they hope to help teens make the choice to refrain from having sex until marriage. They believe sex education encourages teens to engage in sexual activity. The reduction in pre-marital sexual activity resulting from chastity education will, it is hoped, reduce the number of unwanted pregnancies (and abortions) each year.

In addition, many pro-life groups seek legislation against euthanasia, the "mercy killing" of medical patients who are unable to survive without life support systems or who are terminally ill. Other pro-life groups also oppose capital punishment.

Some pro-life groups argue that abortion is never, under any circumstance, justifiable. They recognize that some abortions are sought to prevent the death of the woman, or because the fetus is severely malformed or diseased, or because the pregnancy is a result of rape or incest. Nevertheless they do not view these circumstances as a justification for abortion. Others disagree with this viewpoint, believing that abortion may be justifiable in some of these extreme circumstances.

The pro-life movement includes many factions. It is not a monolithic group. However, adoption as an alternative to abortion is a solution accepted by virtually all pro-life advocates.

The pro-life movement founds and supports numerous crisis pregnancy clinics and shelters to aid women who experience unwanted pregnancies. These establishments may provide pregnancy testing, prenatal health care, transportation, shelter and assistance during pregnancy, information about governmental assistance for needy women, information about adoption, parenting skills classes, counseling, and other services designed to support the continuation of the pregnancy.

The pro-life movement also wishes to prohibit the use of fetal tissue from aborted fetuses in medical research. Researchers have discovered in recent years that fetal tissue may aid in treating Alzheimer's disease. Parkinson's disease, diabetes, radiation-induced anemia, and other diseases. However, most pro-life advocates feel that the regular use of aborted fetuses for research would create a moral justification for abortion in the minds of women seeking abortions and doctors performing them. The possibility of saving the life of another person could not only encourage abortion, but could also form an inappropriate economic bond between abortion clinics and biomedical research centers. Most pro-life groups do not oppose the use of fetal tissue obtained from miscarriages and stillbirths.

Pro-life groups sometimes resort to drastic measures to express their opinions. Some tactics utilized in recent years include blocking abortion clinics with human walls to keep women from visiting the clinics, aggressive sidewalk "counseling," picketing abortion clinics, making threatening phone calls to doctors who perform abortions, and bombing or setting fire to abortion clinics.

The Pro-Choice Position

The pro-choice position is as varied and complex as that of the pro-life groups. The fundamental belief with which all factions concur is that the decision of whether or not to abort should be left to the pregnant woman. Pro-choice advocates agree that a woman should have autonomy over her own body; they see religious and governmental intervention as a violation of her right to control her destiny. Unlike pro-lifers, many pro-choice supporters believe that the rights of the woman should come before the rights of the fetus, which they view as an undeveloped mass of tissue that, until the final stages of pregnancy, is unable to survive independently of the woman. They feel that the fetus is a part of the woman's body and that she should have as much control over that part of her body as she does over any other.

Some who support the pro-choice movement feel that, for their own moral reasons, they could never choose the abortion option. However, they feel that the choice to abort is a personal one and one's opinions should not limit the rights of another.

In addition, population growth often enters into the pro-choice argument. This growth, particularly in third world countries, is seen as the cause of serious environmental problems and a major contributor to disease, poverty, and famine. They feel that abortion by choice is a necessary option in this endangered environment.

Pro-choice groups advocate the use of birth control, family planning, and sex education as a means of preventing unwanted pregnancies and sexually transmitted diseases. Abortion is viewed as another viable option. With this in mind, clinics have been established that provide family planning and contraceptive counseling, a variety of contraceptive methods, gynecological exams, tests for pregnancy, prenatal medical care, testing and counseling about sexually transmitted diseases such as AIDS, gonorrhea, syphilis, and others, and potential health problems such as diabetes and high blood pressure. Abortion services are also offered. (Federal law, however, prohibits clinics that receive funding under the Title 10 Health Service Act to provide abortions.)

Like pro-life groups, many pro-choice groups also resort to drastic measures to make their point. Pro-choice groups often organize escort services to help women get through the "wall" of pro-lifers at abortion clinics, which often results in violent clashes between the two groups. Many pro-choicers also protest and picket and, in some circumstances, have chained themselves to buildings to gain media attention.

Timeline

Early 1800s

There are no state laws prohibiting abortion in the United States. Abortion is permitted without consequence until the fourth or fifth month of pregnancy, until the first movement of the fetus can be detected. Abortion after this period is considered a crime by common law.

1821

The first state law concerning abortion is enacted by the Connecticut legislature. Connecticut's law prohibits the practice of administering poison to induce abortion. Many women have died as a result of the ingestion of poison; the new law is designed to protect women from this harmful practice.

1840

Eight states have laws maintaining safety standards during abortion procedures. The mortality rate associated with surgical abortion is about 30%, mostly due to infection.

Mid-1800s

It is estimated that one in every four pregnancies is terminated.

1857

Dr. Horatio Storer, gynecologist/obstetrician, along with the newly formed American Medical Association, begins a national drive to criminalize abortion. Doctors become involved in the attempt to change public opinion concerning abortion.

Late 1800s

Over forty anti-abortion statutes are passed in the United States. Abortion is illegal unless a physician decides that aborting the fetus is necessary to preserve the life of the woman or, in some circumstances, for other therapeutic reasons. In several states, the decision to abort requires the concurrence of two physicians.

1879

The Connecticut legislature passes a law prohibiting the use of contraceptives.

1900–1950

Approximately one in four pregnancies is terminated despite anti-abortion laws. This is the same as the abortion rate one hundred years earlier. Many women seek illegal abortions or go to doctors who stretch the definition of "therapeutic reasons."

1916

Margaret Sanger opens the first birth control clinic in Brooklyn, New York. The organization grows into what is today known as The Planned Parenthood Federation of America, Inc., one of the leading advocates of the pro-choice movement.

1936

*U.S. v. One Package.*The U.S. Supreme Court strikes down laws prohibiting the import of contraceptives by physicians.

1950–1970

Due to medical advances it becomes much more difficult for doctors to justify abortion for therapeutic reasons. Therefore, abortions become more difficult to obtain.

1955

About 100 in 100,000 abortions (legal and illegal) result in the death of the woman.

In 1965, the U.S.

Supreme Court

expands the

interpretation of the

Fourteenth

Amendment and the

Bill of Rights to

include the right to

privacy in the marital

relationship.

1959

The American Law Institute develops three major defenses for clients charged with criminal abortion:

- The continuation of the pregnancy would gravely impair the physical or mental health of the woman.
- The pregnancy would produce a child with serious mental or physical defects.
- The pregnancy is a result of rape or incest.

Juries are likely to exonerate defendants employing these defenses.

1965

Griswald v. Connecticut. The U.S. Supreme Court expands the interpretation of the Fourteenth Amendment and the Bill of Rights to include the right to privacy in the marital relationship by ruling that the 1879 Connecticut law prohibiting the use of contraceptives is unconstitutional.

1971

United States v. Vuitch. The U.S. Supreme Court upholds a Washington D.C. law that prohibits doctors from performing abortions except when the pregnancy endangers the life or health of the woman.

1972–1976

About 4 out of 100,000 abortions result in the death of the woman. *(In 1955, the rate was 100 in 100,000.)*

1973

Roe v. Wade. The U.S. Supreme Court announces that the U.S. Constitution protects a woman's right to decide whether or not to terminate a pregnancy. The Court determines the abortion decision to be a private one, protected under the constitutional right to privacy established in the Griswald case and other cases. The Roe decision states that:

- The right to an abortion is not absolute. State laws may regulate medical standards to protect the health of the woman.

- The state may insist that abortions are performed only by licensed physicians.

- During the first three months of pregnancy (first trimester), a woman is entitled to choose whether or not to have an abortion.

- Before the fetus is viable, that is, able to survive outside of a woman's body, the state may only regulate abortion to preserve the health of the woman.

- When the fetus is viable, the state may prohibit abortions except when the termination of the pregnancy is necessary to preserve the woman's life or health.

1964–1976

Nearly 300,000 abortions performed yearly are funded by Medicaid, a state and federally funded program that provides funds to pay medical costs for needy people.

1976

Planned Parenthood of Central Missouri v. Danforth. Parental and spousal consent requirements are held unconstitutional because they delegate to third parties an absolute veto power which the state itself does not possess. The requirement that the woman certify that her consent is informed and freely given is ruled constitutional, as are record keeping and reporting requirements. The ban on saline amniocentesis is struck down because it is shown to be the most common and the least dangerous method used after the first twelve weeks of pregnancy. The choice of method must be left to the physician.

1977

Maher v. Roe. The Supreme Court upholds a Connecticut regulation denying the use of state Medicaid funds to provide elective abortions (that is, those performed for any reason other than to save the life or health of the mother).

12

1979

Colautti v. Franklin. A Pennsylvania law requires the physician to determine that the fetus is not viable before performing an abortion. If the physician finds that the fetus "is or may be viable," he or she is required to perform the abortion as if the fetus were intended to be born alive. The law is ruled unconstitutional on the grounds of vagueness. The meanings of "viable" and "nonviable" are unclear and must be left to the good-faith judgment of the physician without imposing criminal liability.

Bellotti v. Baird. The Supreme Court declares unconstitutional a Massachusetts law requiring unmarried minors to obtain parental consent and approval of a judge before obtaining a legal abortion, because this law infringes on the right to abortion established in *Roe v. Wade* (1973).

1981

H. L. v. Matheson. The Supreme Court upholds a Utah law requiring doctors to notify the parents of minor females (women under eighteen) who wish to obtain abortions if they are living at home and are dependent on the parents. The parents do not have veto power over the minor's decision to abort, according to the ruling.

1983

City of Akron v. Akron Center for Reproductive Health. The Akron, Ohio ordinance required:

- A twenty-four-hour waiting period.
- All abortions be performed in full-service hospitals.
- Minors under fifteen have parental or judicial consent.
- Information be given to the woman regarding informed consent, fetal anatomy, risks and consequences.
- A statement be given to the woman that "the unborn child is a human life from the moment of conception."

All challenged portions of the ordinance were ruled unconstitutional. This ruling is subsequently overturned in 1992.

Planned Parenthood of Kansas City, Missouri v. Ashcroft. A Missouri law required that all abortions after the first trimester be performed in full-service hospitals, that two doctors be present at the abortion of a viable fetus, that a pathologist's report be obtained for every abortion, and that minors under eighteen have parental consent or judicial authorization. The hospitalization requirement is ruled unconstitutional, but all other parts are ruled constitutional.

1985

A Lutheran pastor, Michael D. Bray, is sentenced to a ten-year term in federal prison for his involvement in the bombing of ten abortion clinics.

1986

Thornburgh v. American College of Obstetricians and Gynecologists. The Pennsylvania Abortion Control Act requires:

- That a woman be given specific state-produced information before the abortion, including descriptions of the fetus, physical and psychological risks, etc.

- That physicians use the abortion method most likely to result in fetal survival unless it would cause "significantly" greater risk to a woman's life or health.

- The presence of a second physician at post-viability abortions.

- Detailed reporting that is open to public inspection.

- One parent's consent or a court order for a minor's abortion.

The Court ruled all of the above provisions unconstitutional except the parental consent issue, which was remanded to a lower court for review. This decision was overturned in 1992.

1988

The French government approves for use RU-486, a drug developed by Dr. Etienne-Emile Balieu and manufactured by the French pharmaceutical corporation Roussel-Uclaf. RU-486 prevents uterine cells from reacting to the hormone progesterone. Progesterone

In 1989, the U.S.

Food and Drug

Administration

(FDA) places a ban

on the commercial

import of RU-486.

allows an embryo to attach to the uterus. Thus, the embryo is aborted when the uterine cells do not respond to progesterone. RU-486 is administered with prostaglandin, which increases the frequency and strength of the uterine contractions necessary to expel the embryo. The drug had been approved for use in France for up to forty-nine days of pregnancy (seven weeks). RU-486 may also be effective in treating breast cancer, brain tumors, Cushing's syndrome (a rare terminal glandular disorder characterized by osteoporosis, diabetes, infections, and hypertension), and other hormone-related diseases.

1989

The U.S. Food and Drug Administration (FDA) places a ban on the commercial import of RU-486. Many researchers have been denied the drug by the FDA. Roussel-Uclaf has been reluctant to provide the drug for research in the U.S.

Webster v. Reproductive Health Services. Missouri's 1986 Abortion law:

- Declares that life begins at conception.

- Forbids the use of public funds for the purpose of counseling a woman to have an abortion not necessary to save her life.

- Forbids the use of public facilities for abortions not necessary to save a woman's life.

- Requires physicians to perform tests to determine viability of fetuses after twenty weeks gestational age.

The Court allowed all provisions to stand.

1990

Since approval by the French government in 1988, RU-486, Roussel-Uclaf's abortifacient drug, has been used to terminate 50,000 pregnancies.

Twenty-four pro-life groups, including the Christian Action Council, launch an international boycott of corporations that donate money to Planned Parenthood organizations.

1991

Rust v. Sullivan. In 1988, under the Reagan administration, the U.S. Department of Health and Human Services adopted an administrative regulation forbidding the provision of abortion information by family planning clinics funded by Title X of the federal Public Health Service Act. The regulation, known as the "gag rule," requires clinic staff members to answer all abortion-related questions with the statement, "The project does not consider abortion an appropriate method of family planning," and to provide all pregnant clients with a referral list of prenatal care providers that "promote the welfare of the unborn child." This rule is challenged on the grounds that it denies necessary information to the patient, and requires a breach of medical ethics by the practitioner. The challenge is denied and the regulation is upheld.

According to the National Abortion Federation, property damage to abortion clinics from fires and bombings rises from $116,000 in 1990 to over $1 million.

1992

Planned Parenthood of Southeastern Pennsylvania v. Casey. The Supreme Court upholds Pennsylvania abortion restrictions that include:

- Requirements that minors obtain consent from either a parent or a judge before obtaining an abortion, and that a twenty-four-hour waiting period be observed after abortion alternatives have been presented.

- A married woman inform her husband of her intent to have an abortion.

- State-authored material be given to the woman regarding fetal development.

- Records of abortions be provided to the state including the names of referring physicians.

The Court upholds all provisions except the husband-notification requirement which was struck down.

1993

Bray v. Alexandria Women's Health Clinic. Planned Parenthood/ Metropolitan Washington, D.C. and other abortion clinics had challenged Operation Rescue's activities in blocking access to health care facilities. The challenge was upheld by the lower court based on a federal civil rights statute forbidding conspiracies depriving persons or classes of persons their constitutional rights. This 1871 law is known popularly as the "Ku Klux Klan Act."

- The Supreme Court holds that the federal statute cited does not protect women seeking abortions as a class. In reaching its decision, the court held that Operation Rescue was not motivated by "class-based discriminatory animus," but rather for concern for the "innocent victims of abortion."

- President Clinton reverses the 1988 administrative regulation known as the "gag rule" that forbade abortion information be given to patients at federally funded health care clinics.

Abortion Facts

- Every year, approximately 6.1 million American women become pregnant. Slightly more than half of those pregnancies are unintended (3.6 million).

- Nearly 3 million sexually active women do not use birth control devices on a consistent basis.

- One fourth to one half of all abortions in the U.S. are performed on women whose birth control device has failed.

- Fifteen percent of all pregnancies in the U.S. happen despite the use of contraceptive devices.

- About 16,000 women have abortions each year because they become pregnant as a result of rape or incest. This is about 1% of the total number of annual abortions.

Of 6.1 *million annual*

pregnancies, about 3.7

million women have

babies, .9 *million have*

miscarriages, and the

remaining 1.6 *million*

have abortions.

- According to a 1988 Family Planning Perspectives survey, 76% of women who had abortions said having a baby would change their lives in some unwanted way. Sixty-eight percent said they couldn't afford a child, and 51% said they had problems in the relationship with the father or didn't want to be single mothers; 31% said they chose to abort because they didn't want others to know they had sexual relations, and 23% because their husband or boyfriend wanted the abortion. Fetal abnormalities accounted for 13%, threats to mother's health for 7%, and the choice to abort due to rape or incest accounted for 1%. (Participants could give more than one answer.)

- Over 4,300 abortions are performed each day in the United States.

- Unmarried women are five times more likely than married women to have an abortion.

- Women who report no religious affiliation have a higher rate of abortion than women who report some affiliation. However, one sixth of all abortion patients describe themselves as born-again or evangelical Christians, and nearly one third say they are Catholic.

- Of 6.1 million annual pregnancies, about 3.7 million women have babies, .9 million have miscarriages, and the remaining 1.6 million have abortions.

- Worldwide, more than 60 million abortions are performed each year.

- Each year nearly three out of one hundred women in the U.S. between the ages of fifteen and forty-four have an abortion; 40% have had at least one previous abortion, and 45% have had a previous birth.

Facts About Teen Pregnancies

- Approximately 40% of American women become pregnant at least once before the age of twenty. More than one million teens become pregnant each year in the U.S.

- The rate of teen pregnancy in the U.S. is one of the highest in the western world. It is twice as high as in the U.K., France, and Canada, three times as high as in Sweden, and seven times as high as in the Netherlands.

- More than 80% of teen pregnancies are unintended, and more than half of these unwanted pregnancies will end in abortion.

- Of U.S. teens seeking abortion, three fourths say they cannot afford to have a baby, and two thirds think they are not mature enough to have a baby.

- A 1990 Center for Population Options report showed that $21.55 billion was the 1989 cost to U.S. taxpayers to provide public services required to maintain families started by teens.

The Risks

- About 1% of all abortion patients experience a major complication associated with the abortion procedure, such as serious pelvic infection, hemorrhage requiring a blood transfusion, or unintended major surgery.

- The risk of death associated with childbirth is about eleven times higher than that associated with abortion. About one in 200,000 women dies as a result of complications resulting from legal abortions.

- 90% of abortions take place in the first trimester of pregnancy (first thirteen weeks) when the risk is lowest.

- The risk of death associated with abortion increases with the length of pregnancy, from 1 death for every 500,000 abortions at 8 weeks or less, to 1 per 30,000 at 16 to 20 weeks, to 1 per 8,000 at 21 or more weeks.

Abortion Around the World

AUSTRALIA

South Australia and the Northern Territory have both passed liberal legislation regarding abortion based on the 1967 British Abortion Act (See Great Britain).

AUSTRIA

Abortion is permitted for any reason within the first trimester (first thirteen weeks). Restrictions apply after this period.

BELGIUM

Belgium prohibits abortion unless the procedure prevents death or serious injury to the woman.

CANADA

In 1988, the Supreme Court of Canada offered a decision similar to the U.S. Supreme Court's *Roe v. Wade* decision. The Court declared the right to have an abortion is an aspect of the "right of security of the person" specified in the 1982 Canadian Charter of Rights and Freedoms. There is much controversy in Canada over the issue of abortion.

CHINA

The Chinese policy of one child per family includes financial incentives for families who follow the government regulations and compulsory abortions for families who don't.

The rate of abortion of female fetuses and the drowning or abandonment of female babies has increased, because many families desire a male child. The failure to produce a male child is seen as tragic in Chinese tradition, because there will be no child to carry on the family name. In China, about 14 million abortions are performed each year.

The Netherlands has

the most liberal

abortion laws in

Europe and the

fewest abortions

(0.16 per woman).

FRANCE

Abortion is permitted for any reason during the first ten weeks of pregnancy. The French equivalent of Social Security covers 70% of the cost of abortions that are not medically indicated.

GREAT BRITAIN

The 1967 British Abortion Act permits abortion until fetal viability if two doctors agree that the risk to the mental or physical health of the mother or family would be greater if the pregnancy were to continue than if it were terminated. The deadline for abortion is the twenty-fourth week of pregnancy.

INDIA

In 1971, India introduced the Medical Termination of Pregnancy Act, which permits abortion if the fetus is likely to be born with severe mental or physical abnormalities or to preserve the mental/physical health of the woman. As in China, male offspring are preferred and significantly greater numbers of female fetuses are aborted.

IRELAND

Abortion is prohibited unless it is deemed necessary to prevent death or serious injury caused by pregnancy. About 2,000 Irish women travel to England for abortions each year.

JAPAN

Abortion is used as a primary means of birth control. The country has liberal abortion laws that permit abortions for protection of the woman's health and life, or because the fetus is severely malformed or diseased.

THE NETHERLANDS

Abortion is available for any reason during the first twenty-four weeks (first two trimesters). The Netherlands has the most liberal abortion laws in Europe and the fewest abortions (0.16 per woman).

In Sweden, abortion is permitted during the first eighteen weeks of pregnancy for any reason.

NORWAY

Abortion is permitted until twelve weeks of pregnancy for any reason. After this period, restrictions apply.

POLAND

Abortion is outlawed.

ROMANIA

Abortion was legalized in 1989 when the National Salvation Front came into power.

SPAIN

Legal abortion is limited to pregnancies resulting from rape or incest and pregnancies involving health endangerment or serious fetal defect or disease.

SWEDEN

Abortion is permitted during the first eighteen weeks of pregnancy for any reason. After this period, restrictions apply.

Sources

Adler, Nancy E., et al. "Psychological Responses After Abortion." *Science*, 6 April 1990.

Alan Guttmacher Institute. *Facts in Brief: Abortion in the United States, 1990.* Washington, D.C.: Alan Guttmacher Institute, 1990.

Anderson, Christopher, and Peter Coles. "Drug Debate Expands." *Nature*, 29 November 1990.

Baker, James N., et al. "The Church Strikes Back." *Newsweek*, 18 December 1989.

Benson-Gold, Rachel, and Daniel Daley. "Public Funding of Contraceptive, Sterilization, and Abortion Services, Fiscal Year 1990." *Family Planning Perspectives*, September/October 1990.

Biskupic, Joan. "Fracas Over Abortion Advice." *Congressional Quarterly Weekly Report*, 22 September 1990.

Byrne, Harry J. "A House Divided: The Pro-Life Movement." *America*, 12 January 1991.

Callahan, Daniel. "An Ethical Challenge to Pro-choice Advocates." *Commonweal*, 23 November 1990.

Carlson, Margaret. "Abortion's Hardest Cases." *Time*, 9 July 1990.

Dolan, Barbara, et al. "The Doctors Take On Bush." *Time*, 5 August 1991.

Dumas, Kitty. "Bill Would Allow D.C. Abortions." *Congressional Quarterly Weekly Report*, 14 July 1990.

Erhel, Catherine. "The Abortion Fight—Again." *World Press Review*, June 1991.

Fish, Sharon. "The Scandal of Fetal-Tissue Research." *Christianity Today*, 19 November 1990.

Flanders, Carl N. *Abortion*. New York: Facts on File, 1991.

Goldsmith, Edward, and Nicholas Hildyard, eds. *The Earth Report: The Essential Guide to Global Ecological Issues*. Los Angeles: Price, Stern, Sloan, Inc., 1988.

Greenberger, Marcia D., and Katherine Connor. "Parental Notice and Consent for Abortion: Out of Step with Family Law Principles and Policies." *Family Planning Perspectives*, January/February 1991.

Heaney, Robert P. "RU-486 and Abortion Strategies." *America*, 12 January 1991.

Henshaw, Stanley K., et al. "Characteristics of U.S. Women Having Abortions, 1987." *Family Planning Perspectives*, March/April 1991.

Hentoff, Nat. "Abortion Gag Rule." *Progressive*, February 1991.

Horgan, John. "Right to Lie?" *Scientific American*, April 1990.

Hutchison, Sue, and James N. Baker. "The Right-to-Life Shock Troops." *Newsweek*, 1 May 1989.

Johnson, Otto, ed. *The 1992 Information Please Almanac*. 45th Edition. Boston: Houghton Mifflin Co., 1992.

Kaplan, David A., et al. "Abortion: Just Say No Advice." *Newsweek*, 3 June 1991.

Kelly, James R. "The Koop Report and a Better Politics of Abortion." *America*, 2 June 1990.

Kelly, James R. "Abortion: What Americans Really Think and the Catholic Challenge." *America*, 2 November 1991.

Kissling, Frances. "Ending the Abortion War: A Modest Proposal." *The Christian Century*, 21 February 1990.

Lacayo, Richard. "Whose Life Is It?" *Time*, 1 May 1989.

——. "The Shifting Politics of Abortion." *Time*, 23 October 1989.

Lawton, Kim A. "Operation Rescue HQ Closed." *Christianity Today*, 5 March 1990.

——. "Christian Action Council Announces Boycott." *Christianity Today*, 10 September 1990.

National Abortion Federation. "Safety of Abortion." *National Abortion Federation Fact Sheet*, April 1990.

——. "Women Who Have Abortions." *National Abortion Federation Fact Sheet*, October 1990.

——. "Teenage Women, Abortion, and the Law." *National Abortion Federation Fact Sheet*, January 1992.

——. "What Is Abortion?" *National Abortion Federation Fact Sheet*, February 1992.

Neiburg Terkel, Susan. *Abortion: Facing the Issues*. New York: Franklin Watts, 1988.

Nicholson, R.H. "Abortion Remains a Live Issue." *Hastings Center Report*, September/October 1991.

Post, Stephen G. "Fetal Tissue Transplant: The Right to Question Progress." *America*, 12 January 1991.

Rosen, Jeff. "Altered States." *The New Republic*, 1 July 1991.

Rovner, Julie. "Ban on Abortion Counseling Faces Review by Justices." *Congressional Quarterly Weekly Report*, 2 June 1990.

——. "Issue Entangles Defense Bill, Family Planning Measure." *Congressional Quarterly Weekly Report*, 15 September 1990.

——. "Anti-Abortion Forces Prevail In Pentagon Bill Skirmish." *Congressional Quarterly Weekly Report*, 22 September 1990.

——. "Abortion, Procedural Wrangles Sink Family Planning Bill." *Congressional Quarterly Weekly Report*, 29 September 1990.

——. "Abortion Issue Roils Debate On Labor-HHS Measure." *Congressional Quarterly Weekly Report*, 13 October 1990.

Salholz, Eloise, et al. "The Battle Over Abortion." *Newsweek*, 1 May 1989.

Sollom, Terry. "State Legislation on Reproductive Health in 1990: What Was Proposed and Enacted." *Family Planning Perspectives*, March/April 1991.

Smolowe, Jill. "Gagging the Clinics." *Time*, 3 June 1991.

Toufexis, Anastasia. "Battle over the Abortion Pill." *Time*, 6 August 1990.

Tribe, Lawrence H. *Abortion: The Clash of Absolutes*. New York: W.W. Norton & Co., Inc., 1990.

Ulmann, Andre, et al. "RU 486." *Scientific American*, June 1990.

Weis, Judith S. "RU-486 and Freedom of Scientific Inquiry." *BioScience*, June 1991.

Wharton, Mandy. *Abortion*. New York: Gloucester Press, 1989.

Wickenden, Dorothy. "Drug of Choice." *The New Republic*, 26 November 1990.

Woodward, Kenneth, and Mary Talbot. "An Archbishop Rattles a Saber." *Newsweek*, 25 June 1990.

Zurer, Pamela. "Scientists Urged to Face Growing Public Role in Research Decisions." *Chemical & Engineering News*, 5 August 1991.

the deficit

the deficit is the difference between revenue and spending levels. We spend more than we take in. A lot more—in 1992, deficit spending amounted to nearly $400 billion dollars, the largest gap between revenue and spending ever recorded by any nation in history.

1992 Outlays:	$1,475,439,000,000
1992 Revenues:	$1,075,706,000,000
Deficit:	**$399,733,000,000**

The 1992 interest on

the debt is $300

billion, more than we

spend on education,

law enforcement,

housing, and the

environment

combined.

The National Debt

The national debt is the money we have borrowed, both from American and foreign sources of capital, to cover what we spend over and above our revenues. It is the sum of the annual deficits, plus interest. We borrow from domestic sources of capital by selling treasury bonds and the like. These bonds are essentially loans to ourselves and we pay interest on them. We also sell treasury bonds to foreign governments or foreign private capital, or we borrow inter-governmentally, as with the borrowing of the Social Security Fund surplus.

The national debt has grown from $290 billion in 1960 to $4.4 trillion in 1993. The 1992 interest on the debt is $300 billion, more than we spend on education, law enforcement, housing, and the environment combined.

The projection of the amount of the debt for the year 2000, if present trends continue, is $13 trillion. According to some recent predictions, the debt will be larger than the gross national product (GNP) by 1995. GNP is defined as the dollar amount of the total annual output of goods and services of a country expressed in terms of its market value. The term gross domestic product (GDP) has a similar usage, but is derived from a slightly different formula. It is usually slightly less than the GNP.

Once before, at the end of World War II, the debt was larger than GNP (122%). By 1975, it was down to 35% of GNP. As of 1992, it was 69.5% of GNP and rising.

The interest on the national debt is approximately 21% of the national budget. It must be paid or we will not be able to continue to borrow from private sources of capital to cover our deficit. Treasury bonds will no longer be an attractive investment if the interest is not paid.

By some economists' accounts, the mounting debt as a percentage of GNP will make investors wary of U.S. credit-worthiness. Interest rates will thus increase to make the investment attractive in spite of growing fears of U.S. insolvency. The interest obligation will then grow at compounded rates. Some predict that it will take 100% of federal revenues from personal income taxes to pay it by 1995, if present trends continue.

The Federal Budget Deficit

1992 Federal Outlays

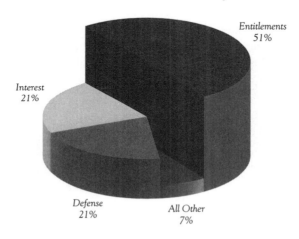

Entitlements
51%

Interest
21%

Defense
21%

All Other
7%

1992 Federal Revenues

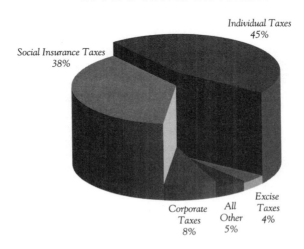

Individual Taxes
45%

Social Insurance Taxes
38%

Corporate
Taxes
8%

All
Other
5%

Excise
Taxes
4%

This prediction of higher interest rates as a result of higher debt is not occurring in today's economy, once again confounding the predictions of many economists. However, should interest rates climb on U.S. treasury bonds to cover the deficit, interest rates may also climb in other sectors of the economy. When mortgages become more expensive, fewer people can afford to buy homes and the housing market contracts. The housing market is one of the key elements in any economy. Higher interest rates will also cause businesses to borrow less and expand less, and the job market will not grow at a sufficient rate to meet the needs of the expanding population.

If more of the work force is displaced by these economic shifts, the entitlement programs must spend more to assist those out of work and in need. Entitlement programs are those programs that pay automatically to anyone who meets eligibility requirements. They include Social Security, unemployment insurance, Medicare and Medicaid, and some other welfare programs.

During the eighties, while income and standard of living rose for many, the number of people living in poverty also increased. The growth of the elderly population also increases demand for entitlements. Thus the annual deficit and total debt grows.

In any economy, there is only so much money to lend, which is determined in part by the amount of money businesses and individuals have saved. Loans of capital to the government deplete this reserve of savings. Even if companies and individuals can afford the interest rates, there is a shrinking base of capital from which to borrow, and loans become harder to get.

Economists do not agree on the short-term and long-term effects of the budget deficit, and economists' predictions are, in any case, notoriously inaccurate. Recently, a bond manager at a leading mutual fund company tracked the success of Wall Street economists in forecasting interest rates. Many hours of analysis and computer time contribute to these forecasts, as they are critically important to both short-term and long-term investors. According to historical data collected in this study, the best investment policy would have been to do the exact opposite of what the consensus recommended. When the economists said "sell," the wise investor bought and achieved excellent results. A running joke among forecasters is that a dartboard pick of economic trends is as reliable as the economists' carefully considered forecasts.

Forecasting economics is not as precise as plotting the path of the planets in the solar system. The economy is infinitely more complex; every action taken to affect it, no matter how successful or unsuccessful in the short term, will also have unpredictable long-term effects. Some argue that the government can run a deficit continuously, as long as the deficit grows at a slower rate than the economy, particularly if this spending is for capital investments such as infrastructure. Capital investments are expected to produce increased productivity and revenue in the long term, thus contributing to growth. Deficit-cutting measures (raising taxes and/or reducing spending) may actually be recessionary, in that less money is circulating in the economy. Currently, however, the deficit is growing faster than the economy. The money that is being spent by the government is largely borrowed money and finally, the money is being used for operational expenses (entitlement programs), rather than capital investment. All of these factors lead most observers to conclude that the deficit is a dangerous and potentially devastating risk.

Substantial unresolved issues include:

- How much of a deficit is too much?
- Should the government control the deficit by raising taxes, cutting spending, or both?
- Whose taxes should be raised, and whose services should be cut?
- Should deficits be allowed only for capital investments, rather than operational expenses?
- Perhaps most important, does deficit spending encourage the growth of a free-wheeling governmental machine that can perpetually increase spending without the implicit referendum of a tax increase? If revenues cannot contain spending, government itself is unrestrained.

These questions have important philosophical, economic, and regional ramifications. In addition, the actual consequences of fiscal policies, both short- and long-term, have proven impossible to predict.

The laissez-faire, or

hands-off, role for the

government in the

economy is generally

accepted through the

eighteenth and

nineteenth centuries in

the U.S., with some

important exceptions.

Timeline

1776

The same year the U.S. declares independence from Great Britain, Adam Smith, a British economist, writes *The Wealth of Nations*. In this extremely influential book, Smith postulates that the marketplace is guided by an almost magical "invisible hand." Smith's major tenets are outlined below:

- The actions of the marketplace are naturally self-regulating. Prices and quantities of goods and services will be determined by supply and demand.

- Manufacturers of goods will seek to maximize their profits.

- As profits increase, wages increase. More people, attracted by higher profits and/or higher wages, will participate in the market, either as the makers of goods or as their employees.

- As the supply of goods and labor increases, the law of supply and demand will come into play.

- Prices, profits, and wages will fall, until the market reaches a state of equilibrium.

- Equilibrium is the natural state of a market economy, with plenty of goods, healthy profits, prices of goods kept reasonable through competition, and work available for everyone.

According to Smith, the government role in the economy is limited. Within Smith's paradigm, government involvement will artificially affect the magical mechanism of the marketplace. How can the government know better than consumers what consumers want? Or at what wage workers are willing to work?

This laissez-faire, or hands-off, role for the government in the economy is generally accepted through the eighteenth and nineteenth centuries in the U.S., with some important exceptions.

Article 1, Section

VIII of the

Constitution grants

the federal

government power to

lay and collect taxes.

Some manufacturing and agricultural enterprises are partially protected by tariffs in order to allow young American farms and businesses to grow.

In addition, Smith could not have foreseen the industrial or technological revolutions that were shortly to follow. The rapid growth in population also is a major factor in complicating economic processes.

As well as manipulations of the economy in the fields of manufacturing and agriculture, we have also supplemented market forces in such realms as defense, law enforcement, education, and road and other infrastructure building.

This manipulation is seen as necessary to fulfill the needs and desires of the growing country, but it is always disputed by those who feel a free-market economy should be untouched by government.

1700s–1800s

Another example of early government intervention in the economy, in addition to imposing tariffs on imports, is anti-monopoly legislation, enacted to ensure that there is sufficient competition within the U.S. for the magic of the marketplace to work. Banking regulations are enacted to protect depositors from fraud and mismanagement. Infrastructure building is usually a combination of public and private enterprise.

1783

U.S. debt, accrued to pay for the Revolutionary War, amounts to $8 million owed to France and $250,000 to Spain. These loans are repaid by 1835.

1789

The U.S. Constitution is ratified. In Article 1, Section VIII, the federal government is granted power to lay and collect taxes, pay its debts, and to provide for the common defense and general welfare of the U.S. It is also permitted to borrow money on the credit of the U.S. This does not include an income tax.

In 1895, the

Supreme Court

abolishes the new

income tax as

unconstitutional.

1816

The debt to pay for the War of 1812 is $129 million, or 13% of GNP. After the war, budget surpluses are used to repay the debt by 1835.

1860

The first U.S. income tax is levied to pay for the Civil War.

1865

The Union government owes more than $2.6 billion for the Civil War. The debt is repaid by the 1890s.

1872

The first U.S. income tax levy is repealed.

1894

Congress passes a law permitting the income tax.

1895

The Supreme Court abolishes the new income tax as unconstitutional.

1909

The first corporate tax is levied.

1913

The Sixteenth Amendment to the Constitution is passed, enabling Congress to collect taxes on all incomes without apportionment among the states and without regard to any census or enumeration.

The Revenue Act of 1913 marks the first time an income tax is initiated in peacetime, without the specific purpose of paying a war debt.

torn by the issues

The New Deal

dramatically

increases the role of

the federal

government in the

economy.

1917

During World War I, debt increases from 3% of GNP to 40% of GNP.

1921

The Budget and Accounting Act creates the Bureau of the Budget.

1929

The stock market crashes, followed by a national banking crisis. The Great Depression begins. GNP will shrink by as much as 30%, and unemployment will reach 25%.

The federal government begins to take emergency measures to correct the worsening economy.

1932

In response to the depression, the U.S. voters elect Franklin Delano Roosevelt as president, and his program, dubbed the New Deal, dramatically increases the role of the federal government in the economy. Some major programs are:

- Works Progress Administration: Public works projects are funded, including roads, dams, and schools, as a means to employ the growing number of jobless Americans.

- Farm Subsidies: Farmers are paid to reduce output, and prices are set artificially high to keep marginal farmers from going out of business.

- The Civilian Conservation Corps: Young men are hired to plant trees and do general conservation work in national parks. Other public works programs are created to increase employment.

- The Federal Deposit Insurance Corporation (FDIC): Bank deposits are insured even if a bank fails.

- The Social Security Administration: The elderly are protected from destitution.

In 1936, John Maynard Keynes challenges Adam Smith's assumption that economies will naturally reach a state of equilibrium that includes full employment.

- President Roosevelt and his policies are tremendously popular with a beleaguered population.

1934

The federal government runs a deficit of $3.5 billion, up from a surplus of $734 million in 1929. This dramatic change in fiscal policy has two primary causes:

- The urgent need to alleviate the economic crisis.

- Changes in the analysis of economic problems.

1936

John Maynard Keynes publishes *The General Theory of Employment, Interest, and Money*. This work, which provides the basis for much of modern economic theory, challenges Adam Smith's assumption that economies will naturally reach a state of equilibrium that includes full employment.

Keynes argues that an economy will achieve equilibrium at less than full employment. When such an equilibrium occurs, argues Keynes, the government must take the initiative to reduce unemployment by adjusting fiscal policy. In other words, governments can reduce taxes or increase spending to inject money into the economy. As more money circulates in the economy, more goods and services are demanded. This, in turn, will increase production and provide new jobs.

1937

The economy takes another turn for the worse. Roosevelt asks for and receives an additional $5 billion from Congress.

1939

The economy begins to recover when World War II creates a tremendous demand for U.S. industrial output.

1941

During World War II, the national debt reaches 125% of GNP.

torn by the issues

1946

The Full Employment Act is passed. The underlying Keynesian assumption of this legislation is that it is the responsibility of the government to provide for high employment, stable prices, and economic growth.

1964

President John Kennedy's economic stimulus package, requiring a deficit of $10 billion, has little noticeable effect because the recession it was enacted to fight has largely ended.

1965

The deficit is $1.6 billion, down from $48.7 billion in 1945. President Lyndon Johnson implements his Great Society Programs, intended to eradicate poverty from our society. These programs are extremely costly. At the same time, federal spending on the Vietnam War increases.

1968

The deficit is $25.2 billion

1969

In spite of high spending for Great Society Programs and the Vietnam War, the deficit is remarkably low at $507 million, once again defying economic logic.

Inflation becomes a growing problem. Johnson's programs put more money into the economy but did not increase production of goods. High demand with low supply creates high prices. This is called inflation: too much money chasing too few goods.

Mild inflation can damage the economy by causing uncertainty. Businesses and people will not know how much they will need to spend in the future. This uncertainty inhibits investment and growth. Severe inflation has much more drastic effects. The German Weimar Republic, in a state of hyperinflation, fell to Hitler .

In 1946, the Full Employment Act is passed. The underlying Keynesian assumption of this legislation is that it is the responsibility of the government to provide for high employment, stable prices, and economic growth.

President Gerald

Ford gives a tax

rebate, and later cuts

taxes, to stimulate the

economy. The deficit

increases by $127

billion over two years

and inflation worsens.

1972

President Richard Nixon briefly imposes wage and price controls to counter the inflation. They are soon abandoned.

1973

The price of oil, an important commodity, rises dramatically, due to political turmoil in the Middle East. Because everyone uses oil, and because energy is vital to virtually every business, an increase in the price of oil causes the price of all other goods and services to rise. Inflation continues.

1975

President Gerald Ford gives a tax rebate, and later cuts taxes, to stimulate the economy. The deficit increases by $127 billion over two years and inflation worsens.

1976–1980

President Jimmy Carter faces a new economic phenomenon: Stagflation (simultaneous high unemployment and high inflation). This problem perplexes economists. Economic theorists recommend conflicting solutions. The president chooses to resolve unemployment first through federally funded jobs programs. The deficit, inflation, and interest rates soar. Social Security and other entitlements are indexed to inflation to prevent recipients from falling into poverty, and the government thereby loses control of a major portion of its expenditures.

1981

The deficit is $74 billion. President Reagan espouses a doctrine called supply-side economics. Guided by this theory, the government will reduce taxes and regulations so that people and companies will be encouraged to produce more. This will lead to more business growth, more jobs, and more tax revenue. President Reagan cuts taxes, particularly on the wealthy who will then have more money to invest. He also hopes to revise the income tax system. It is hoped this policy will induce individuals to work harder, be more productive, and to save more for investment purposes.

At the same time, President Reagan continues to increase government spending on defense. By cutting other domestic spending, particularly on social programs, President Reagan believes he can balance the federal budget. The economy does not produce the revenue expected, and the deficit grows dramatically.

High rates of inflation require high rates of interest. Hence, all government borrowing in the late 1970s and early 1980s is extremely expensive. Interest payments on the debt begin to grow dramatically, driving up the deficit even further.

Defense spending increases are largely offset by domestic spending cuts, although entitlements grow.

After the 1981–1982 recession, the deficit defies economic logic and continues to grow. The causes are lower tax revenues due to tax cuts, increases in entitlement payments, the defense build-up, and interest on the growing national debt.

1985

The deficit is $222 billion. The Balanced Budget and Emergency Deficit Control Act of 1985, also known as Gramm-Rudman-Hollings, sets specific deficit targets declining to $0 by 1990. If Congress fails to meet the targets, there would be automatic, mandatory, across-the-board cuts in spending. Subsequently, the act is watered down, and it ultimately fails to contain spending. Procedural loopholes and overly optimistic revenue projections are cited as the cause of the failure.

1987

The Balanced Budget and Emergency Deficit Control Reaffirmation Act of 1987 sets new targets for eliminating the deficit.

1990

The Budget Enforcement Act changes the emphasis from elimination of the deficit to control of spending, removes some of the loopholes from the budget process, and makes some politically difficult decisions go away by moving some expenditures "off-bud-

President Bush's

1993 budget

predicted that as of

September 30, 1993,

the deficit would be

$400 billion and the

debt would be more

than $3 trillion.

get." This technique is used for certain one-time costs, such as the savings and loan bail-out, or revenue-producing programs such as the postal service.

1992

President Bush's 1993 budget predicted that as of September 30, 1993, the deficit would be $400 billion and the debt would be more than $3 trillion.

Trends

- Between 1970 and 1990 there was approximately a 25% increase in federal employment. This corresponds roughly to the 25% increase in U.S. population during the same period.

- Between 1960 and 1990 there was an increase of approximately 25% in total government expenditures as a percent of GNP.

- Between 1960 and 1990 there was not much change in the federal debt as a percentage of GNP. In 1960, however, the debt was falling. It fell to a low of 36% of GNP in 1975. It has since been steadily rising, in direct proportion to the growth of entitlement spending: between 1990 and 1997, a 30% increase is projected.

Important Terms

The Business Cycle & Fiscal Policy

Capitalist economies depend on constant growth. Growth provides new jobs for the workforce, which grows as the population grows, and an ever-increasing standard of living that provides more demand for more product and thus more growth. Apparently, recurring recessions are also inherent in this system, as the market seeks equilibrium

torn by the issues

Federal Budget Summary (1945–1992)

	Receipts	Outlays	Deficit	Total Debt % of GNP
1945	$45,259	$92,712	$47,453	122.5%
1955	$65,451	$68,444	$2,993	71.0%
1965	$116,617	$118,228	$1,611	47.9%
1975	$279,090	$332,332	$53,242	35.6%
1985	$734,057	$946,391	$212,334	46.0%
1992	$1,075,706	$1,475,439	$399,733	69.5%

(All dollar figures are in millions)

after growth periods. This repeated pattern of growth and recession is known as the business cycle.

Recessions usually occur after a number of years of growth. They range for a few months to a few years in duration. The U.S. has experienced major recessions in 1819, 1837, 1857, 1893, 1907, 1914, 1920–1921, 1929–1941, 1973–1974, 1981–1982, and 1991, with many less serious recessions in between.

The government increasingly attempts to use fiscal policy as a means of controlling the economy, so recessions don't turn into devastating depressions, as happened in 1929–1941. In theory, injecting money into the economy through government spending, or by taxation relief, will help lift the economy out of recession. If people have more money, they want more product. This stimulates business growth. The downside is that the money the federal government is currently spending is borrowed money, money it doesn't have.

Reducing the amount of money in circulation, through cutting spending, will theoretically reduce inflation. (If people have less money, they demand less; thus prices go down.) However, recessionary conditions will sometimes result. Economic theory and resulting fiscal policy is an inexact science at best; at worst, consequences can be disastrous.

One deficit-fighting strategy is for the government to print money to pay its debts. This is perhaps the most inflationary and dangerous approach. This strategy was employed by the German Weimar Republic after World War I. In 1923, the German government's deficit was 88% of revenues. Instead of borrowing to pay for the cost overruns, the government printed more money. The result was hyperinflation; prices increased by more than one trillion percent between August 1922 and November 1923. A loaf of bread cost 0.29 marks before World War I, 1200 marks in the summer of 1923, and 428,000,000,000 marks by November 1923. Modern Germany has a constitutional provision that permits government deficit spending only for productive investments.

Off-Budget

Off-budget items are those excluded by law from budget totals. As the deficit increases, there seems to be an increasing tendency to move items off-budget, so the numbers don't appear to be so ominous. In 1989, the postal service was deleted from the budget, thereby "saving" $1.8 billion. It is supposed to pay its own way as a revenue-producing entity. In 1991, it ran a deficit of $1.3 billion.

The war in the Persian Gulf in 1991 was omitted from the budget as a one-time expense. The savings and loan bail-out is off-budget as a one-time expense. The original estimate for the savings and loan bail-out was $50 billion dollars. This estimate has recently been revised upward to $500 billion. Other items that are off-budget are:

- Direct loans, such as loans given by the Small Business Administration.
- Loan guarantees, such as those given to lending institutions for student loans.
- Federal Housing Authority (FHA) loans, Veterans Administration loans, Rural Electrification loans, and the like. The student loan default bill is currently $13.5 billion.
- Pension benefit guarantees.

There have recently been ominous predictions that an impending bail-out of under-funded pension programs will be as expensive as the savings and loan bail-out.

Others predict possible bail-outs of the banking and insurance industries in the future.

Productive (Capital) vs. Operational Expenses

Most states in the U.S. balance their budgets each year. These states require that the budget be balanced for operational spending, but permit the state to issue bonds (borrow funds) for capital spending. It is assumed that capital spending, for items like roads, ports, and airports, will improve the economy of the state and increase tax revenues. States can also charge tolls and user fees for most capital spending. Capital spending is intended to eventually pay for itself.

All economists advise caution in pursuing solutions to deficit problems. Most have two important caveats. The first is that deficits should be allowed to exist only for productive capital investments (not operational expenses). The second is that the deficit cannot grow faster than the economy as a whole. If the deficit grows more quickly than

As the deficit increases, there seems to be an increasing tendency to move items off-budget, so the numbers don't appear to be so ominous.

the economy, then it will only be a matter of time until interest payments alone will consume all revenues.

Right now, both these warnings go unheeded: the deficit is growing rapidly to support entitlements, which are government operations, rather than capital investments, and the deficit is growing faster than the economy.

Foreign Debt

As the U.S. economy increasingly relies on borrowing foreign capital to cover its deficit, we begin to lose control of our own destiny. It will become more difficult to persuade foreign interests to invest in the U.S. as the ability of the U.S. government to pay its debts becomes questionable. Moreover, as more foreign investors buy U.S. companies, foreign companies may not have the same loyalties to U.S. workers as do American companies; they are more likely to seek cheaper labor elsewhere. Even our own companies are shifting jobs to foreign labor markets to stay competitive.

In addition, foreign ownership will mean foreign profit. Foreign-owned assets in the U.S. have quadrupled since 1980. They include Rockefeller Center, Columbia Pictures, Burger King, Brooks Brothers, Holiday Inn, and many lesser known companies.

Many countries, including Great Britain, have been forced to plead for relief from their obligations when they could no longer service debt. In such cases, the debtor country must often develop economic policies according to strict guidelines set by the International Monetary Fund. The U.S. has not had to submit to these controls thus far, and we do not look forward to this prospect, as we are accustomed to the independence afforded by world leadership.

Discretionary & Mandatory Spending

Discretionary spending is spending that the government can easily control through annual increases or decreases in appropriations. Entitlements and interest, also known as mandatory spending, are not discretionary. Because discretionary spending items come before

Congress in the annual budget process, almost all attempts to cut the budget in the last several years have come from discretionary spending. Domestic discretionary spending includes defense, some welfare programs, education, transportation, energy, infrastructure building and maintenance, and so on. Aid to foreign countries accounts for most nondomestic discretionary spending.

Defense spending is the largest area of discretionary spending.

Defense spending is the largest area of discretionary spending. Most agree that the diminished threat from the former Soviet Union renders cuts appropriate. However, because approximately 119 million Americans work in defense and related industries, the threat of cuts always evokes outcries of protest from the affected communities. Our legislators, for the most part, are in favor of cutting spending, except "in their own backyards."

The waste that is incurred in federal spending has been widely reported, but rarely more frequently than in Defense Department contracts. The $500 hammer, bought by the Navy, is a well-known example:

Base cost..$71.00	
(for an ordinary hardware-store hammer)	
Order charge $41.00	
Charge to determine if it worked................................$93.00	
Charge for manufacturing overhead.........................$102.00	
Charge to ensure availability of spare parts............... $37.00	
Charge for packing..$3.00	
Charge for contractors' administrative costs............. $90.00	
Charge for a finder's fee $56.00	
Charge for the capital cost of the money $7.00	
Total Cost **$500.00**	

All Americans would like to see this kind of waste eliminated from the federal budget. Accomplishing this task seems to be impossible within our present political system. A commission hired by the Reagan administration to study waste in government reported that $500 billion in waste could be eliminated immediately. Given a few years for implementation, they predicted that $1 trillion could be cut. These findings have been largely ignored.

Some politicians would like to see any savings realized by cuts in defense spending used to bolster the domestic programs that were reduced during the 1980s. However, this is prohibited by the Budget Agreement of 1990 until at least 1994. All savings from defense cuts must go to reduce the deficit. In any case, these savings will not be realized if entitlements are permitted to rise unchecked according to currently established formulas.

Since 1960, defense spending as a percentage of GNP and as a percentage of federal outlay has gone down.

Defense Spending

	As a Percent of GNP	As a Percent of Federal Outlay
1960	9.5	52.2
1965	7.5	42.8
1970	8.3	41.8
1975	5.7	26.0
1980	5.0	23.1
1985	6.4	26.7
1990	5.5	23.9
1992	5.2	20.8
DECREASE: 40%		**DECREASE: 55%**

Entitlements

An entitlement is an automatic payment by the government to individuals who meet certain eligibility criteria. Projections of future spending levels in entitlement programs are difficult and usually inaccurate. Entitlement programs include Social Security and Medicare, which are the fastest growing segments of the federal budget. In 1992, they accounted for 51% of federal outlays.

torn by the issues

An entitlement is an

automatic payment

by the government to

individuals who meet

certain eligibility

criteria.

Entitlement spending is not appropriated annually. These programs are politically difficult to cut or alter in any way, and they require major legislation to do so. In contrast, discretionary programs can be cut (or increased) with much less publicity and far fewer political repercussions.

Social Security is the broadest-reaching entitlement program. Social Security was designed to be "off-budget," which means that Social Security taxes are collected separately, placed in a trust fund, and not counted with the rest of the budget.

However, Social Security fund surpluses are borrowed to help cover the deficit.

Benefits have been continuously increased. Increases are always politically popular. They have been indexed to inflation and to the cost-of-living index. In addition, as people live longer after retirement, more people are receiving benefits for longer periods of time. The ratio of contributors to recipients shrank from 17 to 1 in the 1950s to 3 to 1 in the 1970s.

Medicare and Medicaid are also entitlement programs. Medicaid cost was approximately $72.5 billion in 1992, and Medicare cost was approximately $119 billion. Social Security and Medicare are perfect examples of the inability or unwillingness on the part of Congress to accurately predict future spending levels. The growth of the elderly population relative to the working population, the development and increased use of expensive medical technologies, and the huge increase in malpractice litigation were not considered when these programs were created.

Welfare and unemployment programs are the third major category of entitlement spending. The federal government provides income support that includes unemployment compensation (estimated at $36.4 billion in 1992), housing assistance ($19.5 billion), food and nutrition assistance ($33.6 billion), and other income security ($45.1 billion). Together these programs account for a small proportion of the federal budget. Even large-scale changes to these programs will not provide the means to control the deficit.

Interest

Interest on the debt is one of the fastest-growing obligations of the federal government. It must be considered mandatory spending because any default on interest payments would result in tremendous international economic and political difficulties and much higher costs in future borrowing.

Public Debt: 1940–1991

	Debt in Billions	Per Capita
1940	$43.0	$325
1950	$256.1	$1,688
1960	$284.1	$1,572
1970	$370.1	$1,814
1980	$907.1	$3,985
1991	$3,502.0	$13,992

The Balanced Budget Amendment

One solution to the deficit and debt problem is a balanced budget amendment to the U.S. Constitution. This amendment would require Congress to balance the annual federal budget except in cases of dire emergency. Supporters of the amendment say it is the only way the federal government can find the discipline to balance the budget and reduce the debt. Opponents argue that it will not permit the government to exercise discretion in combating recessions. Others feel that it will be ignored in times of emergency and will be rendered meaningless as a spending constraint, violable at any time for any reason.

The Effects of Disasters

One solution to the deficit and debt problem is a balanced budget amendment to the U.S. Constitution.

In the late 1980s and early 1990s, two major events demonstrated that the government has responsibilities that can impede efforts to balance the budget. Operation Desert Shield/Storm, although substantially paid for by U.S. allies, showed that the U.S. has an important role in global politics as the last remaining superpower. Other countries look to the U.S. to provide leadership in resolving conflicts. Continuing unrest in Eastern Europe, the Middle East, the former Soviet republics, and Africa is likely to demand U.S. response and thereby consume U.S. resources. Increasing financial contributions from other countries to support these peace-keeping missions will help to alleviate this burden and may serve to support the U.S. role as the major peace-keeping force in the world.

The savings and loan crisis has also impeded efforts to balance the budget. Because one of the causes of the Great Depression was a massive failure of the banking system, the federal government has created deposit insurance organizations to provide limited guarantees for deposits in member banks. This prevents depositors from losing their entire savings if a bank fails. The failure of hundreds of savings and loan institutions in the late 1980s drained the reserves of the insurance organizations. In order to meet its obligation, the government took funds from general revenue; the cost is estimated to reach $500 billion. Many predict a similar bail-out of underfunded pension plans in the near future.

The banking and insurance industries could require similar expensive bail-outs should they fail.

The failure of
hundreds of savings
and loan institutions
in the late 1980s
drained the reserves
of the insurance
organizations.

Bank Failures

Selected Years

Year	Closed or Assisted Banks
1938	81
1955	5
1960	2
1975	14
1982	42
1989	207
1991	127

Sources

Brashear, David. *Government in Crisis: What Every American Should Know About the Federal Budget Deficit.* Alexandria, VA.: Chesapeake River Press, 1991.

Carson, Robert. *Macroeconomic Issues Today: Alternative Approaches.* 5th ed. New York: St. Martin's Press, 1991.

Collender, Stanley E. *The Guide to the Federal Budget: Fiscal Year 1993.* Washington, D.C.: Urban Institute Press, 1992.

Figgie, Harry E., and Gerald Swanson. *Bankruptcy 1995: The Coming Collapse of America and How to Stop It.* Boston: Little, Brown and Company, 1992.

Friedman, Benjamin. *Day of Reckoning: The Consequences of American Economic Policy.* New York: Vintage Books, 1989.

Heilbroner, Robert, and Peter Bernstein. *The Debt and the Deficit: False Alarms/Real Possibilities.* New York: W.W. Norton and Company, 1989.

Morris, Charles R. "It's Not the Economy, Stupid." *Atlantic Monthly*, July 1993.

Office of the President. *Budget of the United States Government, Fiscal Year 1993.* Washington, D.C.: U.S. Government Printing Office, 1992.

Plano, Jack C., and Milton Greenberg. *The American Political Dictionary.* 8th edition. New York: Harcourt Brace Jovanovich, 1989.

Schiller, Bradley R. *The Macroeconomy Today.* 4th edition. New York: Random House Business Division, 1988.

U.S. Department of Commerce, Bureau of the Census. *Statistical Abstract of the United States, 1992.* Washington, D.C.: U.S. Government Printing Office, 1992.

Wright, John. *The Universal Almanac, 1993.* Kansas City, Kansas: Andrews and McMeel, 1993.

gun
control

gun control

the desire to control violence through the regulation of

the tools of violence is not a new idea. Governments throughout

the ages have disarmed citizens in an effort to curb the all-too-

human tendency towards violence. It should be pointed out that

throughout history, the inclination of governments to disarm their

citizens has often been motivated by the need of tyrannical regimes protect themselves from rebellion, rather than by an interest in protecting citizens from one another.

The inordinate level of violence in the United States, and the perceived need to protect one's self against this violence have fueled the debate over gun control. The debate begins with the varying interpretations of the Second Amendment. The two sides of this argument take their respective constitutional bases from either the first or second half of the amendment. The pro-gun control view is grounded in the first clause (sometimes called the preamble) of the Second Amendment:

> *A well-regulated militia, being necessary to the security of a free state,…*

Gun control advocates feel this qualifying phrase limits the possession of firearms to militias, and that legislatures are empowered to control the possession of firearms by individuals. It is believed by gun-control advocates that restriction of gun ownership would lower the level of violence in this country.

The anti-gun control view is based upon the second clause of the amendment:

> *…the right of the people to keep and bear arms, shall not be infringed.*

The anti-gun control contingent usually cites this clause without the qualification of the preamble, as they do not believe the preamble restricts the right of every citizen to freely keep and bear arms.

The ongoing gun-control debate has involved statistical manipulation and emotional propaganda on both sides. It should be made clear, however, that both the pro-control and anti-control sides insist that they are concerned above all with the safety and well-being of law-abiding citizens.

torn by the issues

Gun Control: Pro & Con

The Anti-Control Argument

- The right to own a gun is seen as intimately related to the right to defend one's body and property. In addition, an armed citizenry is seen as one of the principal safeguards against possible tyranny by the state.

- Violent criminals do not, by definition, obey laws. They do not obey existing gun registration laws and would not do so in the future. Instead these laws only serve to prevent timely access to guns by law-abiding citizens, for self defense. Most existing laws are not enforced or are under-enforced in any case, so it seems pointless to add more to the books.

- Domestic homicides are usually committed by career criminals who already own a gun, or by their abused spouses. Children should be protected from access to guns by their parents. This is not a matter for law enforcement. Suicides will happen in any case, whether or not there is a gun available. In general, comparative studies of communities with strict gun laws and those with looser control show no significant difference in homicide rates.

- More firearms are used to thwart crime than are used to commit crimes, and victims resisting with firearms were less likely to be injured during the course of an attempted crime than those who used a less dangerous weapon or no weapon at all.

- There are not enough police to protect everyone, at any given time, so while a police presence may be a deterrent, they can't really effectively protect citizens all the time. They usually appear after the fact to report on the crime and apprehend the criminal.

- High rates of gun possession in many Western European countries do not result in high homicide rates.

- There should be a different approach to violent crime than one of gun regulation. It is a law enforcement issue; there should be less plea bargaining, more prosecution, conviction and incarceration. There should also be stricter parole guidelines, more prison space, and broader use of the death penalty.

- Regarding the banning of semi-automatic assault weapons, anti-control advocates maintain that there is nothing but a cosmetic difference between these and ordinary rifles and handguns. All shoot only one bullet with every squeeze of the trigger, as opposed to automatic weapons, which shoot continuously as long as the trigger is held. There is little opposition to the control or prohibition of automatic weapons like machine guns. The National Rifle Association (NRA) did not oppose the restrictive machine gun legislation of the National Firearms Act of 1934, and has never indicated any desire to repeal the law. Military-style assault weapons account for only about 1% of all weapons seized from criminals by law enforcement agents.

The Pro-Control Argument

- More stringent federal legislation requiring registration and pre-purchase waiting periods will reduce the number of firearms in the hands of violent criminals. It will reduce the access to firearms by children. It will reduce the number of spontaneous suicides. It will reduce the number of domestic homicides. It will reduce the amount of violent crime in general. It will assist in apprehending criminals.

- Self-defense is one of the strongest motivations for acquiring a handgun, but statistics show that attempts at self-defense are often ineffective. Victims who resist violence are at greater risk of being killed or injured than those who do not resist.

- It is the responsibility of the police to protect citizens and control crime. If citizens "take the law into their own hands," a chaotic, violent, and dangerous social climate is the result.

- In Western Europe and various other nations with strict gun laws there is far less incidence of homicide and violent crime, even though per-capita gun possession is higher.

- All of the Supreme Court rulings with regard to the Second Amendment have supported the notion that states have a right and a responsibility, under the Second Amendment, to restrict the sale, possession and use of firearms.

- Gun control bills currently under consideration by Congress target certain types of firearms. Those under consideration for regulation are mostly handguns and firearms falling under the category of "Assault Weapon." One bill currently being proposed (H.R. 669) defines an assault weapon as any semi-automatic, center-fire rifle that accepts a detachable magazine with a capacity of twenty or more rounds, and shotguns with barrels less than nineteen inches long with folding stocks or magazine capacities of more than six rounds. It is felt that these weapons with a military appearance and the capability of firing multiple rounds are not needed for hunting or self-defense purposes, but are only used for criminal purposes.

- President Bush, in 1989, suspended the importation of forty-three types of assault weapons including:

  - AKS type, which includes AK-47

  - Uzi carbines

  - FN-FAL types (NATO weapons)

  - FN-FNC types

  - The Steyr-Aug and others

- Regulation advocates would like to include such weapons as the Mac-10 and Mac-11, Tech-9, The AR-15 (civilian model of the US Army M-16), and the Striker 12, a drum-fed, twelve-round shotgun.

The Second Amendment

A well regulated militia, being necessary to the security of a free state, the right of the people to keep and bear arms, shall not be infringed.

The Second Amendment to the Constitution of the United States, and its interpretation by historians and the U.S. judicial system, are pivotal to the arguments on either side of the gun control issue.

Interpretation concerns the two distinct clauses in the amendment and their relationship to one another. Is the preamble, or first half of the amendment, a qualifying clause relative to the second half of the amendment, or does each clause address its own issue?

Secondary issues are:

- The use of the word "people," and its intended meaning as individual or collective.
- The definition and use of the word "militia."

Those against the government regulation of firearms interpret the word "people" in its individual sense, to mean that every person has the right to keep and bear arms. The historical support for this interpretation relies on the arguments presented by the various framers of the Constitution during the period in which the amendments were being written. Richard Lee, in *Letters from the Federal Farmer*, wrote that in order to "preserve liberty," everyone should "always possess arms and be taught...how to use them."

Patrick Henry stated that, to preserve liberty, "every man be armed" and that "everyone who is able may have a gun." He further stipulated that public liberty should be jealously guarded by armed force; that "whenever you give up that force, you are ruined."

Tench Coxe and James Madison were perhaps the most rigorous in their defense of individual rights. Coxe wrote in *Remarks on the First Part of the Amendments to the Federal Constitution*: "As civil rulers, not having their duty to the people duly before them, may attempt to tyrannize, and as the military forces which must be occasionally raised to defend our country, might pervert their power to the injury of their fellow citizens, the people are confirmed in their right to keep and bear their private arms."

Madison, in *The Federalist*, wrote: "A government resting on a minority is an aristocracy, not a republic, and could not be safe with a numerical and physical force against it, without a standing army, an enslaved press, and a disarmed populace," and that Americans need never fear their government because of "the advantage of being armed, which the Americans possess over the people of almost every other nation."

Those in favor of government regulation of firearms, have historically insisted that the first half of the amendment limits and qualifies the second half. This interpretation means that the right of the people to keep and bear arms is limited to the states' right to maintain militias. Therefore, the pro-gun control argument contends that "the people" have the right to keep and bear arms only as members of a well-regulated militia. This theory assumes that the word "people" was used in the collective, rather than the individual sense.

Anti-gun control advocates feel that the arguments put forth by the founding fathers support the right of the individual to keep and bear arms, and that the first part of the amendment is merely an amplifying clause, rather than a limitation on that right. Pro-gun control advocates insist that the preamble limits that right, and that regulations restricting the possession of firearms were felt, by the framers, to be necessary for the maintenance of a peaceful and orderly society.

Another important issue in the gun control debate is the definition of the word "militia." According to pro-gun control interpretations, the militia is viewed as the collective citizenry which is obligated to defend its environment by armed force. This does not necessarily imply that each of its members should be in private possession of firearms. This interpretation implies that the arms in question would be regulated, supplied, stored, or otherwise maintained by government or an agency of government. A study of pre-Constitutional history will reveal numerous arguments supporting the concept that only the landed citizenry has the right to bear arms in defense of the commonwealth. It was felt by some that only a "freeman," or a man capable of supporting himself through his own labors, and on his own land, would possess the necessary courage and virtue to motivate him to defend the commonwealth in time of aggression. Whether it was intended for the "militia" to include all able-bodied men, or only those who owned property was seen as a legitimate subject of debate at that time.

Several precedent arguments can be found in both European law and English common law concerning the right of the individual to bear arms. Machiavelli contended that the defense of a nation should be the responsibility of every citizen, but that professional armies were to

The pro-gun control argument contends that "the people" have the right to keep and bear arms only as members of a well-regulated militia.

There have been five

decisions on the

Second Amendment

handed down by the

Supreme Court of the

United States since

the ratification of the

Constitution.

be avoided so as to reduce the temptation of governments to use them in tyrannical acts against their own citizens, as has happened frequently throughout history. According to this view, a citizen did not make the martial arts his sole occupation, but was nonetheless obliged to take up arms in defense of himself or his nation, when necessary.

The culture and social framework of this country has changed dramatically since the Second Amendment was written. We no longer maintain state or local "militias," as we found they were inefficient and unreliable compared to a national standing army. After the Civil War, the federal army replaced the states' militias and they disbanded. The reference in the Second Amendment to the existence of state militias and the right of citizen members of these militias to keep and bear arms, has necessarily been reevaluated in light of the changes that have taken place in this society since revolutionary times.

Gun Control & the Supreme Court

There have been five decisions on the Second Amendment handed down by the Supreme Court of the United States since the ratification of the Constitution:

1876

U.S. v. Cruikshank

The Court concluded that the "right of bearing arms for a lawful purpose is not a right granted by the Constitution, nor is it in any manner dependent upon that instrument for its existence." (Gun control advocates, when quoting this decision, tend to omit the latter half, which implies that the right to keep and bear arms predates the Constitution.)

1886

Presser v. Illinois

The Court reaffirmed the Cruikshank decision and affirmed that although the states have the right to form militias, they are also free to regulate the rights of citizens to bear arms, within the parameters of state constitutions. (The National Guard has been formed within these guidelines.)

1894

Miller v. Texas

The Court upheld its earlier decisions on states' rights to regulate firearms sales and possession.

1934

U.S. v. Miller

The Court, in response to a challenge to the National Firearms Act of 1934, affirmed the right of the federal government to regulate the transportation and possession of firearms, and made clear their assertion that the constitutionally protected right to bear arms is only in connection to service in a militia.

1990

Perpich v. Department of Defense

The Court clarified the meaning of the term "militia" in the Constitution. The NRA had asked the Court to find that the National Guard is not the militia, as that term is used in the Second Amendment. The Court did not do so, and instead held that, when not in federal service, state Guard members "continue to satisfy (the) description of a militia."

U.S. v. Verdugo-Urquidez

Chief Justice Rehnquist, in the majority opinion, observed that the phrase "right of the people" occurs several times in the Bill of Rights. In all cases, in the Court's opinion, the phrase refers to individual Americans, thereby upholding the right of individual Americans to bear arms.

Quilici v. Morton Grove

In 1981, the village of Morton Grove, Illinois, enacted an ordinance prohibiting the possession of handguns for everyone except police officers, prison officials, military personnel, licensed gun collectors, and others needing guns for their work. Both Federal

The NRA had asked the Court to find that the National Guard is not the militia, as that term is used in the Second Amendment. The court did not do so....

District Court and the Federal Court of Appeals upheld Morton Grove's right to enact such an ordinance in the challenge of *Quilici v. Morton Grove*. The Supreme Court declined to hear the case upon appeal, leaving the lower federal courts' rulings as the operative interpretation. Several small communities have since enacted similar legislation.

Timeline

1181

England requires Anglo-Saxon yeomen to bear arms in the common defense.

1400s

Victorious European armies, on various occasions, summarily execute firearm-using enemy soldiers for using barbarous and ungentlemanly weapons.

1541

The Bill for Crossbows and Handguns is enacted in England during the reign of Henry VIII. This law restricts the use of firearms to noblemen and commoners with an annual income of one hundred pounds or more. Only the privileged could keep, carry, and use firearms for hunting and self-defense. As a concession to the militia, commoners with less wealth could use firearms, but for practice only. In an obvious effort to outlaw concealable weapons, it also rules that no one may carry or use a gun of less than three-quarters of one yard in length. This law is enforced for over two hundred years.

1546

French monarch Francis I prohibits, by edict, the possession of firearms by anyone, under penalty of death. Fifteen years later, however, the French aristocracy was, through the use of edict, still attempting unsuccessfully to disarm the populace. In 1561, all citizens of Paris were required to remit their firearms to city hall within twenty-four hours, while requiring gun makers to supply inventory and sales lists. Gun makers were also prohibited from selling firearms to anyone whose names and addresses were not known to them.

1611

Virginia's Governor Lord De La Ware, in his *Martial Laws of Virginia*, orders all targeteers to carry wheel lock or flint lock pistols as part of their civic responsibility to help defend the colony.

1614

French historian Gabriel Hanotaux writes: "All contemporaries are in agreement in declaring that, in France, arms are no longer given to the people, for fear that they will rise up against their oppressors."

1622

After the Indian massacre of that year, the Virginia colony requires every able-bodied man between sixteen and fifty years of age to serve in the militia as defense against further Indian uprisings. A Royal British Proclamation is issued against the practice of giving firearms, as an item of trade, to Indians.

1628

Plymouth Colony formally expels Thomas Morton for selling firearms to Indians.

1630

The Privy Council formally prohibits firearms trade to Indians. The Puritans of this period punish firearms smugglers by whipping and branding.

1631

A Massachusetts court requires every town to enroll all men, except ministers and magistrates, in the militia. A later addition to this order required all men to possess a firearm. All who did not comply were hired out as servants.

1637

The Massachusetts colonial government, as a result of a religious controversy, orders seventy-six followers of Anne Hutchinson and the Reverend John Wheelwright disarmed. This is an example of an early colonial government reserving the right to disarm those whom it regarded as dissenters, while maintaining the right to arm and maintain a militia.

1638

Dutch colonial leaders in New Amsterdam order capital punishment for traders who supply firearms to Indians. Ten years later, Governor Peter Stuyvesant attempts to use the law on several convicted traders but is forced to reduce the sentence due to citizen protest.

1640

The colony of Virginia passes legislation prohibiting blacks from owning firearms. This presumably was seen as a way of protecting white slave owners against slave uprisings.

1670

English law associates the right to keep and use arms with the right to hunt. The nobility sought to retain the monopoly on game hunting by levying stiff fines for the unauthorized killing of game. The Robin Hood story is based on the resistance of the English peasantry to this restriction of hunting privileges and firearm ownership.

torn by the issues

By *the early*

eighteenth century,

gunsmiths are a

significant element in

the economy of

practically every

American town.

1689

The English Bill of Rights provides, for Protestants only, the right to bear arms "for their defense."

1695

The Irish Parliament enacts a law to disarm the Catholic populace, with justices and sheriffs empowered to carry out searches to insure compliance. There are, however, provisions for Catholic noblemen to possess "a sword, a case of pistols, and a gun."

1700s

By the early eighteenth century, gunsmiths are a significant element in the economy of practically every American town.

Firearm technology advances (the flint lock and the rifled bore) markedly improve the quality of American-produced firearms.

1712

In An Act for the Better Ordering of Negroes and Slaves, the colony of South Carolina prohibited blacks from carrying a firearm beyond the limits of the master's plantation without the master's written permission, and white men were ordered to keep their firearms in the most private rooms of their homes.

1715

At the beginning of the reign of George I, the Scottish highlanders are prevented from possession of any sword, knife, gun, or pistol or any other warlike weapon. As in the case of Ireland, an exception was made for the upper classes, who were allowed to retain a specific number and type of weapons.

1718

English inventor James Puckle attempts to patent a cannon that will fire conventional round projectiles at Christians and square

In 1794, a Prussian

law is enacted

requiring those

entitled to own

firearms to unload

them before entering

their houses and to

keep them out of the

reach of children.

ones at Turks. Many critics object to the use of unorthodox projectiles on the battlefield which they view as further evidence of the unmanliness of firearm use. With this view undoubtedly in mind, the British, during America's Revolutionary War, charge Revolutionary War hero Joshua Barney with violation of the rules of war when he fires a crowbar into the rigging of an English warship.

1768

William Blackstone, in *Commentaries on the Laws of England*, asserts that it is lawful for a man "to repel force by force; and the breach of the peace which happens is chargeable upon him only who began the affray." This idea was to become the cornerstone of various American gun-related laws over the next two centuries as well as the basis for the self-defense plea in countless murder charges.

1775

On April 19, British soldiers engage a small group of Massachusetts militiamen in a skirmish that will mark the beginning of the American Revolution. The success of this and similar militias will be the conceptual cornerstone of the preamble clause of the Second Amendment. (See Second Amendment notes.)

1792

The U.S. Congress passes the Militia Law requiring every white, free, able-bodied American male (blacks and Indians were excluded) between the ages of eighteen and forty-five to serve in his own state's militia. Each man was to provide his own weapons and ammunition. A later addition to this legislation authorized the president of the U.S. to call upon the state militias for federal use.

1794

Prussian law is enacted requiring those entitled to own firearms to unload them before entering their houses and to keep them out of the reach of children. Gunpowder, falling under the same prohibitive restrictions as poisons and dangerous drugs, is to be sold only to persons "above suspicion."

In 1854, [it is
reported that] "since
California opened her
mines to the world,
she has invested
upwards of six
million dollars in
bowie knives and
pistols."

1816

Remington Arms Company founded.

1832

Samuel Colt builds his first revolver.

1834

The Indian Intercourse Act provides legal authority for American natives to acquire firearms.

1836

Colt opens his first factory in Paterson, New Jersey. Due to the high cost of his revolvers and subsequent low volume of sales, he is forced into bankruptcy in 1842. In the following few years, Colt redesigns his dragoon revolver and resumes operation in 1855 at what is then the largest private armory in the world.

1849

The 30th Congress, realizing that it will be less expensive to provide weapons to emigrants relocating to the Oregon, California, and New Mexico Territories than it would be to send troops along to protect them, authorizes a release of $50,000 of government funds to arm the settlers.

1854

The *Annals of San Francisco* records: "It has always been a practice of a large proportion of the citizens to carry loaded firearms or deadly weapons concealed about their person, this being, as it were, a part of their ordinary dress."

The following year, Hinton R. Helper reported in *The Land of Gold*, "By a calculation, based upon fair estimates, I learn that since California opened her mines to the world, she has invested upwards of six million dollars in bowie knives and pistols." Twenty years later a writer for the *Wichita Eagle* remarked that "Pistols are as thick as blackberries."

1854–1857

The Sir St. George Gore hunting expedition travels throughout the West. Gore kills 1000 American bison during the course of one day with single shot rifles by using tripods and the help of his servants to hand him a freshly loaded weapon after each shot. Between the European arrival in America and 1887, over 100 million buffalo were killed.

1857

City officials of Baltimore, Maryland authorize police use of firearms for "emergencies." An officer could return fire when fired upon, but could not shoot a suspect that was running from him. In New York City, Officer Eugene Anderson is the first NYC policeman admitted to the force's roll of honor, having been killed that year in a gunfight with a burglar.

Due to the perceived expense of underwriting official police departments, combined with the general public's fear of armed authority, only eight cities in the United States have organized police departments by the outbreak of the Civil War. The overall level of public violence engendered by the Civil War leads to a change in public attitude making possible the rapid rise of organized police departments after the war's end.

1860–1871

Some 500 firearm-related patents are filed in the U.S. including patents from Colt, Remington, Winchester, Gatling, Spencer, Derringer, Smith and Wesson, Savage, and many others. The 1860 U.S. census lists 239 firms engaged in the production of small arms.

Cartridge munitions became popular during this period with Winchester and the Union Metallic Cartridge Company plants both producing one million cartridges a day by 1875.

Rising concurrently with the expanding post-Civil War gun market of the 1870s are the forerunners of the "Saturday Night

In 1872, Aaron
Montgomery Ward
starts his mail order
business, selling,
among other items,
various types of
firearms.

Special." This genre of handgun became known as "suicide specials," bearing such names as "Tramps Terror," "Red Jacket," and "Little Giant," and sold for as little as two dollars each. The extremely low cost of these weapons made them ideal give-away premiums for the purchase of anything from carriages to religious weekly subscriptions. Catalogues advertise pocket pistols, house pistols, muff pistols for the ladies, cane guns, alarm guns to frighten burglars away, and even one firearm designed to look like a pocket watch.

The set gun, or trap gun, finds its way onto the market in the 1880s as the latest in home and business protection. It is triggered by the tripping of a cord strung across an entry path to surprise housebreakers. It became popular with shopkeepers of the era in spite of being condemned by many as immoral and inhumane.

1866

In An Act to Prevent the Furtive Possession and Use of Sling Shot and other Dangerous Weapons, New York prohibits the carrying of sling shot, billy, sand club, metal knuckles, any dirk or dagger, sword cane or air gun, but omits handguns from the list.

1867

The Army Appropriation Act is passed, disbanding the southern militias. President Andrew Johnson signs the bill in spite of the fact that he believes it unconstitutional.

1871

The National Rifle Association is founded to foster gun shooting competition.

1872

Aaron Montgomery Ward starts his mail order business, selling, among other items, various types of firearms. Sears follows suit in 1886.

1876

The Winchester Company's repeating rifle is debuted and rapidly becomes the most popular long gun of the American frontier. The Winchester became so popular that citizens of Idaho named a town after it. At Custer's defeat at Little Big Horn, government troops were armed with single-shot Springfield rifles, while 25% of the Indians possessed Winchester repeating rifles.

1882

A *New York Daily Tribune* survey reported 750,000 pistols, 400,000 shotguns, and 500,000 rifles being purchased annually by Americans.

1893

The first Grand American Trapshooting Contest is held at Dexter Park, New York. The practice of clay target shooting as an alternative to live-bird target shooting grows in popularity, due in great part to the lobbying efforts of the Society for the Prevention of Cruelty to Animals (founded in 1866). The SPCA, from their earliest days, campaigned against the sport of live pigeon shooting.

1900

The U.S. census reports $18.5 million spent on arms and ammunition by Americans in that year.

1903

The Mondell Act creates the National Board for the Promotion of Rifle Practice. At the board's first meeting, it recommends that federal facilities be opened to civilians for rifle practice.

A *New York Tribune* article reports police estimates of 20,000 citizens regularly carrying handguns concealed on their persons.

1905

Congress passes Public Law 149 authorizing the sale of surplus arms and ammunition to rifle clubs. The NRA becomes the chief organizer of these sales.

torn by the issues

The State of New York amends its restrictive penal code relative to sale and possession of dangerous weapons to include prohibition of the possession, by aliens, of firearms in any public place. This provision is retained in the Sullivan Act. (See below)

1911

Volume I of the *Journal of the American Institute of Criminal Law and Criminology* publishes an article which asks the question: "Is the pistol responsible for crime?"

A series of shootings, beginning with that of Mayor of New York William J. Gaynor on August 9, 1910, culminates in the signing into law of the Sullivan Act on May 29, 1911, which severely restricts the sale, possession, and carrying of deadly weapons, including handguns. The unlicensed carrying of a concealed weapon becomes a felony. In the four years preceding the Sullivan Act, more than 10,000 revolvers were confiscated by the New York City Police, an average of more than seven a day for that period.

1912

The City of New York's police and coroner statistical data for the year following the Sullivan Act's passage show a 40% decrease in suicide and 1% increase in homicide.

1913

The state of Oregon, in An Act Forbidding the Sale, Barter, Giving Away, Disposal of or Display for Sale of Pocket Pistols and Revolvers and Fixing a Penalty for the Violation Thereof, requires registration of handguns and affidavits to the applicant's good moral character from at least two reputable persons.

1916

The National Defense Act provides $300,000 to be used for the promotion of civilian marksmanship.

The City of New York's police and coroner statistical data for the year following the Sullivan Act's passage (1912) show a 40% decrease in suicide and 1% increase in homicide.

1919

Chicago Crime Commission is created in response to the rising crime rate. By 1921, Chicago police are making three concealed weapon arrests per day, and Chicago businessman John R. Thompson publicly offers $1000 "to anyone who would give one good reason why the revolver manufacturing industry should be allowed to exist and enjoy the facilities of the mails."

1922

The *American Bar Association Journal*, in an essay titled "For a Better Enforcement of the Law," states: "We recommend that the manufacture and sale of pistols . . . shall be absolutely prohibited, save as such manufacture shall be necessary for governmental and official use under legal regulation and control."

Reconsidering the gun control argument from the victim defense viewpoint, the ABA reverses its position in 1926 to support the Uniform Firearms Act then being considered in the House of Representatives. The number of handguns in private possession at this time is estimated to be approximately 10 million.

In the first three months of that year, New York City authorities issued some 35,000 pistol permits in response to citizen concern over rising street crime, a 430% increase over 1916 registration figures.

Colonel John M. Thompson demonstrates his .45 caliber sub-machine gun (dubbed the "tommy gun") to the Chicago Police.

The manufacturers, Colt and Auto Ordinance Company, in an effort to reduce unwanted inventory, sell their "tommy guns" indiscriminately.

1924

After unsuccessfully attempting to comply with laws regulating the sending of handguns through the mails, Sears, Roebuck and Company drops all handguns from its catalogues.

As a measure to aid the faltering police in their city, the authorities in Philadelphia announce that they are issuing pistols to their 1600 firemen.

1925

The NRA takes over the 100,000 member Winchester youth marksmanship program.

1927

The Miller Bill is signed into law prohibiting handgun sales via the mails.

1932

In a radio address directed at the White House Conference of Child Health, George Aubrey Hastings, sponsored by the National Anti-Weapons Society, states: "Pistols and guns do not fit into the pattern of a safe, healthy, and happy environment. They belong to an environment which breeds delinquency, accidents, and crimes in sudden anger." Senator Arthur Capper of Kansas, speaking for the same organization, states, in reference to parents allowing their children to play with toy guns: "I do not think this is cute. I think it is the real American tragedy."

1934

The NRA membership has now grown to some 35,000, spread among 2000 clubs across the United States, having become the largest association of firearms users in the country.

Congress begins its hearings on the National Firearms Act before a House Committee. The original intent of this legislation was to curtail, through the manipulation of the Federal Interstate Commerce Laws, the sales of several categories of firearms and related devices used almost exclusively in the commissions of crime (large caliber pistols and revolvers, sawed-off rifles and shotguns, machine guns and silencers). After a lengthy and heated battle resulting in various amendments to the original, it is signed into law by President Franklin D. Roosevelt.

1938

The Federal Firearms Act becomes law, establishing registration procedures for arms manufacturers engaged in interstate commerce. These procedures included provisions for accounting for serial numbers and barring convicted felons from purchasing firearms.

1939

A Gallup poll reveals 79% of those responding felt that all owners of pistols and revolvers should be required to register with the government.

Between 1937 and 1939, gun regulations in Great Britain, Germany and France become considerably more restrictive than their American counterparts.

1941

The United States enters World War II. The national production of firearms expands accordingly, boosting Remington's production by 2000%. Smith and Wesson produced more during WWII than they had in the preceding 90 years.

1958

The number of gun collectors in the U.S. has grown from 50,000 in 1939 to 650,000 in 1958.

1961

Fourteen million hunting licenses are sold, doubling the amount sold in 1937.

1962

Sales statistics show toy guns as the largest category of toys for boys, with annual sales exceeding $100 million.

1964

Stanley Meisler reports on the "Dodge City Syndrome" (*The Nation*, 4 May, 64), a growing medical concern: "gunshot wounds of lower extremities or the Fast Draw Syndrome."

1965

The number of NRA-affiliated clubs exceeds 11,000.

During the 22-year period between 1946 and 1968, Americans purchased 45 million small arms from American producers and another 10 million imports.

1968

The Gun Control Act is signed by President Lyndon Johnson, providing stricter control of both foreign and interstate traffic in the firearms trade, drastically reducing the mail-order business. To this end it requires retail purchasers to be residents of the state in which the purchase is being made, and to sign a written statement that they are not minors, narcotics abusers, felons, mentally ill or fugitives from justice. It also gives the Secretary of the Treasury the authority to ban the importation of certain firearms.

President Johnson names the National Commission on the Causes and Prevention of Violence. Its findings suggest that firearms are a major factor in suicide, crime, and collective violence.

The NRA's registered membership reaches 1,000,000.

1981

The village of Morton Grove, Illinois, enacts An Ordinance Regulating the Possession of Firearms and Other Dangerous Weapons, banning the possession of a specific group of dangerous weapons, including any handgun that had not been rendered permanently inoperative, for anyone except the police, prison officials, on-duty security guards, licensed gun collectors and gun clubs. (For further information, see the Supreme Court section).

1982

In response to the Morton Grove ordinance, the city council of Kennesaw, Georgia, passes an ordinance requiring all local citizens to keep at least one firearm in their homes.

A report on the effects of gun control, commissioned by President Carter in 1978, and completed in 1982, finds no conclusive evi-

A report commissioned by President Carter in 1978 shows that waiting periods, various licensing systems, and registration appeared to have no discernible effects.

In 1989, Patrick

Purdy opens fire on a

school yard in

Stockton, California,

killing six children

and wounding thirty-

five. He uses a semi-

automatic rifle to fire

105 shots in about

four minutes.

dence that America's 20,000 gun-control laws have reduced criminal violence. For example, the Gun Control Act of 1968, which banned most interstate gun sales, had no discernible impact on the criminal acquisition of guns from other states.

Subsequent studies revealed that strict penalties for carrying an illegal gun seemed to reduce robbery rates. Waiting periods, various licensing systems, and registration appeared to have no discernible effects.

1985

The Federal Firearms Owners Protection Act, known also as the McClure-Volkmer Act, is passed, effectively repealing certain restrictive measures of the 1968 legislation. This legislation allows for the interstate transportation of handguns by retail purchasers as long as the firearm is transported in a locked trunk.

1986

The International Association of Chiefs of Police, collectively upset over lobbying efforts to protect the use of machine guns and Teflon-coated bullets, bans the NRA from setting up a booth at their annual convention. IACP Director Jerald Vaughn calls the NRA "one of the most potentially dangerous organizations in the United States today." The NRA's membership declined from 3 million in the late 1970s and early 1980s to 2.7 million by 1986.

1989

James S. Brady, former aide to Ronald Reagan, who was shot by John Hinckley during a 1981 assassination attempt on Reagan, testifies before the U.S. Senate Judiciary Committee to promote legislation restricting the possession of handguns. This bill (H.R.7) was defeated in the House of Representatives in 1988 but passed in May of 1991 by a margin of 239 to 186.

Patrick Purdy opens fire on a school yard in Stockton, California, killing six children and wounding thirty-five. He uses a semi-automatic rifle to fire 105 shots in about four minutes. The rate of fire could have been duplicated by many single-shot rifles or handguns.

The Bush

administration requests

$589 million to fight

violent and organized

crime in 1993, an

increase of $99

million, or 20% over

1992.

However, the large magazine capacity of his gun allowed for a longer period of continuous shooting without reloading. The national media implies incorrectly that Purdy had used an automatic AK-47 rifle, and that these guns could be bought over-the-counter. This incident fuels the subsequent debate regarding semi-automatic assault weapons.

President George Bush approves a temporary ban on Chinese-made AK-47 assault rifles. Immediately afterwards, as during the aftermath of the 1986 ban on machine-guns, gun collectors begin buying up the remaining stock still in stores.

California passes the Assault Weapons Control Act (the Roberti-Roos Act) banning new sales of automatic and semi-automatic "assault weapons" and requiring registration for already owned weapons on the list. Under consideration, at the federal level, for inclusion into the category of "assault weapon," are firearms with cosmetic similarities to military weapons and firearms using loading clips that contain more than five rounds.

1992

The *Journal of the American Medical Association* documents the high incidence of firearm violence among young urban blacks and widespread availability of handguns among high-school students of all races. Their and other statistics seem to indicate that gun violence is a national health hazard.

The Bush administration requests $589 million to fight violent and organized crime in 1993, an increase of $99 million, or 20% over 1992.

To provide adequate prison space to insure that convicted felons will serve the full term of their sentences, the Bureau of Prisons will add 4200 new prison beds in 1993, a 9% increase over the bed space available in 1992.

To curtail the illicit movement of firearms, explosives, and ammunition, the BATF will devote $8.1 million and 101 agents to its International Trafficking in Arms program.

The FBI will field over 2000 agents in 1993, 385 of which will be assigned to work with BATF and state and local law enforcement agencies to fight violent crime.

The 1992 National Crime Victimization Survey covering 1981 through 1992 indicates that crime rates per 100,000 are edging down as Federal law enforcement appropriations rise.

Citing the statistical evidence that increased incarceration rates are resulting in lower crime rates, the NRA actively advocates tougher anti-crime laws such as:

- Abolition of parole and all other forms of early release.

- Limitation of good time credits to a maximum of 15%, which means criminals will have to serve at least 85% of their sentence.

- No plea-bargaining.

- Sixteen- and seventeen-year-old juveniles be tried as adults.

Gun Facts

- Half of all American households contain firearms.

- There are approximately 40 million handguns in circulation in the U.S., a number which increases by 2.5 million annually.

- There are more than 160 million privately owned long guns in the United States.

- There are about 65 guns for every 100 men, women, and children in the U.S.

- Gun ownership is more prevalent among males, whites, southerners, veterans, Protestants, and rural and small-town residents, and is fairly evenly distributed by income.

- Between 1960 and 1980, the death rate from firearms increased 160%.

- Unintentional shootings cause 100,000 injuries annually.

- More than $1 billion is spent annually in the United States on medical costs associated with the treatment of individuals who have been shot.

- Firearms kept in homes for self-defense are six times as likely to be used in an accidental or deliberate homicide involving a friend or relative than against an intruder.

- Less than 2% of all homicides in the U.S. are considered legally justifiable as self-defense or property defense.

- Robbery victims who make some attempt at defending themselves are eight times more likely to be killed than victims who put up no defense.

- Approximately 65% of all murders in the United States involve family members or friends.

- Between 70% and 90% of domestic homicide offenders have been arrested previously or have been the object of a disturbance call to police. In more than half the cases, police had been called five or more times. Statistics show that homicides between intimates are typically part of an ongoing and persistent pattern of violence.

- Half of all interspousal homicides are committed by wives against their husbands, and half by husbands against wives.

- For every case of self-protection-related homicide, there are forty-three suicides, criminal homicides, or accidental gunshot deaths in homes where guns are kept.

- Of the 30,000 annual suicides in the U.S. about half are committed with firearms. A study done from data collected between 1979 and 1981 showed that while gun controls did reduce gun suicide, overall suicide rates were not affected. That is, people who had decided to commit suicide found another way. Firearm homicide is greater than firearm suicide for every ethnic group except whites, for whom suicides outnumber homicides by almost 50%.

- Black men aged twenty-four to thirty-five have a gunshot mortality rate of 135 per 100,000, more than three times that of the group at next highest risk.

Half of all interspousal homicides are committed by wives against their husbands, and half by husbands against wives.

A *record of arrest is*

not sufficient to deny

a person the right to

purchase a firearm

under most existing

regulations.

- There are currently over 20,000 gun-related ordinances in effect in the U.S.

- A record of arrest is not sufficient to deny a person the right to purchase a firearm under most existing regulations.

- The NRA proposes mandatory instant record checks on gun purchasers and no waiting period. The Brady Bill recommends a waiting period of seven days and does not require a record check.

- The .22 caliber revolver that John Hinckley used in his assassination attempt on President Ronald Reagan and subsequent wounding of James Brady was purchased in a Texas pawn shop for $33, five months before the crime was committed. A waiting period and a check for criminal record would not have prevented that purchase.

- Homicide rates per 100,000 have been found to be four to five times higher in the United States than in Western Europe.

- The four nations with the highest number of firearms relative to population size—Switzerland, Israel, Denmark, and Finland—have some of the lowest crime rates in the world.

- The Italian-made Carcano rifle that was used to kill John F. Kennedy was purchased through the mails for $12.78 plus shipping costs.

- Handguns, representing only 20% of all firearms, account for 53% of all murders and 95% of all robberies in the United States. They are popular with criminals because they are concealable.

- In 1989, forty of the sixty-six law enforcement officers killed in the line of duty were killed with handguns.

- Between 40% and 70% of the handguns owned by felons are stolen weapons. (Between 30% and 60% are legally registered.)

- Career criminals commit 75% to 80% of the violent crimes in the U.S.

- The Bureau of Alcohol, Tobacco, and Firearms estimates there are at least one million semi-automatic assault weapons in private hands in the United States.

- One percent of homicides involve military-style "assault" rifles.

- Civilian women trained at the Chattanooga, Tennessee Police Academy pistol range, after one hour of target practice and two hours of classroom instruction, consistently outshot police cadets who had received eight times as much formal instruction and practice.

- In 1966, in a highly publicized program, the Orlando, Florida Police Department trained several thousand women to use guns. The rape rate decreased 88% during the following year, a larger decrease than any previous year of study.

- Florida reported a 61% increase in gun incidents in schools between 1986 and 1988; 86% of the weapons that were traced came from the students' homes.

- In 1988, gun accidents were the fourth leading cause of accidental death for children fourteen years of age and under.

- An estimated 135,000 boys carried handguns to school daily in 1987. Another 270,000 carried handguns to school at least once.

- Guns are the leading method used by teenagers to commit suicide (60%).

- Nine out of ten attempted suicides involving handguns are completed.

- A 1990 Gallup poll indicated that 87% of Americans are in favor of a seven-day waiting period for the purchase of a handgun.

- About 32% of assaults involve the use of a firearm.

- A gun is used in 11% of all rapes.

- With currently more than three million members, the NRA is the largest consumer organization in America.

- Of the half-million police officers currently working in the combined jurisdictions of the U.S., only one quarter of that number (accounting for shift divisions, vacation and sick leave, etc.) are on duty at any one time.

- Half of those on duty are assigned to clerical duties and are not on the street. This leaves a total of 62,500 officers to protect 250 million citizens during any given moment. This is one police officer for every 4000 people.

Both pro-gun control

and anti-gun control

forces claim that the

majority of

professional law

enforcement

organizations are on

their side.

- In the *Uniform Crime Reports for 1983*, The F.B.I. stated that it has "long been recognized that murder is a societal problem over which law enforcement has little or no control."

- In New Jersey, the state has required a background check for handgun purchasers for twenty years. More than 10,000 convicted felons have been refused a legal gun purchase under this system. There is no data showing how many of these individuals subsequently acquired a gun illegally.

A *Felon Survey*

- One third carry a gun all the time, and 20% carry only when they intend to commit a crime.

- The average gun-wielding felon is most likely to view after-the-fact punishments to be insignificant compared to the possibilities of needing a gun and not having one.

- About half of those surveyed indicated that they are more worried about meeting an armed victim than they are about running into the police. 27% felt, however, that committing a crime against an armed victim is an exciting challenge.

- When asked what they would do if they wanted to carry a handgun but could not obtain one, 72% indicated they would carry a sawed-off shotgun or rifle instead.

- Of those in this sample who stole the guns that they used (40% of the total sample), 37% stole from stores, 15% from a policeman, 16% from a truck shipment, 8% from a manufacturer, and 24% from residential burglaries.

- Half of those who purchased their guns purchased them illegally through unregulated channels, and half through regulated channels.

- In another convicted felon survey, only 15% stated that they had ever applied for a permit to own a gun, even though almost all were convicted in states which had provisions for registration.

Police Surveys

Half of those who purchased their guns purchased them illegally through unregulated channels....

- Both pro-gun control and anti-gun control forces claim that the majority of professional law enforcement organizations are on their side.

- The leadership of the International Association of Chiefs of Police voted in February of 1989 to oppose the distribution and sale of assault weapons to the general public. They define assault weapons as firearms with such a high capacity for firepower that their function as legitimate sports and recreational firearms is substantially outweighed by the danger that they can be used to kill or injure human beings. Jules Bernstein, legislative counsel for the National Association of Police Organizations stated: "For cops, this is an occupational and health issue."

- The National Sheriffs Association went on record in 1989 in support of the Brady Bill.

- The Fraternal Order of Police issued a statement in 1989 in support of the Brady Bill: "If the seven-day waiting period will save just one life—the life of a law enforcement officer or a citizen—then (the law) will have been successful. Our prediction is that a cooling-off period will save hundreds of lives."

- The National Association of Police Organizations stated, in support of the Brady Bill: "The Brady Bill is occupational safety legislation for law enforcement officers."

- A Boston police study revealed that 83% of the officers polled were against any ban on the private possession of handguns. The carrying of handguns on one's person for protection was approved by 50% of those surveyed. The other half of those surveyed disapproved of the carrying of handguns.

- A Crime Control Research Project survey in 1977, sponsored by the Second Amendment Foundation together with the American Law Enforcement Officers Association, found that:

  - Of the officers surveyed, 86% said they themselves would keep firearms for the protection of family and property.

- Almost all (95%) indicated that in the event of federal handgun laws being enacted, felons would still be able to secure handguns from organized crime.

- An anti-gun-control-sponsored survey of police chiefs, sheriffs, and federal and state police heads in the United States produced the following results:
    - Approximately 87% indicated that they agreed with the concepts of the McClure-Volkmer Act of 1985. (For McClure-Volkmer Act, see Timeline for 1985).
    - Most (93%) said that, in their experience, criminals tend to get their guns illegally rather from licensed dealers.
    - Most (98%) felt that citizens, whether for home or business, have the right to purchase firearms for self-protection.
    - Most (91%) indicated a disbelief that gun bans reduced gun crimes.

Sources

Abrams, Daniel. "Law and Justice." *USA Today*, May 1990.

Alderman, Ellen, and Caroline Kennedy. *In Our Defense: The Bill of Rights in Action*. New York: Avon Books, 1991.

Biskupic, Joan. "Bush Action on Gun Imports Cheers Backers of Curbs." *Congressional Quarterly*, 18 March 1989.

Brill, Stephen. *Firearms Abuse: A Research and Policy Report*. Police Foundation, 1977.

Cassidy, William, and Sarah Brady. "The Case for Firearms and the Case Against Them." *Time*, 29 January 1990.

The Center to Prevent Handgun Violence. *Legal Action Report*. Washington D.C: July 1991.

"Crime in America." *The Economist*, 22 December 1990.

Franklin, Talcott J. *"Saving Seven Days' Time While Fighting Crime."* Research Reports; Second Amendment Foundation, 1990.

Gottlieb, Alan M. *Gun Rights Fact Book*. Bellevue, WA: Merrill Press, 1988.

"Guns are a Health Hazard." *The New York Times*, 28 June 1992.

Kates, Don B., Jr., and Patricia Terrell Harris. "Eight Myths of Gun Control." *National Review*, 21 October 1991.

Kennett, Lee, and James LaVerne Anderson. *The Gun in America: The Origins of a National Dilemma*. Westpoint, CT: Greenwood Press, 1975.

Kopell, David B. "Hold Your Fire." *Policy Review*, Winter 1993.

Lenzi, Jack. "Semi-Automatics Constitutionally Protected." *American Rifleman*. September 1989.

Long, Emmett, ed. *Gun Control*. New York: The H.W. Wilson Co., 1989.

Mackenzie, Hillary. "David and Goliath." *Maclean's*, 6 May 1991.

"NRA Challenges California Gun Ban," *The American Rifleman*. April 1990.

Nisbet, Lee, ed. *The Gun Control Debate: You Decide*. Buffalo, NY: Prometheus Books, 1990.

Orrick, Sarah, ed. "The 1990 Omnibus Crime Bill: Pros and Cons." *Congressional Digest*, November 1990.

U.S. Department of Justice, Federal Bureau of Investigation. *Uniform Crime Reports*. U. S. Government Printing Office, 1990.

Wright, James D., and Peter H. Rossi. *Armed and Considered Dangerous: A Survey of Felons and Their Firearms*. New York: Aldine De Gruyter, 1986.

the U.S. has the most technologically advanced and

expensive health care system in the world. As a culture, we have

become accustomed to the constant availability of these advanced

methods of treatment, whenever we feel inclined to use them, but

we have been largely shielded from the cost of these services.

Insurance coverage for health care has become commonplace for

Between 30 and 40

million Americans

can no longer get the

health care that they

have come to believe

is their birthright.

many of us, and employers are expected to pay the cost of this coverage as a part of their operating expenses.

The employer's role as provider of health care coverage is a relatively recent one. It began during World War II when wage increases were frozen and health insurance was an inexpensive way to improve employees' wage packages without violating the law. It was called a "fringe benefit," and quickly became a popular addition to a wage package.

Those who are not covered by an employer can theoretically seek assistance from government programs. However, many are finding themselves ineligible for these programs. Rising doctors' fees, hospital fees, and insurance premiums combine to make health care inaccessible for many people. In 1993, there are approximately 37 million Americans without health insurance. They often do not seek health care until they have an acute need. The cost of treatment delivered in emergency rooms is significantly higher than the cost of preventive care, and when it is not paid, the taxpayer ultimately absorbs it.

Meanwhile, doctors and hospitals have almost no incentive to keep fees in line, because insurance companies and government programs traditionally do not question them, and have the deep pockets to pay them. As consumers with employer-paid health insurance, we rarely restrict ourselves from seeking services. We are usually not inclined to question a doctor's recommendations, and we feel we are entitled to any existing health care service on demand if a doctor has prescribed it. Insurance companies, public and private, pass their rising costs along to corporate and individual consumers, and again, they are expected to absorb these costs no matter how great.

Particularly between 1960 and the present, health care and health care insurance systems have evolved in an environment that shields all participants from the actual costs in a way that no other system in our free-market culture does. There are almost no checks on costs anywhere in these systems, resulting in the two most obvious symptoms of the health care crisis:

- Between 30 and 40 million Americans can no longer get the health care that they have come to believe is their birthright. They can't get these services because provider fees are too high, insurance premiums are too high, or because they do not have an employer who will pay these costs for them.

- The federal budget deficit is so large, and growing so rapidly, that some observers are predicting the economic collapse of the U.S. by the end of the century. The deficit is in large measure a result of a health care system that exists without either free-market or government-imposed controls.

In the U.S., research and development funding is plentiful for health care because we are a wealthy country. This makes our medical technology the envy of the world. However, the cost of using this advanced medical technology is becoming prohibitive for most citizens. The growing deficit indicates that it is becoming prohibitive even for the government to support.

Doctor and hospital fees grow unchecked because we are a free-market country with a huge government-funded health care program that supplements an equally huge private insurance industry. The costs of services, including medical research programs, can rise unquestioned because they are subsidized by the seemingly bottomless pit of tax-supported and corporate funding. In 1960, patients paid 56% of health costs out of their own pockets. By 1991, that dropped to 22%, but the more insurance Americans had, the more doctors and hospitals resorted to the use of expensive technologies.

Each year health-care costs rise at a rate that would be unacceptable in any other segment of our economy. Physicians' incomes have far outstripped the average rates of increase for incomes over the past twenty years. Since 1970, total health care expenditures have risen 60% faster than general inflation.

Employers' average annual health-insurance costs per employee have increased from $1,645 to $3,605 in the last six years. Health benefits represented almost 20% of corporate profits in 1970. By 1990, these costs represented more than half the value of businesses' pre-tax profits. If current trends continue, health care spending will equal almost 75% of corporate pre-tax profits. This is the reason why recent surveys of owners of large companies show considerable support for government intervention in the health care crisis. What the nature of that intervention should be is widely disputed.

The American people in general respond favorably to the idea of a nationalized health care system that will provide them the security of guaranteed coverage, but the tax burden necessary to pay for such a program is usually considered unacceptable. European economies are

Doctor and hospital fees grow unchecked because we are a free-market country with a huge government-funded health care program that supplements an equally huge private insurance industry.

straining under these extremely high rates of taxation on individuals and businesses alike, and Americans traditionally regard these levels of taxation as destructive to the economy and the free market system. At the same time, Americans are accustomed to unlimited medical care. Any nationalized plan requires some limits on fees and services, as well as higher taxes. Americans are resistant to these changes.

Another point raised by analysts of the current crisis is the fact that free market forces depend on informed purchasers who know what they are choosing to buy or not to buy. In the case of health services, these choices are usually handed over to doctors as a part of the traditional relationship of trust between doctor and patient. There is a temptation to offer more services than are necessary, and to charge higher and higher fees, because they seem to cost the patient nothing. An article in the *New England Journal of Medicine* in 1990 reported the results of a study showing that higher health expenditures in the U.S. are explained entirely by higher fees. The study showed that the quantity of physician's services per capita is actually lower in the U.S. than in Canada, but U.S. fees for procedures are more than three times as high as in Canada.

Physicians' fees represent one fifth of U.S. medical expenditures. The mean income of a self-employed American physician is $170,000, about 5.2 times the average. German doctors average about $110,000 annually, which is 4.3 times the average. The salaries of specialists are usually significantly higher.

- Salaries of CEOs of large hospitals currently average $236,000 a year.
- Salaries of CEOs of the largest pharmaceutical companies average $6.6 million in 1992.
- Salaries of CEOs of the largest health insurers average $1.2 million annually.

The basic flaws in the system must be addressed. A privately operated but publicly funded health-care system—without cost controls and without consumer awareness—has resulted in the budget crisis we are facing in the U.S. today. There are no easy answers.

Cost of Services

Most of the scientific breakthroughs and advances in medical technology have improved the quality of our lives and increased life expectancy. However, the cost is high. Some of the average costs of new high-tech procedures are as follows:

Cost of Services

Procedure	Cost
Premature birth	$150,000
Liver transplant	$150,000
Bone marrow transplant	$105,000
Kidney transplant	$75,000
Heart bypass	$40,000
Heart transplant	$90,000
Knee surgery	$15,000
Back surgery (disc removal)	$10,450
Hysterectomy	$7,850
Cesarean section	$7,710
Gall bladder surgery	$7,500
Appendectomy	$7,200

As the AIDS epidemic spreads, and as the elderly population grows, the strain on public and private health insurance providers grows.

As the AIDS epidemic spreads, and as the elderly population grows, the strain on public and private health insurance providers grows. Aetna's average lifetime medical claim for AIDS is about $60,000 per person and rising. One million to 1.5 million people are estimated to be infected by the HIV virus currently. The elderly population, which requires more health care than other segments of the population, grew by 37% from 1950 to 1980.

U.S. Health Care Costs from 1960 to 1990

	1960	1990
Total (in billions)	$27.1	$666.20
Private insurance and out-of-pocket (in billions)	20.5	383.60
Public insurance (in billions)	6.7	282.60
Health costs per capita	$143.00	$2,566.00
Health costs as a % of GNP	5.3%	12.2%

Timeline

1940–45

Employment-based insurance begins. Wartime regulations limit the amount employers can increase cash wages, so medical insurance is added as a non-cash addition to wage packages.

1960s

For-profit hospitals begin to proliferate. Before this time, hospitals were usually not-for-profit and balanced their budgets with private donations.

1965

Health care spending is less than 10% of corporate operating costs. Health care expenditures as a percentage of GNP are 5.9%.

Medicare/Medicaid is established as a government program providing health care to the elderly and the needy. Congress demands that the methods of billing and payment be identical to the private market, so that fees for services from doctors and hospitals are not questioned, limited, or regulated.

1968

President Johnson calls for reform of these Medicare/Medicaid programs because they offer no incentive to provide care efficient-

Since 1980, the

proportion of the

population under 65

without health

insurance has

increased by 25%.

ly. Johnson warns that without reform, reimbursement costs could reach $100 billion by 1975. His warning is ridiculed.

1975

Actual Medicare/Medicaid costs exceed $130 billion. A malpractice crisis disrupts the medical community when no existing insurance companies will provide malpractice insurance at any premium.

1980

Third-party payers, that is, insurance companies and the government, begin to take steps to lower and control costs.

1981

The Omnibus Budget Reconciliation Act is passed, resulting in a reduction of federal Medicaid payments of 3% in 1982, and 4.5% in 1984. Between 1981 and 1985, more than 1 million people lose their Medicaid eligibility. Of the remaining 20 million Medicaid recipients, most have reduced health-care coverage.

1983

Approximately 17% to 25% of the population under 65 are uninsured or underinsured.

Medicare introduces cost-control measures, forcing hospitals to reassess the cost of providing care to non-paying patients. In the past the costs incurred by these patients were covered through cost-shifting to paying patients. With new cost-control ceilings on services, more private, for-profit hospitals turn the poor or underinsured away, increasing the burden on public hospitals.

1980s

Recession in the early 1980s causes high unemployment and subsequent loss of insurance coverage for many Americans. Since 1980, the proportion of the population under 65 without health insurance has increased by 25%. Health-care cost inflation is outstripping the rest of the economy, rising up to 20% annually.

1986

The government spends $300 billion on defense and $400 billion on health care.

1988

Hospitals spend more than $1.3 billion on marketing and advertising.

Chrysler estimates its health care cost at $700 per vehicle; in France, it is $375; in Germany, $337; in Japan, $246; and Canada, $233.

1990

General Motors Corporation spends $32 billion on health benefits, more than it spends on steel.

1992

Health care expenditures are 13.4% of GNP; 36 million people are uninsured.

2000

Health care costs are projected to be 16% of GNP, based on current growth rates.

More Facts

- More than 40% of U.S. health care expenditures are paid by individuals. This share has increased since 1980. The remaining expenditures are divided evenly between government and business.

- Medicaid covers only about 40% of the people who live in poverty in the U.S.

- European countries with essentially universal health care spend at a fairly stable rate of 6% to 9% of GNP. The U.S. rate is 13% and rising. The lower European rate is partly due to the practice of global budgeting, which sets an annual limit for spending in any particular area of health care. This limitation in spending creates waiting lists for some non-emergency treatments in some instances. There are also substantially lower administrative costs than are incurred in the U.S.

- A recent Gallup poll reports that 91% of CEOs of the nation's largest firms felt a fundamental change is needed in the current health care system. Most (75%) favor reforming the current employment-based system, about half (53%) are willing to accept national health care if the current managed care system fails to contain costs in the next few years, and 79% support expanding public programs for the uninsured.

- Health insurance coverage varies by industry. More than 60% of workers in the agriculture, forestry, and fishing industries are uninsured. About 39% in the construction industry and 36% in retail trade lack coverage. Manufacturing has the lowest rate, with 14% uninsured.

- Medicare/Medicaid together are the fourth-largest item in the federal budget.

- Life expectancy has increased in this century from 47 years to 75 years. One fifth of the elderly will spend five years or more in a nursing home. Nearly all will exhaust their financial resources long before their stay is ended. The largest proportion of Medicaid spending is for nursing home care. In a recent Gallup poll, 72% of respondents said that long-term care of the elderly should be financed by the federal government, even if it requires a tax increase.

- During the two years leading to the 1986 elections, the health-care industry channeled more than $8.5 million through various political action committees to members of Congress. In general, the health care industry does not support any controls of fees or services.

- Average health insurance costs per employee have increased from $1,645 to $3,605 in the last six years.

In 1965, Medicare

was projected to cost

$9 billion a year by

1990. By 1983,

costs had already

exceeded $61 billion.

Who Are the Uninsured?

Employed persons and their dependents represent 77% of the approximately 37 million uninsured. Approximately 50% of the employed uninsured have insurance available through their employer, but they choose not to purchase it because of its cost. The other 50% of the employed uninsured work for employers who do not offer a group health plan. Individuals must then shop for a private health care plan, which is often unaffordable for people with low or even moderate incomes. Only 36% of firms with fewer than twenty-five employees make coverage available.

The remaining uninsured include those with incomes at or below the poverty level who are not eligible for Medicaid because of increasingly restrictive eligibility standards. The federal government sets the poverty level at $13,358 per year for a family of four. But in most states, people earning less than half that are not eligible for Medicaid. More than half the poor in America are without Medicaid coverage. The "near-poor," those within 100-200% of poverty level, are not eligible for Medicaid and often cannot afford private insurance. Also included in the uninsured are people between jobs, who have chosen not to avail themselves of individual coverage because of the cost.

Technology—When to Use it

In addition to the fee increases, a subtler problem has arisen: the technology available to diagnose and treat illness is more expensive than almost anyone can afford. When there is seemingly unlimited government or insurance company funding, extremely costly services are routinely used to prolong life for very elderly or terminally ill persons. These technologies are also routinely used to administer extra testing as insurance against malpractice suits. The complicated ethical, moral, and spiritual aspects of these practices are being much discussed during the current health care debate.

Cost Shifting

In 1965, Medicare was projected to cost $9 billion a year by 1990. By 1983, costs had already exceeded $61 billion. Ten years after

Medicare/Medicaid programs were enacted, hospital charges had risen by 300%.

In spite of this escalation, or perhaps because of it, Medicaid and Medicare reimbursement levels have declined, and now cover only a part of the cost of care rendered. The American Hospital Association estimates that 62% of hospitals in the United States lost money treating Medicare patients in 1991. These costs are shifted to those patients with private insurance plans, and the cost of these plans goes up accordingly.

Malpractice Litigation

The number of malpractice suits is growing. Damage awards have reached staggering highs. Physicians and hospitals pass on the cost of liability insurance by increasing charges for medical services. Further, due to the threat of malpractice suits, physicians practice defensive medicine, often performing extensive diagnostic tests or taking extraordinary measures that may not necessarily add to the quality of care but which serve to protect the physician from actions brought on behalf of the patient. These procedures add enormous costs to the treatment of any illness. If only 20% of all diagnostic tests are unnecessary, it is still $21 billion spent unnecessarily. In 1984, the Harvard School of Medicine estimated the annual cost of defensive medicine at $42 million. The American Medical Association (AMA) estimates that $15.5 billion are added to overall costs due to the practice of defensive medicine and that such practices account for 30-40% of all diagnostic procedures.

Malpractice insurance premiums vary by area and medical specialty. In the New York City area, the average annual rate in 1992 was $86,661.

State Mandates

During the last twenty years, states have imposed over 1000 laws mandating the inclusion of specific coverage and providers within health insurance plans. The mandates range from fertility coverage, to acupuncture, to chiropractic and podiatry, to a variety of mental health treatments. Not only are many of these benefits expensive, but

Malpractice insurance premiums vary by area and medical specialty. In the New York City area, the average annual rate in 1992 was $86,661.

because state laws are complicated and varied, the administrative costs are high and are added to the cost of premiums. These mandates do not apply to larger, self-insured employers, but small employers cannot escape them. Small employers are left with the more costly mandated insurance packages they neither want nor can afford.

Underwriting Requirements

Many of the practices designed to hold down premium costs have resulted in loss of coverage. These practices include:

- Declining either an entire group or uninsurable individuals in the group, when preexisting conditions exist that require costly treatment.
- Cancellation of a group's coverage when one employee experiences a large claim.
- Reinstatement of pre-existing condition limitations when moving to a new carrier or employer.

Lack of Encouragement for Healthy Lifestyles

Most doctors agree that the increased life expectancy realized in this century can be attributed to preventive measures such as improvements in sanitation and immunizations. However, because our system of reimbursement is based on illness rather than wellness, there is little incentive for the promotion of healthy lifestyles. Doctors and patients alike expect the medical establishment to spare no expense, even when a lifestyle change might be the better and less costly cure. Of the $550 billion spent in 1986 on health care, less than 0.3% was spent on health promotion and disease prevention.

Administrative Costs

These include the costs of marketing and administering group and individual health plans, the cost of utilization review by third parties (second opinions), and costs associated with insurers and providers complying with the various state and federal laws, as well as the cost of meeting the requirements of different insurance companies.

torn by the issues

Fraud

According to the National Health Care Anti-Fraud Association, fraud within the health care system may amount to $50 to $75 billion per year of health care expenditures. Potential fraudulent activities cited include clinics billing inflated or false charges, kickback schemes between labs and physicians, and higher charges from physician-owned diagnostic facilities and private for-profit hospitals.

Proposals for Reform

While most health plans have adopted some measures to introduce cost consideration into health care decisions, health-care planners agree that comprehensive reform of the system is crucial, not only for the health and well being of the citizenry, but also for the health of both the private and public sector of the economy. If the rate of spending continues unchecked, it could be devastating to our national economy.

The proposals for reform now under consideration can be summarized as follows:

Incremental Reform

Building on the strengths of the existing system, these proposals address those parts of the system that are not working or that are causing costs to skyrocket. Incremental multi-targeted reforms focus on specific problems. These reforms include the following:

- A basic care package available to all employers and their employees without having to prove insurability.
- Elimination of state-mandated requirements for coverage over and above what is considered basic care.
- A 100% tax deduction for the health insurance costs.
- Restrictions in the cost of initial premiums and renewal increases.
- "Portability," which is the ability to carry coverage from

While multi-targeted

solutions do not

achieve universal

coverage, the cost

savings involved are a

significant

contribution to the

resolution of the

current crisis.

one employer to another without re-satisfying pre-existing condition limitations.

- Purchasing arrangements allowing small companies to enter coalitions with other small companies to get the same cost breaks as larger employers.

- Malpractice reforms that include limiting malpractice awards, removing malpractice disputes from the judicial system to an arbitration forum, and requiring punitive damages to be paid to the state, not the plaintiff.

- Outcomes research, determining what works best for whom at what cost. The Agency for Health Care Policy and Research was created in 1989 for this purpose. Using this information, it is hoped that efficiency and cost-effectiveness will be enhanced, and waste and fraud will be eliminated.

- Reduction of administrative costs through uniform computerization of medical information.

- Prevention as a key to cost containment, including incentives for healthier lifestyles and greater encouragement to medical students to pursue careers in primary care and preventive medicine.

While multi-targeted solutions do not achieve universal coverage, the cost savings involved are a significant contribution to the resolution of the current crisis.

Medicaid Expansion

The current Medicaid program could be expanded to include all individuals whose incomes are below 100% of poverty. Families or individuals whose incomes are below 200% of poverty could buy into Medicaid with fees set on a sliding scale. This would provide coverage for most of the uninsured and would not interfere with most existing plans, but it does not adequately address the problem of soaring costs.

Health Maintenance Organizations

These organizations are already widespread and gaining in popularity. They combine a multi-specialty group of providers with a fixed monthly fee for each patient. The organization bears the risk of losses if its costs are higher than the fee received. Individual subscribers pay only nominal fees for services and prescriptions. These organizations stress preventive care and it is in their own interests to monitor costs and use of services. They are not inclined to accept higher-risk patients.

Preferred Provider Organizations

These are managed care arrangements under which providers (hospitals and doctors) agree to provide discounted fee-for-service health care. PPO subscribers may use any physician or hospital, but if they select a preferred provider, they are charged a lower deductible or receive a more favorable co-insurance rate.

The Personal Choice Option

As outlined by the Heritage Foundation, this proposal requires all heads of households to buy a basic insurance package, the cost of which would be subsidized by tax credits granted to the family. The poor would receive vouchers for this purchase. One important element of this proposal is that health care insurance would no longer be tied to an individual's employer. Consumers could pick and choose between many competitive groups, and this would theoretically bring costs down. This proposal assumes health care costs would decline with consumers becoming more and more cost-conscious. The current tax credit for employer-provided health coverage would be eliminated, and individuals would receive tax breaks to subsidize health care costs.

Preferred Provider Organization subscribers may use any physician or hospital, but if they select a preferred provider, they are charged a lower deductible or receive a more favorable co-insurance rate.

Employer Mandates
(Pay or Play)

These proposals are based on the premise that the vast majority of citizens are covered through the employer/employee health insurance mechanism. Under these plans, employers would be required to provide basic coverage through private insurance companies or pay a payroll tax for coverage under a government plan. The initial tax is estimated at 7%–9% of payroll. Increases may be required in the future, even with rigorous cost-containment mechanisms in place. The unemployed would be covered by the government program. Some proposals include an individual mandate, requiring everyone to participate in the plan offered to them, whether public or private. No one would remain uninsured.

This system would change the way the health insurance industry operates. Coverage would be available to all employees without having to prove insurability. Initial and renewal premium rates would be restricted and satisfaction of pre-existing condition limitations could be carried by the employees to other plans. The most comprehensive of these proposals would incorporate Medicaid into the public program, resulting in a plan that effectively provides universal coverage.

Cost-containment would be addressed by establishing a federal board or commission responsible for developing annual health care spending targets. The board would negotiate prices with representatives of all interested parties to set binding payment rates. If consensus could not be reached this commission would be empowered to set rates.

Very few pay-or-play solutions provide a truly comprehensive plan for addressing the underlying cause of rising health care costs, which is the lack of market controls that normally exist between consumer and producer. They do recognize the importance of developing technology assessment (need vs. cost), malpractice reform, preventive medicine, and managed care as keys to cost-containment.

Many fear that a pay-or-play plan would encourage a significant number of employers to shift to the government program as the less costly of the two options. Some predict as many as 35% of workers currently covered by employers would shift to the government plan, requiring ever-increasing tax revenues. Another cost is in jobs. Many employers indicate they will eliminate jobs or cut back hours to avoid the mandated costs of insuring full-time employees.

torn by the issues

The health insurance

industry would be

severely disrupted by

implementation of

national health

insurance.

Single Payer or
National Health Insurance

These proposals make the government the sole provider of coverage. This is a tax-financed universal-coverage plan similar to those in Canada and most western European democracies. These single-payer plans extend coverage to every citizen at birth for hospital and physician services as well as preventive health care needs. Cost containment is achieved through setting fee structures and budgets for providers, restricting covered services, and restrictive budgeting for the purchase of expensive technologies. Administrative costs are lower in these countries. While U.S. health insurance administrative costs average around 12% for large firms, Medicare's administrative costs are 2.3% of its budget, and administrative costs for the Canadian plan are only 1.4%.

The health insurance industry would be severely disrupted by implementation of national health insurance, although the use of private insurers is growing in European countries as people seek to supplement the basic government coverage.

These single-payer government programs are financed by a combination of income, sales and other taxes. The level of taxation in countries with national health care plans is significantly higher than in the U.S. In some cases, the rate is more than doubled when sales and other taxes are taken into account. Consumers in single-payer countries report some rationing of non-emergency services. However, the quality of basic care has not appreciably deteriorated in these countries. Societal health indicators, such as infant mortality rates, life expectancy rates, disease rates, and the like, compare favorably with those in the U.S. Along with lower administrative costs, health expenditures under these plans account for a significantly lower percentage of GDP.

Health Care Costs as a Percentage of GDP

U.S. 13.2

GERMANY 8.5

FRANCE 9.1

JAPAN 6.6

BRITAIN...6.6

These lower costs are accomplished by providing less care, paying less to providers, and maintaining very low administrative costs.

The Canadian System

This system is funded mainly through sales and income taxes. Premiums are charged in some areas, and these premiums are subsidized for the poor. Employers sometimes subsidize the premiums for their employees, and sometimes additional benefits are offered. Private insurers are available, but they are prohibited from offering plans that compete with the basic government plan. Canada pays a lower percentage of its GNP (about two thirds as much) than the U.S. does for its health care.

Because of strict government budgeting, many hospitals are unable to buy special diagnostic or therapeutic equipment. There are waiting lists for non-emergency procedures. U.S. technology is more advanced and many Canadians come to the U.S. seeking certain kinds of high-tech services. However, all Canadians do have the security of guaranteed basic health care.

The United Kingdom System

The British have a national health care system that provides universal coverage. It is financed by a small compulsory insurance premium (about 5% of wages) for employed and self-employed people, nominal charges (about 5% of cost) for drugs and appliances. The remaining 90% is government-funded. As the government program experiences rising costs and is forced to cut back services, more and more people are buying private insurance to supplement their coverage.

The German System

This system has preserved patient choice, high-quality care and provider autonomy while achieving a fairly stable rate of spending at about 8% of GNP. It is financed mainly by payroll taxes. Purchase of private insurance for expanded coverage is commonplace.

torn by the issues

Income Taxes in the U.S., Britain & Germany (1992)

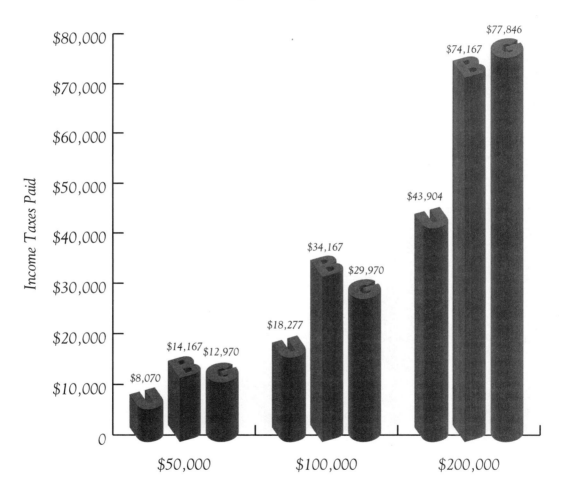

Income Taxes Paid

Income

Managed Competition

One of the current system's largest flaws is the traditional fee-for-services practice whereby a hospital or a physician makes an unquestioned decision about what services are given, and they are paid more for doing more, regardless of whether the care is necessary or appropriate. Managed competition seeks to replace fee-for-service with a market-based system designed to spur cost-conscious, informed choice among consumers and employers and to reward providers who deliver price and quality value.

Individuals, small employers, and large employers alike would band together in health alliances to achieve lower costs through bulk pricing. The federal government would define a "core benefit package" to provide a uniform product, thereby enabling these alliances to comparison shop. Provider plans like HMOs and insurance companies would have to compete for the business of these large alliances, thus providing incentives to keep their bids low. Health alliances (buyers) would contract with insurance companies or managed care providers like today's HMOs (sellers). Employers would contribute to these semi-public corporations, and the unemployed would be offered a subsidized opportunity to choose one of them. Large employers could negotiate with HMOs directly, as they do now, or they could choose to self-insure. Small employers could use the alliance as a collective purchasing agency and pay bulk rates through a competitive, pooled arrangement.

These alliances would have the power to drive hard bargains with health provider networks. There would be competition to see who could offer the best service for the lowest price. Doctors' and hospitals' services and fees would be carefully scrutinized before payments were made. The desire to win the contract with these large alliances would encourage medical networks to hold down charges and maintain quality.

The Clinton Plan

In October of 1993, President Bill Clinton proposed sweeping reforms for the health care system. His plan is basically a managed competition system as outlined above, that would include caps on

The cost (in the
Clinton Plan) is
predicted at
approximately
$1,800 per individual
and $4,200 per
family per year.

spending. It would require consumers to share in the costs, with employers covering 80% in most cases and consumers covering 20%. There would be tax exemptions for the cost of the basic core benefit package. The cost is predicted at approximately $1,800 per individual, and $4,200 per family per year. The cost of the plan, which is estimated at $400 to $500 billion, is to be covered by eliminating waste and fraud, cutting administrative costs, possible sales taxes on tobacco and gasoline, and contributions from employers and employees. The proposed "core benefit package" is as follows:

- **Professional Services:** Doctor's office visits, emergency room care, and ambulance fees.

- **Hospitalization:** Semi-private room.

- **Preventive Care:** Immunizations, prenatal and infant checkups, cholesterol screening, physicals with increased frequency as patient ages. Mammograms for women over 50.

- **Long Term Care:** Nursing homes and rehabilitation centers are covered as an alternative to hospital stays, with a maximum of 100 days in a calendar year.

- **Home Care:** Covered as an alternative to hospital stays. Need for further care would be assessed every 60 days.

- **Eye and Ear:** Routine exams, children's eyeglasses.

- **Outpatient Therapy:** Occupational, physical or speech therapy to restore functions lost because of illness or injury. Need reassessed every 60 days.

- **Dental Care:** Preventive care for children. Adult care would be phased in starting in 2000.

- **Prescription Drugs:** $5 per prescription or a $250 yearly maximum depending on the plan you choose.

- **Hospice:** For terminally ill patients as an alternative to hospital stay.

- **Mental Health:** Initially, 30 days of inpatient care per episode of illness, up to 60 days in a year; up to 30 outpatient visits to a psychotherapist; by the year 1998, 90 inpatient days; no limit on outpatient visits.

- **Substance Abuse:** Similar to mental health.
- **Medical Equipment:** Prostheses and braces that improve function or prevent deterioration.

This and other plans will be discussed extensively by Congress and the voters before a final decision is made. It promises to be a long and heated debate.

Sources

"Access to Health Care: The American Debate." *The Principal Financial Group Newsletter*, September/November 1992.

Congressional Budget Office, U.S. Congress. *Selected Options for Expanding Health Insurance Coverage*. Washington, D.C.: U.S. Government Printing Office, 1991.

———. *Universal Health Insurance Coverage Using Medicare's Payment Rates*. Washington, D.C.: U.S. Government Printing Office, 1991.

Easterbrook, Gregg. "The National Health Care Phobia." *Newsweek*, 6 September 1993.

"Health Care Reform and New Decisions for Business." *Forbes Magazine*, November 1992.

Hurst, Jeremy. "Reform of Health Care in Germany." *Health Care Financing Review*, 1991.

Long, Robert Emmett, ed. *The Crisis in Health Care: The Reference Shelf*. New York: H.W. Wilson Company, 1991.

National Education Association. *The U.S. Health Care Crisis: Symptoms, Causes, Cures*. Washington, D.C.: NEA Research Division, 1992.

Organization for Economic Cooperation and Development. *Health Care Systems in Transition: The Search for Efficiency*. Washington, D.C.: OECD Publication Service, 1990.

Paine, L.W.H., and Siem Tjam. *Hospitals and the Health Care Revolution*. Geneva: World Health Organization, 1988.

Pearman, William, and Philip Starr. *Medicare: A Handbook on the History and Issues of Health Care Services for the Elderly*. New York: Garland Publishing, Inc., 1988.

Roemer, Milton Irwin. *National Health Systems*. Oxford: Oxford University Press, 1991.

Rosenthal, Marilyn M., and Marcell Frenkel, eds. *Health Care Systems and Their Patients: An International Perspective*. Boulder: Westview Press, 1992.

Samuelson, Robert J., et al. "Special Report: Health Care." *Newsweek*, 4 October 1993.

Taylor, Malcolm G. *Insuring National Health Care: The Canadian Experience*. Chapel Hill: University of North Carolina Press, 1990.

U.S. Department of Labor, Health and Welfare Benefits Administration. *A Look at Health Benefits and the Workforce*. Washington, D.C.: U.S. Government Printing Office, 1992.

U.S. Department of Commerce, Bureau of Census. *Statistical Abstract of the United States, 1991*. Washington, D.C.: U.S. Government Printing Office, 1991.

World Health Organization. *From Alma-Ata to the Year 2000*. Geneva: World Health Organization, 1988.

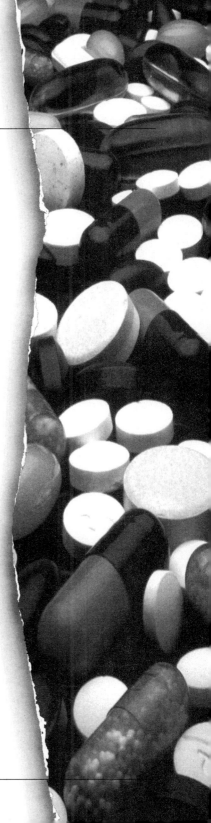

drug abuse

drug
abuse

the use of drugs to alter mood and perception is as old as or older than the institutions of law, medicine, agriculture, industry, and religion. Stone Age cave paintings depict our prehistoric ancestors using plant substances for ritual or social purposes. Currently we define drug abuse as any use of a substance that has a psychological or physiological effect on the human organism other than the uses that are socially, medically, or legally accepted.

Although drug abuse research includes the study of drug addiction, the two terms are not synonymous. Addiction to a substance carries with it a craving, along with a physical dependence, that motivates continuing use of the substance. The addict develops physical tolerance to the effects of the drug, and specific, identifiable symptoms appear when it is withdrawn. By some standards, the definition of drug abuse can include even occasional, nonaddictive use of a substance, if that substance is illegally obtained.

The use of legal drugs such as tobacco and caffeine is not usually included in discussions of drug abuse, as they do not cause dysfunction for the individual and the resulting problems for society. Alcohol abuse is usually considered as a distinct and separate problem because it is somewhat more socially acceptable in this society; also, since it is legally obtainable, its relationship to violent crime is less pronounced.

The Cost of Drug Abuse is High

- Cost to rehabilitate a drug abuser: $3,000 to $14,000 depending on the type of therapy.

- Intravenous drug use accounts for one third of the more than one million people who are now HIV-positive. Average long-term cost of caring for a person with AIDS: $60,000.

- More than 550,000 drug-exposed babies are born each year. Median daily hospital costs are $5,500. Total cost of care for these newborns until age 1: $51 million.

- Nearly 50% of federal prison inmates and 70% of state inmates have a history of drug abuse, and 50% of federal prisoners are serving time for drug-related crimes. Average yearly cost per incarceration: $16,946.

- Drug abuse accounts for a 29% increase in the number of children placed in foster care, from 280,000 in 1987 to 360,000 in 1989. Annual cost of care: $36,000.

- Thirty years ago, the U.S. Supreme Court ruled that drug addiction is a disease, not a crime. This issue and the associated issue of legalization of controlled substances have been matters of great controversy in recent years.

Pro-Criminalization

An overwhelming percentage of Americans are against the legalization of drugs. A recent Gallup poll (January 1990) showed that 80% of those questioned thought that legalizing heroin, cocaine, and marijuana would have disastrous effects on society. Most feel that legalization would create increased availability of drugs at a significantly reduced cost, and that drug use would increase beyond measure. In the same poll, 65% of the respondents thought that drug use in public schools would increase, 67% thought the number of drug addicts would increase, and 63% thought the cases of drug overdoses would increase. The elimination of criminality from the use of drugs, along with cheaper prices and easier access, would dramatically increase the number of first-time users and, subsequently, the number of addicts, a number already far too high.

It is estimated that the current price of heroin sold on the black market is 200 times higher than if it were legal and marketed under a system based solely on supply and demand. Legalization might reduce some drug-related crime, but it would increase the availability and use of drugs.

The annual number of deaths from illegal drugs is estimated at 3000 to 4000. The number of deaths from tobacco and alcohol is over a hundred times as great. If all dangerous drugs were legalized, the number of deaths would match those from legal substances.

It is estimated that the current price of heroin sold on the black market is 200 times higher than if it were legal and marketed under a system based on supply and demand.

Those in favor of

legalization or

decriminalization of

drugs argue that the

removal of drugs

from the black

market would

substantially reduce

the incidence of

violent crime

associated with drug

dealing.

Pro-Legalization

Those in favor of legalization or decriminalization of drugs argue that the removal of drugs from the black market would substantially reduce the incidence of violent crime associated with drug dealing. In addition to this benefit, a significant portion of the billions of dollars going to drug traffickers would instead go to local, state, and federal governments as tax revenues. This money could be spent on education, prevention, and rehabilitation. Government control would allow licensed production and distribution of drugs, effectively insuring the public against impure or overly potent products. Controlled distribution of drug paraphernalia, especially syringes, would reduce the spread of AIDS and other infectious diseases. The current system of drug-prohibition has proved to be incredibly costly and is generally ineffective.

The U.S. has an incarceration rate higher than any other nation in the world. The cost of prosecuting and incarcerating drug cases costs the American economy an estimated $80 billion a year.

The criminality of drug use benefits criminals. Figures range from $10 billion to $50 billion in annual sales of illicit drugs; the sale of illicit drugs is believed to account for over half of all organized crime revenue.

Federal cocaine seizures in fiscal year 1990 amounted to about 10% of the total amount used during that period in the U.S.

Approaches to the Control of Drug Abuse

Although drug use is widespread in human society, the belief that it should be controlled or, in some cases, prohibited by law, is equally widespread. Two reasons are generally given for legal intervention in drug use:

- The negative effects that the uncontrolled use of these substances has upon the user (general poor health, physical and mental diseases, violent behavior, and premature death.)

- The undesirable effects on the culture at large of nonproductive, antisocial, and criminal behavior.

The debate over how to address the problem of drug abuse has been going on in human society for centuries. The question in the U.S. is whether the federal government, the medical profession, or the education institution is best qualified to bring about an end to drug abuse.

Governmental response has, for the most part, leaned toward more and more laws against drugs and increasingly strict enforcement of those laws. This approach assumes that illegal drug use is an antisocial vice, chosen by criminally inclined individuals who must be restrained from this behavior.

The medical profession's response, at least within the past forty years, has been that drug use is nearly universal, that drug addiction is a disease, and that a number of factors determine a predisposition towards abuse. Therapy is thus the obvious avenue of approach.

The proposed budget of the U.S. government for 1993 estimates that the total funds to be allocated for the control of drug abuse will be in excess of $12 billion, of which $8.6 billion is directed to drug law enforcement, $1.8 billion is earmarked for drug-use prevention programs, and $2.3 billion is for addiction treatment services. The percentage increase since 1989 is 88% for law enforcement, 121% for drug-use prevention, and 94% for treatment services. The total cost to the American economy for prosecution and incarceration of drug users and traffickers could be as high as $80 billion.

In 1993, treatment for drug abuse will be provided to over 311,000 drug users, a 19% increase over 1992.

The causes of both drug abuse and addiction have been researched extensively since World War II, giving rise to many theories. Statistical analysis seems to indicate that the stresses inherent in poverty, urban living, and the fast pace of modern life determine to some degree the predisposition toward drug abuse. To date, however, there is no unified theory that could be used to design a comprehensive prevention program that includes all types and classes of drug abusers.

The one underlying factor that can be readily observed, when individual motivations are reduced to their lowest common denominator, is that human beings will tend to enhance, negate, or otherwise alter their physical, mental, and emotional sensations when faced with the various pleasant or unpleasant circumstances of life, and they will readily use drugs, legal or illegal, to do so.

Timeline

10,000–4,000 BC

Primitive peoples use various psychoactive nuts, leaves, berries, and mushrooms for energy, fearlessness, and ritual ceremonies. Opium is used in the Middle East.

800 BC–AD 400

Greek and Roman physicians prescribe opium as medicine.

AD 600

Arabian traders take opium to China and India.

1500–1700

Opium is used in many standard medicines. Thomas Sydenham, a respected seventeenth-century physician, writes that opium is "one of the most valued medicines in the world [and] does more to honor medicine than any other remedy whatsoever." Its use is so extensive that the withdrawal syndrome is noted and described by John Jones in 1700.

Tobacco use is prohibited in several European countries, after it is introduced by traders returning from the colonies in North America. In Germany, the death penalty is introduced for tobacco users in 1691.

The Portuguese begin selling opium to the Chinese on a large scale. The British cultivate large opium plantations in India when they realize the commercial potential of the China trade.

torn by the issues

1531

Along with his discovery of the Inca Empire, Francisco Pizarro learns of the Incan habit of chewing coca leaves for their stimulating, fatigue-dispelling effect.

1611

American colonists in Jamestown import hemp (marijuana) to be cultivated primarily for fiber.

1709

Thomas Dover, a student of Thomas Sydenham, introduces Dover's Powder, a patent medicine, almost one third of which is opium.

1729

The Chinese government outlaws opium.

1803

Frederick Serturner isolates the chief alkaloid of opium and names it morphine, after Morpheus, the Greek god of dreams.

1831

Laboratory scientists discover more than two dozen other opiate alkaloids, including codeine.

1830s

English traders smuggle half a million pounds of opium into China every year.

1839

English traders continue to smuggle opium into China in exchange for silks and spices. The Chinese begin confiscating these shipments, leading to the so-called Opium Wars.

MID-1800s

The hypodermic syringe is used to inject drugs directly into the body. Of the many substances injected experimentally, morphine is found to be an effective pain killer and calming agent and finds its way into medical practice after the Civil War.

1852

The American Pharmaceutical Association is established.

1855

The German chemist Freidrich Gaedke isolates alkaloidal cocaine from coca leaves. During the latter part of the nineteenth century, Angelo Mariani of Corsica produces an extract of the coca leaf that he mixes with wine and calls Vin Coca Mariani, a magical drink touted to free the body from fatigue, lift the spirits, and create a lasting sense of well being. For his effort he receives a medal of appreciation from Pope Leo XIII, who used the drink as a source of comfort in his retirement.

1870

Cannabis (marijuana) is included in U.S. pharmacopoeia, leading to the preparation and sale of various forms of the herb in pharmacies throughout the country. Over one hundred articles recommending its use are published in medical journals between 1840 and 1900.

1874

British chemist C.R.A. Wright discovers diacetylmorphine hydrochloride while experimenting with the effect of combining various acids with morphine. Twenty-four years later, in 1898, Bayer and Company, the famous aspirin manufacturer, begins marketing diacetylmorphine under the trade name heroin. Due in large part to the ignorance of the medical and scientific community concerning both the effective dosages and addictive qualities of heroin, the drug quickly finds its way into routine medical prescriptions and over-the-counter medicines.

1875

The city of San Francisco passes an ordinance banning the smoking of opium in opium dens, but continues to allow the production and sale of over-the-counter medications containing opium. Opium smoking has become widespread in the U.S. among not only the criminal classes, but also the more respectable middle and upper classes. In 1888, an examination of 10,000 prescriptions from Boston-area pharmacies finds that some 15% contained opiates. In 1900, it is estimated that in the small state of Vermont, 3.3 million doses of opium were sold each month. Data collected by the U.S. Public Health Service (in 1924) indicates that more than 7000 tons of crude opium and 800 tons of smoking opium were imported during the four-decade period ending in 1889.

1880

German laboratory scientists synthesize amphetamines.

1883

Dr. Theodore Aschenbrandt, a German military physician, procures a quantity of cocaine, which he gives to Bavarian soldiers during maneuvers. He notes the drug's ability to suppress fatigue. Also during this year, the tariff imposed on imported smoking opium is raised from $6 to $10 per pound in an attempt to curtail importation into the U.S.

1884

Noting Dr. Aschenbrandt's account of his 1883 experiment, Sigmund Freud begins his research on cocaine by testing its effectiveness in rehabilitating morphine addicts and observing the subjective results of ingesting the drug himself. Freud is initially enthused about cocaine, but toward the end of the 1880s withdraws his support in light of increased reporting of compulsive use and undesirable side effects.

During the 1880s, cocaine achieved popularity in the United States as a general tonic, as a treatment for sinusitis and hay fever, and as a cure for opium, morphine, and alcohol habits. The Parke-Davis Company sells coca-leaf cigarettes and cigars, along with

Although opium is

recognized as

addictive prior to

1900, there are no

moral sanctions

against its use.

other products such as "Coca Cordial" (a liqueur-type drink), cocaine tablets, hypodermic injections, ointments, and sprays.

1885

John Styth Pemberton of Atlanta, Georgia, noting Angelo Mariani's success with Vin Coca Mariani, develops a new product that he registers as French Wine Coca—"Ideal Nerve and Tonic Stimulant." The following year, Pemberton adds an additional ingredient, changes the drink from a medicinal preparation to a soft drink, and in 1886 renames it Coca Cola.

1887

Weak opium (less than 9% morphine) is outlawed and the Chinese are prohibited from importing opium. Sears, Roebuck and Company advertises hypodermic kits in their mail order catalogue. The kit includes a syringe, two needles, two vials, and a carrying case and sells for $1.50.

1898

The practice of smoking marijuana is introduced to the American public via Mexico where its use has become prevalent. Up until the end of the nineteenth century, marijuana is used primarily for medical purposes.

1906

The U.S. Congress passes the Pure Food and Drug Act which requires medicine manufacturers to list ingredients. Later amendments require exact amounts of ingredients to be listed as well.

The District of Columbia Pharmacy Act permits any physician to prescribe narcotics for addicts when "necessary for the cure" of addiction. The prescribing of narcotic drugs to non-addicted persons is limited to the treatment of injury or disease.

Although opium is recognized as addictive prior to 1900, there are no moral sanctions against its use. By the early 1900s there are an estimated 250,000 opium addicts in the U.S. (3.4% of the population). Among the many patent medicines containing opiates are

torn by the issues

those sold to women for the alleviation of menstrual discomfort, giving rise to a substantial number of white, middle-class, female opium addicts well into the early 1900s.

Until the passage of the Pure Food and Drug Act, not even infants were protected from narcotized medicines. Among those on the market prior to the Harrison Act (see below) were "Mrs. Winslow's Soothing Syrup" and "Hooper's Anodyne, the Infant's Friend."

1909

Passage of the Smoking Opium Exclusion Act outlaws the importation of smoking opium into the U.S. President Theodore Roosevelt calls for an International Opium Convention to be held in Shanghai.

1910

A national survey conducted by Dr. Hamilton Wright concludes that about 2% of doctors and 1% of nurses are addicted to some form of opiate while only 0.7% of other professional classes are addicted.

1911

The Hague International Opium Convention convenes to negotiate the control of opiates on the international level.

1912

Dr. Charles E. Terry, a Jacksonville, Florida, physician, establishes the first city-sponsored drug clinic for the treatment of addicts.

1914

The Harrison Act is passed by the Congress, requiring the systematic, controlled marketing of opium, morphine, heroin, and cocaine in small over-the-counter quantities. The law requires a physician's prescription for larger quantities and requires anyone who imports, manufactures, produces, compounds, sells, dispenses, or otherwise distributes these products to register with the

In 1909, the Smoking Opium Exclusion Act outlaws the importation of smoking opium into the U.S.

Treasury Department, pay special taxes, and keep records of all transactions. Laws affecting marijuana trafficking and use are omitted from the enacted version. This legislation effectively makes opium and opium-containing products virtually unavailable to hundreds of thousands of people who had developed addictions when the drug was legal. It makes the unauthorized use of opium a "crime," and existing addicts seek black market sources to alleviate their discomfort.

1915

The *New York Medical Journal* refutes the theory that drug abuse is a vice and suggests that it may be a "compromise, or an adjustment to the conditions…of the American way of life."

1919

The Supreme Court fundamentally upholds the Harrison Act in *Webb v. U.S.* in 1919, and *U.S. v. Behrman* in 1922.

The Congress passes the Eighteenth Amendment to the U.S. Constitution outlawing the production, sale, and use of alcohol. By the mid-1920s, there are 30,000 illegal clubs dispensing alcohol in New York State alone. When, after fourteen years, the use of alcohol appears to be going up rather than down, the law is repealed by the Twenty-First Amendment. Within a few years after Prohibition ends, reports indicate that the production and consumption of alcohol have fallen by 50%.

1922

The federal Jones-Miller Act allows fines up to $5,000 and imprisonment up to 10 years for the unlawful manufacture, importation, or exportation of certain habit-forming drugs, notably cocaine and opium products. There are an estimated 110,000 affected addicts in the U.S. by the end of 1922.

1925

The Supreme Court disavows the premises of the Harrison Act in *Lindner v. U.S.*, in which it holds that addicts are entitled to medical care. The ruling, however, has almost no effect, due to the

torn by the issues

unwillingness of physicians to treat addicts under any circumstances. The establishment of the illicit drug black market allows addicts to obtain such drugs fairly easily.

1928

Statistical accounts found in *The Opium Problem*, which Dr. Charles Terry coauthors with Mildred Pellens in 1928, indicates that, in the Jacksonville area, white addicts outnumber blacks by almost two to one (although the population was half white and half black), and female addicts outnumber male addicts three to two.

1929

The Porter Act provides for federal funding to build and maintain two drug treatment farms (in Lexington, Kentucky, and Fort Worth, Texas) to house those undergoing treatment after being convicted of the "crime" of drug addiction.

1930

The Federal Bureau of Narcotics (FBN) is the first federal agency established specifically to control illicit drugs.

1915–1933

Every state west of the Mississippi passes legislation prohibiting marijuana.

1936

The U.S. sends a delegation to the Conference for the Suppression of the Illicit Traffic in Dangerous Drugs held in Geneva, Switzerland. Twenty-six other nations are in attendance. The U.S. seeks to include a requirement for the control of marijuana in the final recommendations. When its proposals concerning marijuana are rejected, the U.S. refuses to sign the treaty.

1930–1937

During its first seven years, the FBN minimizes the marijuana problem, leaving the responsibility for its control to state governments. Government officials in the southwestern states begin to apply pressure for federal anti-marijuana legislation. This lobbying is a result of the fear generated in the white population by the growing Mexican immigrant population, which is largely unemployed during the depression years and uses marijuana extensively.

1937

The federal Marijuana Tax Act imposes strict control and reporting requirements on the production and sale of marijuana, which effectively prohibits its use.

1938

Dr. Albert Hoffman of Sandoz Research Labs isolates D-lysergic acid diethylamide (LSD). It remains in his laboratory unnoticed until April 16, 1943, when, after accidentally absorbing some through the skin of his fingers, he begins to hallucinate, thereby taking the first LSD "trip."

1939

World War II intervenes, cutting off supplies of opium from Asia and interrupting the trafficking routes from Europe. For the remainder of the war, narcotics addiction in the U.S. all but disappears.

1942

The federal Opium Poppy Act regulates legal cultivation of opium poppies in the U.S.

1946–1949

Opium-heroin trafficking networks from Southeast Asia and Europe are reestablished, and illicit narcotics once again begin to reach American ports. The modern "drug problem" begins to take shape when several large American cities begin to report an epidemic of heroin use among young minority males.

torn by the issues

1951

The Boggs Act increases federal penalties for all drug law violators. It also makes penalties for marijuana violations the same as those for narcotic drugs and introduces the concept of minimum mandatory sentences for drug law offenders.

1955

The Joint Committee of the American Medical and Bar Associations (AMA/ABA) on Narcotic Drugs is appointed. Within three years, its Interim Report recommends softer drug penalties and a re-evaluation of clinic use and addiction maintenance.

1956

The Narcotic Control Act further empowers the federal government to mete out harsher sentences to drug law offenders. Capital punishment becomes a judicial option for anyone over eighteen selling narcotics to anyone under eighteen.

1961

The Single Convention on Narcotic Drugs, adopted by the United Nations, states that each participating country may "adopt such measures as may be necessary to prevent misuse of, and illicit traffic in, the leaves of the cannabis plant."

1962

The U.S. Supreme Court rules that drug addiction is a disease and not a crime.

1963

President John F. Kennedy appoints the Advisory Commission on Narcotic and Drug Abuse (the Prettyman Commission) to review the drug problem. Among its recommendations are:

- Decrease use of mandatory minimum sentences.
- Increase research appropriations.

- Transfer the FBN to the Department of Health, Education and Welfare.
- Return final judgment on the legitimate use of narcotics to the medical profession.

1964–1974

Middle-class American youths become involved in heroin use. Substantial numbers of military personnel in Vietnam become regular users of the inexpensive heroin available there. Marijuana, LSD, amphetamines, and sundry other psychotropic drugs are rapidly becoming widely used in the hippie counterculture.

1965

New York City begins a large-scale experimental methadone program for the treatment of heroin addicts.

1966

The Narcotic Addict Rehabilitation Act (NARA) is enacted as a direct result of the Prettyman Commission's recommendation "to provide an alternative method of handling the federally convicted offender who is a confirmed narcotic or marijuana user."

1969

On September 21, the U.S. government launches "Operation Intercept," an effort to stem the flow of illicit marijuana from Mexico through an intensive border inspection procedure. Twenty days later, it is abandoned due to the complaints of Mexican merchants and American tourists.

1970

The Comprehensive Drug Abuse Prevention and Control Act repeals all prior federal legislation on marijuana and reduces federal penalties for possession and sale of marijuana. Possession is reduced from a felony to a misdemeanor offense.

More Americans are evacuated from Vietnam for drug-related reasons than for war injuries.

torn by the issues

1971

On June 17, President Richard M. Nixon addresses Congress, outlining his plans to curtail illicit drugs from entering and being used in the U.S. This is the advent of the war on drugs.

1972

Conservative economist Milton Friedman calls for an end to drug prohibition in *Newsweek* magazine.

1973

Oregon repeals its prohibition on the use of marijuana.

1974

Of $4 million used by the U.S. Justice Department's Drug Enforcement Agency (DEA) for drug purchases in their pursuit of upper-echelon drug traffickers, more than $3.8 million is never retrieved.

1975

The Alaska Supreme Court rules that possession of marijuana for personal use by adults at home is protected by the constitutional right to privacy and hence not subject to any penalty. Similar decriminalization legislation is enacted by the governments of Colorado, Ohio, and California.

1976

Maine repeals criminal penalties for marijuana use.

1977

Mississippi, North Carolina, and New York repeal criminal penalties for marijuana use.

1978

Nebraska repeals criminal penalties for marijuana use.

By 1984 it was

becoming evident that

drug abuse in the

U.S. had not only

not gone away, but

had grown beyond

anyone's

imagination.

1975–1980

The number of persons using marijuana during these years declined by 10 million.

1984

Nancy Reagan launches her "Just Say No" campaign.

1985

"Prescription pot" becomes a reality when the Food and Drug Administration approves commercial production of THC, a derivative of marijuana found useful in treating nausea associated with cancer chemotherapy.

A Department of Defense survey shows that 31.4% of American servicemen in Europe were using drugs such as cannabis, cocaine, and LSD, and one in ten admitted to working under the influence of drugs.

1986

President Ronald Reagan issues an Executive Order requiring federal workers to be tested for illegal drug use. The Anti-Drug Abuse Act strengthens governmental control of drug traffic.

1988

The second Anti-Drug Abuse Act authorizes an additional $2.8 billion over the original $3.5 billion for the war on drugs. President George Bush appoints William Bennett as the first director of national drug control policy. He becomes known in the popular media as the "Drug Czar." Francis L. Young, the chief administrative law judge for the DEA, calls for the legalization of marijuana for medical purposes.

1990

The number of federal, state, and municipal agencies implementing federal drug laws is estimated to be over 17,000. It is estimated that $12 billion belonging to Colombian drug cartels will remain in the U.S. to be laundered and funneled into legal investments such as stocks, bonds, real estate, and treasury bills.

From 1970, when the Comprehensive Drug Abuse Prevention and Control Act was enacted, until 1984, there were only minor changes legislated by the U.S. Congress. By 1984, however, it was becoming evident that drug abuse in the U.S. had not only not gone away, but had grown beyond anyone's imagination.

According to some reports, cocaine is the most profitable article of trade in the world.

In California, the cash value of the cannabis crop is said to be greater than the value of the grape crop—officially the state's leading agricultural product.

By 1986, Congress has resumed its attempt to control drug abuse through legislation with extensive biannual additions to the 1970 legislation. By 1990, the Comprehensive Drug Abuse Prevention and Control Act has been expanded to a volume of material that exceeds all laws passed on drug abuse in the preceding 100 years.

In 1990, the cash value of the cannabis crop in California is said to be greater than the value of the grape crop—officially the state's leading agricultural product.

Drug Use & Statistics

Most of the following statistical data is drawn from the 1990 Household Survey on Drug Abuse conducted by the National Institute on Drug Abuse (NIDA). Because of the illegal status of these substances, the responses may not have been entirely honest, even though anonymity was assured. The actual statistics regarding drug use may be higher. The responses of the population surveyed indicated that:

- Almost 75 million people (30% of the population) have used some type of illicit drug.
- Over 66 million people (26%) have used marijuana. Marijuana was the most commonly used illicit drug.
- The next most commonly used illicit drugs were prescription-type psychotherapeutic drugs obtained illegally and cocaine.
- About 24 million people (10%) have used psychotherapeutic drugs. (Psychotherapeutic drugs are a legally obtainable

class of drugs, a portion of which find their way onto the illicit drug market.)

- About 22.7 million people (9%) have used cocaine.
- About 2.7 million people (1%) have used crack cocaine.
- In excess of 10 million people (4%) have used inhalants (glue and paint fumes, gasoline fumes, amyl nitrates, etc.) as recreational drugs.
- Over 15 million people (6%) have used hallucinogens.
- Almost 14 million people (5%) have used stimulants.
- Approximately 7.5 million people (3%) have used sedatives.
- Over 8 million people have used tranquilizers.
- Almost 6 million people (3%) have used PCP, (an extremely potent form of animal tranquilizer).
- Approximately 83% of the surveyed population have used alcohol.
- Approximately 73% of the surveyed population have smoked cigarettes.
- The figures showed that more than 1.5 million people (0.75%) have used heroin. (The accuracy of heroin use statistics obtained through the National Household Survey on Drug Abuse are considered even less precise than those gathered on other drug use. The actual figures for heroin use are estimated to be significantly higher.)
- About 3.3 million people (1%) have used needles to administer illicit drugs.
- The National Association of State Alcohol and Drug Abuse Directors estimates that there were, at the time of the survey, 1.2 million intravenous (IV) drug users (0.5%) in the United States.
- By 1988, IV drug users had become the second largest group of AIDS victims in the U.S. The Centers for Disease Control estimated as of January 1988 that 23% of all reported AIDS cases were drug users.
- Researchers in the drug abuse field hold that narcotics addicts are responsible for as many as 50 million crimes each year in the U.S.

130

- Males were significantly more likely than females to have used illicit drugs.

- Use of illicit drugs, alcohol, and cigarettes peaked during the late 70s and has been declining.

- The rates of alcohol use have been more stable than for any other drugs, although the percentage of youth (18-25) who reported that they had ever used alcohol decreased dramatically from 1979 to 1990.

- Among members of the survey population, 5% could be classified as heavy drinkers. (Heavy drinking is defined as having five or more drinks per occasion, and five or more occasions during any month.)

Age Groups & Drug Use

In the NIDA survey also reported the following statistics regarding age groups and drug use:

- The prevalence of illicit drug use was highest among young adults aged 18 to 25.

- In 1990, approximately 56% of young adults had used illicit drugs in their lifetime. About 88% had used alcohol, and 70% had smoked cigarettes.

- The percentage of youth and young adults (aged 12 to 25) who had ever used illicit drugs, alcohol, or cigarettes was highest in the late 70s. Rates decreased during the 1980s to match the lowest levels recorded since the study began in the early 70s.

- In 1990, current use among young adults (18 to 25) of any illicit drug was 15%, of alcohol was 63%, and of cigarettes was 32%. This was the lowest rate since the National Household Survey began in the early 70s.

- In 1990, approximately 5% of adults (26 and older) were current users of illicit drugs: 52% were current alcohol users and 28% were current cigarette smokers.

Heroin & Other Narcotics

- The word narcotic is widely misused, often referring to any drug that is considered dangerous. In pharmacology, the word narcotic refers to a very specific group of drugs that includes the natural derivatives of the opium poppy (*Papavar somniferum*) and any synthetic derivatives of similar structure and action.

- Natural narcotics include opium, which is derived directly from *Papavar somniferum*, and morphine and codeine, which are derived from opium. Heroin is a semisynthetic narcotic. Synthetic narcotics with high potency include Methadone and Demerol, and low-potency synthetics include Darvon and Talwin.

- The number of heroin addicts in the mid-80s was estimated to have been between 300,000 and 500,000. In the U.S., it is declining. In some other parts of the developing world, it is increasing.

- Heroin overdose deaths are often the result of using too much or too potent heroin. Even more frequently, they are the result of heroin intake combined with the use of alcohol or another sedative.

Marijuana

- Marijuana is the most commonly used illicit drug. Estimates of current use in the U.S. range from 10 to 20 million people (4% to 8%).

- The percentage reporting use in their lifetime was highest in 1979. The rates of use have decreased substantially since this peak.

- According to surveys conducted by the National Organization to Reform Marijuana Laws (NORML), Americans spend $30 billion on marijuana each year. Estimates by the U.S. Forest Service, a branch of the Department of Agriculture, place the total value of marijuana grown on federal property in excess of $5 billion each year.

- According to DEA statistics, seven states—California, Hawaii,

Kansas, Kentucky, Louisiana, Missouri, and Tennessee—are the primary domestic producers of marijuana, accounting for almost four fifths of total production. It is reported to be America's second-largest cash crop.

- The National Narcotics Consumers Committee (NNCC) estimated that approximately 25% of the marijuana sold on the U.S. market in the year 1987 was domestically produced.

Cocaine

- In 1990, according to NIDA's Household Survey on Drug Abuse, approximately 23 million people, or 11%, had used cocaine in their lifetime.

- Chronic cocaine use typically causes hyperstimulation, digestive disorders, nausea, loss of appetite, weight loss, occasional convulsions, and sometimes paranoid psychoses and delusions of persecution. Cocaine can induce epileptic seizures in a person with no previous epilepsy as well as heart fibrillations that can lead to cardiac arrest.

- Rates of cocaine use were highest in the period from 1979 to 1985, but have since decreased. In 1990, rates of cocaine use were similar to those of the early 70s.

- In lab tests conducted during the 1960s, laboratory monkeys were connected intravenously to lever-operated supplies of cocaine to observe their response to the drug. In most cases, the monkeys pressed the levers repeatedly for days, until they began to have convulsions and died.

- Approximately 50% of the world's illegal cocaine is consumed in the U.S. Cocaine use in this country is considered a major health problem, with estimates of the number of regular users ranging as high as 10 to 20 million, with an additional 5000 trying the drug for the first time each day.

• In 1983, crack cocaine first appeared in the U.S. Crack is a much less expensive version of cocaine, making it much more available to younger and less-affluent sectors of the population. From 1983 to 1988, the incidence of cocaine-related deaths in the U.S. has more than doubled.

Sources

Allinson, Russel R. *Drug Abuse: How It Happens and How to Prevent It.* Lower Burrell, PA: Valley Publishers, 1983.

Ball, Rosen, et al. "The Lifetime Criminality of Heroin Addicts in the United States." *Journal of Drug Issues* No. 12, 1982.

Bonnie, Richard J., and Charles H. Whitebread II. *Marijuana Conviction: A History of Marijuana Prohibition in the United States.* Charlottesville: University of Virginia Press, 1974.

Coleman, Vernon. *The Drugs Myth.* London: Green Print/The Merlin Press, 1992.

Cooper, Mary H. "The Business of Drugs." *Congressional Quarterly,* 1990.

The Drug Abuse Council. *The Facts About Drug Abuse.* New York: Free Press, 1980.

Husak, Douglas N. *Drugs and Rights.* Cambridge: Cambridge University Press, 1992.

Inciardi, James A. *The War on Drugs: Heroin, Cocaine, Crime and Public Policy.* Palo Alto: Mayfield Publishing Co., 1986.

Long, Robert Emmett, ed. *Drugs and American Society.* New York: Wilson Publishers, 1986.

Musto, David F., M.D. *The American Disease: Origins of Narcotic Control.* New Haven: Yale University Press, 1973.

Nadelmann, Ethan A., and David T. Courtwright. "Should We Legalize Drugs? History Answers." *American Heritage*, February/March 1993.

National Institute on Drug Abuse. "Highlights from the 1990 National Household Survey on Drug Abuse." Chicago: World Book Encyclopedia, 1990.

Office of the President. *Budget of the United States Government for 1992*. Washington, D.C.: U.S. Government Printing Office, 1992.

Platt, Jerome J. *Heroin Addiction: Theory, Research and Treatment*, 2nd edition. Malabar, FL: Robert E. Krieger Publishing Co., 1986.

Wilson, James Q. "Against the Legalization of Drugs." *Commentary*, February 1990.

Since its inception in 1935, the Social Security program has been cited as one of the main reasons for the general improvement in the health, well being, and financial security of the elderly in this country. It was created when the U.S. economy was in the depths of the worst depression in its history, and the pains of unemployment and poverty were felt by a much larger portion of the society than had ever suffered that pain before.

There have been

some very strong

criticisms of the way

Social Security is

managed, of the way

it is financed, and of

the very viability of

the program

altogether.

Since 1965, the programs to aid the elderly have included health care under the program called Medicare. Social Security and Medicare have been funded by an ever-increasing payroll tax.

The causes and possible cures for the Great Depression of the 1930s, and for subsequent recessions have been argued ever since by economists, but one thing is certain: the Depression created a climate in this society that allowed and encouraged the federal government to play an increasing role in the economic security of the individual. This same development has characterized the western European democracies of the industrialized world as well.

In 1940, the total federal expenditure was $10 billion. The Social Security Act expenditure was 0.62%, less than 1% of total government expenditure. In 1960, the total federal expenditure was $93.1 billion and the Social Security Act expenditure was 12.67% of that total. In 1990, the total federal expenditure was $1.285 trillion, and the Social Security Act expenditure was 19.6% of that total.

These increases are due to both program expansions and demographic changes.

The Graying of America

Projections for 2030 indicate that 21.2% of the population will be sixty-five and over.

There have been some very strong criticisms of the way Social Security is managed, of the way it is financed, and of the very viability of the program altogether. These criticisms have been reinforced by the growing concern with the national debt, and the fear that the Social Security and Medicare programs promise future retirees benefits that cannot be delivered.

In fact, there are increasing fears that these programs will themselves break the back of the U.S. economy. It is a certainty that if the program is kept as it is, the combined payroll tax that funds Social Security and Medicare may be raised to as much as 40% of payroll to keep the program solvent. (That rate is currently 15.3% of payroll,

An Aging Population

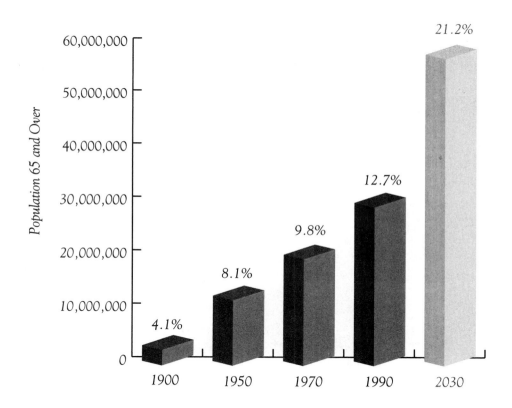

Projections for 2030 indicate that 21.2% of the
population will be 65 and over.

combining employer and employee contributions). Higher levels of taxation are already in place in western European democracies with similar programs. Studies in the European community show that if these programs are left untouched and uncontrolled, they will eat up 100% of the gross national product (GNP). Obviously this is unsustainable.

ANNUAL INCOME	$50,000	$100,000	$200,000
TAXATION NOW			
U.S.:	$8,070	$18,227	$45,241
Germany:	$12,970	$29,450	$77,846
Britain:	$14,167	$34,167	$74,167
Japan:	$7,987	$22,271	$70,929

A considerable proportion of Social Security and Medicare benefits are being paid to wealthy Americans with substantial retirement incomes from other sources. In 1988, approximately 15% of the population over sixty-five had a net worth of more than $250,000. However, limiting, taxing, or denying Social Security benefits to the wealthy is an almost untouchable political issue. People feel that they paid into the system during their working life and that they are entitled to the payout, no matter what their means are upon retirement. The program remains very popular with voters.

In 1992, neither the Republican nor the Democratic presidential platforms offered reforms. Both promised that the program would not be cut. However, when President Clinton took office, he did propose the following options as a part of his budget proposal:

- Freeze cost-of-living hikes for one year for recipients of Social Security and government-employee pensions.
  - Fiscal 1994 savings: $10.9 billion.
  - Four-year savings: $43.5 billion.
- Limit cost-of-living adjustments to the consumer price index increase minus two percentage points.

torn by the issues

- Fiscal 1994 savings: $6.8 billion.
- Four-year savings: $54 billion.
- Increase the portion of benefits included in figuring adjusted gross income for higher-income retirees from 50% to 85%, which would tax more Social Security benefits.
  - Added revenue in 1994: $5.6 billion.
  - Added revenue over four years: $26.4 billion.

Most observers agree that the problems with the program's fiscal sustainability must be confronted and understood, so that there can be intelligent, compassionate, and responsible reform in the near future.

In the 1600s, poor-relief is seen as threatening recipients with "pauperization," rendering them incapable of self-reliance.

Timeline

Early 1600s

The small settlements in the U.S. have no laws for the public provision of assistance to the destitute. The people in need include all categories of poor, young and old. People who find themselves in need of assistance in these small communities are cared for by families, friends, and churches.

1630s

Laws emerge to restrict entry into communities by those considered undesirable (poorer immigrants, criminals, and those of incompatible religions). Unrestricted entry is seen as threatening to the community's ability to "take care of its own."

1630–1700

As population grows, diversifies, and becomes more mobile, "poor laws" are enacted, modeled after the English Poor Law of 1601. These include compulsory taxation on the local or town level and are an acknowledgement of the community's responsibility for the

During the 1800s, as

relief expenditures

grow, controls

deteriorate and

political corruption

appears.

destitute. This responsibility is declared to extend no further than the community's own poor, whose individual cases are well known and understood. Those who are seen as idle or unproductive, but able-bodied, are bound as indentured servants, jailed, run out of town, or otherwise subjected to harsh punishments. Poor-relief is seen as threatening recipients with "pauperization," rendering them incapable of self-reliance. Laws were designed to discourage this pauperization of individuals.

Population growth tends to threaten the individualized form of relief that was possible in small communities.

1700s

Almshouses appear to house the destitute. As the population continues to grow, relief expenditures are often the largest item in town and city budgets, rising sharply in the post-Revolutionary War years.

1800s

Public outdoor relief, relief to those not housed in an institution, grows due to overcrowding of almshouses. State, as opposed to local, monies are requested and received. As relief expenditures grow, controls deteriorate and political corruption appears. Officials distribute funds illegally, particularly in the larger cities, to gain political support.

1890–1930

Public outdoor relief is authorized in twenty-four states, but administered in only a few. As late as 1928, major cities such as New York and San Francisco are still legally prohibited from dispensing outdoor relief. The perceived pauperizing effect of undiscriminating relief and the widespread political corruption lead reformers and taxpayers alike to question the viability of public relief.

Private charities proliferate but they require more and more assistance from public funds. In general, they are seen as more responsible agencies than their public counterparts (public outdoor assistance) because the public programs produce costly payrolls for administrators, rather than depending on volunteers, and are subject to inevitable political corruption. More frequent investigation of individual cases is seen as necessary to prevent fraud and corruption, and social workers emerge as a professional class. Investigation of individual cases, supervision of the people who distribute money, and coordination of the various sources of charity become the emerging trends in poor-relief, public and private.

1898

The first school of social work is opened, and by 1900 paid professionals are beginning to replace the volunteer worker of the 19th century.

Economic depressions in 1870 and 1893, as well as heightened immigration, industrialization, and urbanization all threaten the traditional society and heighten insecurity among the populace, even as the economy grows.

The perceived differences between poverty alleviation and poverty prevention are a product of political philosophies developed previously in England and Europe that had evolved over the centuries in this country. Poverty prevention, that is, insurance against loss of income, was traditionally seen as an individual's own responsibility. However, this insurance, in the form of pensions, begins to be offered to public employees and to veterans, as a reward for public service.

Early 1900s

A proliferation of retirement systems for public employees appears. First, state and local retirement systems are offered to police, firemen, and teachers. Statewide and citywide systems follow during the period from 1911 to 1915. Finally, a federal civil service system is initiated in 1920.

The interest of social scientists in the elderly poor as a separate class emerges in the early twentieth century. The first public inquiry into the extent of old age poverty is authorized in 1907 in Massachusetts. The rise in the nation's economic well-being in the late nineteenth and early twentieth centuries, along with increasing population and life expectancies, lead many to re-examine the specific problem of the elderly. Life expectancies are increasing significantly beyond retirement age for a growing percentage of the population, and, with the rise of industrialization the family is becoming more and more fragmented and mobile. The elderly suffer more and more insecurity.

1910

The Massachusetts Commission, the first to study old age dependency, found that in 1910, of the 177,000 elderly in that state, 80% were self-supporting, 2% were in almshouses, 3% were supported by organized private or public charity, and the remainder were supported by family and friends.

1920s

A federal pension system specifically for veterans and soldiers becomes the largest pension system in America and probably the most expensive one in the world. It is liberalized repeatedly, increasing three- to four-fold from 1910 to 1932 alone.

During these years, about one-fifth of all persons covered by retirement pension schemes are covered publicly. These programs are always politically popular among the various segments of the society that benefit from them. The attitude toward poverty prevention (or social security) is changing.

The growing number of professional social workers begins to have more and more of an influence on government policy formation.

1900–1929

Before the Great Depression, the general public outcry for social security insurance is almost nonexistent. Most of the proposals for federal social insurance programs are not received well in the prosperous America of the 1920s. They are considered un-American, socialistic, communistic, alien, and destructive to the traditional values of self-reliance. (Social insurance programs existed in thirty-five other countries by 1929.)

The labor union movement is completely opposed to social insurance, as it would compete with the labor union pension plans.

torn by the issues

Labor unions accumulated considerable wealth as a result of membership contributions to these pension programs. Samuel Gompers, head of the American Federation of Labor, vows in 1916 to assist in a "revolution against compulsory insurance." No bills for compulsory insurance are introduced to the U.S. Congress at this time. Prevailing public opinion, based on studies done in many states, is that compulsory insurance would be, in the words of the Massachusetts Commission on Old Age Pensions, "unthinkable and distasteful." It was supported by neither major lobby groups nor popular opinion.

1923

There are approximately 42,000 paupers over the age of sixty-five in almshouses in the U.S. This is 1% of the elderly population nationwide. There is little public notice of this group of paupers, but social workers are becoming more and more vocal about the sometimes sub-human conditions to which these elderly poor are subjected.

Since colonial days, almshouses had been designed as housing for "defectives." Most of these buildings are very old, many lack modern sanitation, or electricity, and some are still contracted out to the lowest bidder. Most do not segregate residents on the basis of sex, health, or for any other reason.

1929

Private institutions for the care of the elderly are widely available, but not affordable by many elderly. The county almshouse is still the only form of permanent assistance to the elderly poor in virtually all states. The trend in the late 19th century is toward specialization of approaches to poverty relief. As children, the insane, the blind, and others with particular problems are removed to specialized institution, the almshouses are left largely to the elderly.

A study in New York finds that 93% of the elderly are self-supporting or are supported by family and friends. Forty-three percent are self-supported by private savings or private pensions, and 50% are supported by friends and family. Along with the proliferation of pension plans for public employees and veterans, disability payments are introduced. Because people are living longer, the lifetime ceiling on pensions is eliminated. Growing public assistance to special classes of the elderly such as the destitute, retirees from public employment, veterans, and disabled workers, naturally evokes interest on the part of other elderly, particularly those who consider themselves poor or near-poor, who desire similar attention be given to their circumstances.

1900–1935

A growing number of advocates of social insurance begin to appear. These advocates come mainly from the ranks of the social worker profession, joined by other progressives, intellectuals, and social scientists. A nearly universal problem among the aged is seen developing as a result of industrialization, urbanization, and population growth. According to social insurance advocates, the movement from farm to city and the change in employment from agricultural to industrial renders the elderly worker obsolete.

On the farm, the elderly can continue to work by scaling down work effort and hours worked, but they still contribute to the productivity of the family. They are considered a vital part of the work unit—the family—even in old age, because of their superior experience.

In industrial employment, the wage contract is impersonal and insecure. Compulsory retirement, the preferred vigor of the younger worker, and inflexibility of hours and tasks make employment, once lost due to old age, difficult to find again. Livelihood is tied to wages. With wages cut off, and family support non-existent, any savings are quickly wiped out. The ultimate destiny of many in the elderly population is the dreaded almshouse.

The private insurance and pension business is growing rapidly. This is seen in the prevailing public opinion as philosophically preferable to compulsory public insurance, as well as more profitable. However, many of the poorer members of society cannot participate in these plans.

torn by the issues

1930

The U.S. (and most of the world) enters into the most prolonged economic depression in history; one-fifth of all commercial banks fail, many people's savings are uninsured and lost, unemployment reaches one-quarter of the labor force, and millions of people who have never before resorted to public assistance find themselves on the dole.

The Great Depression is a poorly understood economic phenomenon but many people consider it an unavoidable failure of the free market system that will periodically recur.

Many who had had complete confidence in the private sector as a source of economic reward and incentive suddenly lose faith in it as a provider of protection or security. There is a climate conducive to federalization of many programs as a guarantee against personal and collective economic disaster.

1933

Fifteen million people are on public relief of one kind or another.

Many state and county pension programs curtail or cease payments because of the shrinking of tax revenue.

Dr. Townsend, a retired physician from Los Angeles, gains attention when he circulates a petition to Congress proposing monthly benefits to everyone over 60 in the amount of $245. (This was an adequate monthly income in those days.) It was to be financed through a combination of sales and inheritance taxes. The only stipulations are that eligible recipients have to leave the work force immediately and spend the whole payment in the month it is received. According to Townsend, this will release four million jobs held by the elderly and stimulate the economy. The Townsend movement gains widespread support very quickly and within two years, it has 3.2 million paid supporters.

1934

Nineteen million people (15% of the population) are receiving emergency relief (direct relief or work relief) from various levels of government.

In 1930, many who had had complete confidence in the private sector as a source of economic reward and incentive suddenly lose faith in it as a provider of protection or security.

Other plans emerge to meet the growing crisis. The one proposed by the federal government, the Social Security Act, is more moderate than the Townsend Plan and other plans being proposed. The Social Security Act is essentially an insurance plan that minimizes the break from the time-honored tradition of self-sufficiency.

A bill passes unanimously in the U.S. Congress to give state pension programs funding assistance. Destitution among the elderly is growing and many younger family members, on the dole themselves, are unable to support their elderly friends and relatives as readily as they have in the past.

1935

President Roosevelt signs into law the Social Security Act—it passes through Congress in eight months with very little opposition. Warnings about future viability are ignored in the midst of the economic pain. The bill is a comprehensive system of compulsory federal old age insurance that is coupled with a tax-offset system of unemployment insurance and grants to states for old-age poverty relief.

1937

Collection of payroll taxes begins. Assessment on taxable earnings is set at 1% of the worker's salary up to a wage ceiling of $3000. The employer is also assessed a matching rate of 1%. Eligibility will be a matter of right for workers, not need. The Social Security check is intended to replace 40% of the workers' pre-retirement earnings, to be supplemented with savings and private pension plans.

The first payouts are scheduled for 1942, after a trust fund had built up sufficiently to cover all payments to eligible retirees. The trust fund is always to be funded at 100%. That is, there will always be a fund, fed by the payroll tax, equal to the promised benefits. This guards against changes in the economic and the demographic climate.

1939

Significant changes to the original act are adopted. Eligibility is expanded to include dependents and survivors, and the initial pay-out date is moved back to 1940. The restrictions on the reserve fund are relaxed (and have been reduced ever since).

1940

When payments start, there are 177 workers per beneficiary. All the computations and projections are based on this ratio. (By 1990 the ratio will drop to 3.2 workers for every beneficiary.)

In subsequent amendments (1940 to present), Congress generally raises benefits and expands coverage without providing adequate financing. The amount required to be kept in the reserve fund for future payout is lowered again and again. These are always politically popular activities—guaranteed vote getters.

1950

The program is overhauled and updated. Benefits increase as much as 70%, payroll taxes are raised, and coverage expands to many other previously ineligible segments of the workforce. Some farm and domestic workers, the self-employed, and state and local government workers are some of the 9.2 million newly eligible persons added to the rolls.

1954

The wage base, payroll tax rate, and coverage are raised, and 7.5 million newly eligible persons are added to the rolls.

1956–59

The wage base is increased, the tax rate is increased, and a separate disability tax is added to make persons disabled before retirement age eligible for benefits.

1964

The Old-Age, Survivors, and Disability portions of the Social Security Act become the nation's single most important entitlement program accounting for 37% of all welfare expenditures (compared with only 6% in 1950).

1965

Major medical care, under the Medicare program, is provided under the Social Security Act. Revenues from the new tax added to the existing social security tax are to be placed in a trust fund separate from the Social Security fund.

1969–72

Rising inflation leads Congress to raise benefits three times: 15% in 1969, 10% in 1971, and 20% in 1972.

1972–76

Congress ties future benefit increases to the consumer wage and price index. Optimistic members of Congress believe that a healthy economy and rising wages will generate adequate reserves to cover future increases. Conservative members of Congress are important advocates of indexing, or tying benefit increases to the larger national economic picture; they feel indexing will protect the system from the pressure of benefit-hungry constituents. (Cost-of-living adjustments became automatic in 1975.)

To facilitate enactment of the 1972 amendments, (which are so technically flawed that they nearly bankrupt the system within five years), the Chairman of the House Ways and Means Committee, Wilbur Mills, assured members of Congress that more money would be taken in than would be paid out for the next seventy-five years.

1977

Within a few months of the passage of the Social Security Act Amendment of 1972, it was clear that the assurances of Mills and others were erroneous, but action is not taken to correct the error until 1977. The reluctance on the part of the public to come to grips with the fiscal unsoundness of the program is fostered by the belief that the government can guarantee a program's solvency.

	Cost of Living	Real Wages	Unemployment
Congressional Projections (1972-1976):	+14.5%	+11.7%	4.2%
The Real Numbers (1972-1976):	+36%	+1.2%	6.5%

This demonstrates how inaccurate political projections can be. The fix is based on more overly optimistic projections:

	Cost of Living	Real Wages	Unemployment
Congressional Projections (1977-1982):	+28%	+13%	5.9%
The Real Numbers (1977-1982):	+50%	-7%	7%

The nation's largest peacetime tax increase sets new taxable wage bases and tax rates for Social Security over an eleven-year period, tripling both. Automatic cost-of-living adjustments in Social Security benefits are reformulated to reflect fluctuations in the economy.

1975–80

The wage and price indexing of benefits (with automatic cost-of-living adjustments) becomes very costly and is admitted to have been a mistake. The expanding program outstrips all predictions of cost and growth, and the viability of the program is in doubt.

1979

Approximately 90% of the elderly receive Social Security benefits. (In 1940, it was about 40%.)

It soon becomes evident that the 1977 measures to strengthen the program and keep it solvent are not enough. President Carter urges Congress to eliminate or cut back certain unnecessary aspects of the program. He proposes cuts in educational benefits to dependent children aged eighteen and over, a cut-off in surviving parent benefits after the youngest child has reached age sixteen, and elimination of the minimum benefit guarantee, which provides a payment of $122 a month, regardless of employment history.

His efforts make little headway in a Congress that is loath to make any changes to the program except to increase taxes and benefits. There is no apparent recognition among members of Congress or the public of the drastically rising costs of the program, and no willingness to confront the problem.

Payroll taxes are raised five times in ten years, and each increase is supposed to put the issue to rest.

1980

Outlay totals $149 billion. In 1935, the estimate of outlay for 1980 was $1.3 billion. Life expectancy after sixty-five was three and a half years in 1935. It is now seventeen to twenty-two years. This increase in length of retirement years was unforeseen by the creators of the original program.

A politically palatable measure is adopted to delay the system's financial crisis. Money is borrowed from the disability trust fund to make sure there will be enough to pay beneficiaries for the coming year.

1981

Outlining his program for economic recovery, President Reagan proposes short- and long-term approaches to the Social Security problem. Among his proposals are elimination of the minimum benefit program, as Carter had proposed, and elimination of windfalls available to certain beneficiaries, such as retired government workers with generous federal pensions. The beneficiaries, called double dippers, work only a short time in employment covered by Social Security, then retire and reap double benefits. While the House and the Senate go along with this plan initially, both reverse themselves later in the year, voting to restore the minimum monthly benefit. President Reagan proposes further significant changes to the system, but is met with such resistance from the public, particularly organizations representing the elderly, that he withdraws his proposals and offers to compromise on all counts.

Congressional leaders, both Republicans and Democrats, seek to accommodate President Reagan on this issue, seeing the need for Social Security reforms as critical, but the issue has become so politicized that major changes seem unlikely. Another short-term funding solution is approved, to tide the program over until the mid-1980s. Further borrowing is permitted from the Disability and Hospital Insurance Funds.

1983

Another major overhaul of the system is approved. It is intended to maintain solvency until the end of the century. Social Security payroll taxes are increased, and a new schedule is set for periodic increases throughout the 1980s. The decisions to tax the benefits of high-income recipients and to transfer funds from general revenue to bolster the system's trust funds are fundamental changes.

1990

Approximately 12% of the population is elderly, compared to 3.4% in 1880. This marked aging of the population was unforeseen by the creators of the program.

By the year 2050,

the bulk of the baby

boom generation will

be retiring. They will

be healthier and live

longer than any

generation before

them. They will

expect constant

medical care.

In 1940 there were 177 workers to support each retiree. In 1990 the ratio is three workers for every retiree. This drastic change in the worker-retiree ratio also was unforeseen by the creators of the program.

1992

Neither the Republican nor Democratic platform of the 1992 presidential race includes recommendations for Social Security reforms or cutbacks. However, President Clinton's budget package of 1993 does include reductions in the cost-of-living increases and increased taxation of the benefits of elderly recipients.

Some 40 million people are receiving benefits today. The cost is $251 billion, which includes huge administrative costs. This will more than double in the next ten years. This is 4% of the GNP and 19% of the Federal Budget.

Number of Workers per Beneficiary

1940 – 177	1970 – 3.5
1945 – 35.7	1975 – 3.1
1950 – 13.8	1980 – 3.2
1955 – 8.2	2000 – 3.2
1960 – 4.9	2020 – 2.3
1965 – 3.9	2030 – 2.0

2020

There will be an estimated 65 million recipients.

2050

There will be more than 80 million recipients, involving $20 trillion or more in expenditures.

The bulk of the baby boom generation will be retired and receiving Social Security benefits. They will be healthier and live longer than any generation before them. They will expect constant med-

torn by the issues

ical care as a part of their benefit package, which will further pro-long their lives. Due to the declining fertility rate, the generation that will be working and paying into the system will be relatively smaller than the baby-boom generation. There will be two workers for every recipient, as opposed to three workers for every recipient in 1990, and 177 workers for every recipient in 1940. This makes the system, as it was designed in 1935, unworkable. Many observers feel that the system will go bankrupt, with benefit obligations of $6 trillion (including Medicare obligations).

The federal government has used the trust fund surpluses, accumulated during these years that the baby boom generation has been working, to service the huge deficit in the federal operating budget. It has left IOUs in the trust funds, thereby misrepresenting the actual size of the deficit to the American public. Observers from across the political spectrum have no suggestions as to how it will make good on these IOUs and rescue the bankrupt program.

The federal government has used the trust fund surpluses, accumulated during these years that the baby boom generation has been working, to service the huge deficit in the federal operating budget

Suggested Reforms

Raise Taxes

Based on demographic projections for coming years, Social Security taxes will have to double or triple to cover the program's cost.

Combined employer/employee rates are now set at 15.65%. Predictions of future increases range from 25% to 40%.

Developed western European countries with nationalized health care and old age pension programs live with a much higher level of taxation than do Americans at the present time, but a larger percentage of their taxes are returned, in the form of "cradle-to-grave" security benefits than in the U.S. They also report lower infant mortality rates, lower crime levels, fewer homeless, and other positive aspects of their systems. These programs, however, contribute to somewhat lower levels of economic growth and standards of living than in the U.S.

There appears to be

broad-based support

for these programs, but

little understanding of

how they work, or

what they cost.

There is a much lower level of defense spending, as a percent of GNP, in these countries, and yet taxes are still considerably higher than in the U.S. This change in national priorities (lowering defense spending, increasing social spending for the sake of cradle-to-grave security, and increasing taxes considerably) is a choice Americans may wish to make in the future, but at present most Americans are outraged at the current level of taxation and are philosophically committed to the notion of self-reliance.

Alter the Benefit Formulas

Reduce benefits and eliminate certain dependents' benefits, particularly for wealthy recipients. In 1987, a recipient with a monthly income of $3000 could receive a median benefit of $754. Does he need it? Should he receive it? The suggestion to cut the benefits of wealthy Americans is unpopular with some elderly citizens' groups and was not mentioned in the presidential campaigns of 1992, except by third-party candidate, Ross Perot.

The resistance of advocacy groups representing the elderly to reform of Social Security needs to be addressed. The security of their children is at stake. At present, these groups resist all efforts to discuss the issue publicly. In 1982, when reform of the program became necessary because of its impending bankruptcy, a coalition of one hundred national elderly and other groups insisted that any cut in benefits, including taxation of the benefits of the upper-income elderly was a breach of faith. There appears to be broad-based support for these programs, but little understanding of how they work, or what they cost.

The following cost analysis was taken from a 1985 study performed by the U.S. Chamber of Commerce:

- A worker starts to pay into the system in 1937. He pays the maximum social security taxes for forty-five years and retires in 1982. His payments total $12,828. His benefits begin at $734 per month. His wife can collect half his benefit, an additional $367 monthly. Their total first-year benefit comes to $13,217, or more than he had contributed in forty-five years of employment.

- His life expectancy is 14.2 more years, and his wife's life expectancy is 18.5 years. If rates keep increasing at current trends, the couple's lifetime benefit would amount to approximately $375,000—all from a contribution of $12,828.

The National Council of Senior Citizens claimed in 1982 that an infusion of general revenues and borrowing would make the system "good as new." At the same time, the Leadership Council of Aging Organizations announced that "Social Security is not going bankrupt, nor is it in danger of doing so; scare tactics suggesting impending doom frighten older people unnecessarily and undermine young people's confidence in the system." No serious proposals were offered to improve the program's financial solvency.

Encourage the Use of Private Pension Plans

This is suggested as an alternative to the federally funded Social Security program.

If the choice were available, many might choose private plans because the payout from private plans would be greater. Social Security contributions are not invested and bear no interest. Private pension plans are managed money and they do grow and bear interest.

Contributions by employees to private-sector pension plans would increase the GNP and thus support economic growth. This is apparently a politically unpopular proposal. Neither party proposes or endorses it. If this is not encouraged by employers or other advisors, many people do not even realize it is an attractive option.

Many worry that if the compulsory aspect of social insurance were removed, many people, particularly those with lower incomes and less margin for saving, would simply not invest in pensions at all. Upon retirement, they would have to apply for some kind of public assistance. The compulsory contribution program is a hedge against that probability. Many privatization plans recognize this, and allow for a compulsory tax but provide free choice among public and private alternatives.

Contributions by employees to private sector pension plans would increase the GNP and thus support economic growth. If this is not encouraged by employers or other advisors, many people do not even realize it is an attractive option.

*T*his earnings test does

not apply to

nonearned income

from interest or

dividends from

investments, which

benefits wealthy

retirees with

substantial assets and

penalizes retirees who

need to work to

support themselves.

Reform Health Care

Some blame much of the funding crisis on the Medicare program or on health care delivery systems in general. The combination of a market-based medical system and a federally funded insurance program have been a deadly combination, producing an increasingly ominous lack of responsibility on the part of consumers and deliverers alike.

Some feel the medical system should be nationalized, so that all medical costs would be established and controlled by law, and no one would be without medical care. Others insist that nationalization would be far too costly and would automatically lower the quality of medical care.

Advocates of privatization believe that if all federal involvement in health care were abolished, medical care systems, including private insurance companies and health care deliverers, would regulate themselves according to market forces. However, the cost of much of the high-tech medical care available today would be out of reach for many people.

Most proposals for dealing with the skyrocketing costs of medical care include both public and private elements. In 1992, both the American College of Physicians and the American Academy of Family Physicians endorsed plans whereby the federal government would cap health spending by setting limits on doctor and hospital fees. They feel this is necessary, even though they themselves are risking pay cuts. A wide range of citizens' groups have endorsed the plan, including the American Association of Retired Persons, and Chrysler Corporation.

The American Medical Association has criticized the plan as a precursor to nationalized health care.

Eliminate Earnings Test
or Raise Ceiling

This proposal would allow the younger recipients to go back to work without losing their benefits. The earnings test allows retired people to earn income up to a ceiling of approximately $9,700. If a beneficiary earns more than that, Social Security payments are

Advocates say that

the taxes generated

by retirees returning

to work would far

exceed the additional

benefits that would be

paid.

reduced. This prevents many elderly from taking even part-time or low-paying jobs to supplement their Social Security income. This earnings test does not apply to nonearned income from interest or dividends from investments, which benefits wealthy retirees with substantial assets and penalizes retirees who need to work to support themselves. Advocates say that the taxes generated by retirees returning to work would far exceed the additional benefits that would be paid. The people involved could add to their benefits, improve their standards of living, and contribute to the community as well. The older worker is seen as a valuable commodity in the growing service, retailing, and health-care industries. It is estimated that 700,000 people would go back to work, adding to the shrinking labor force, paying taxes, and contributing to the GNP.

Following are two applications of the earnings test:

- A widowed homemaker is entitled to $3,600 annual benefit. She earns $16,200 a year as a bookkeeper, but that requires her to forfeit $2,000 of her annual benefit.

- A retired chief executive officer of a small corporation has a retirement income of $150,000 a year in pension, interest and stock dividends. Because these categories of income aren't counted against the earnings limit, he also collects a maximum social security benefit of $13,056 a year.

From the Director's Overview
— 1993 Federal Budget —

Mandatory or entitlement programs were 28% of the budget in 1962. They are 52% today. Within the mandatory total, funding for the non-poor has increased far more than for the poor.

A major reason for both the near-term and long-term deficit problem is the continuing unrestrained growth of the so-called mandatory programs. These are programs that do not come up for review or decision by the Congress or the President. They are not discretionary in that they do not require annual appropriation. And they are not available for vote or veto. They just keep growing automatically and are referred to as uncontrollable.

Comparisons:
1960–1990

Total Government Expenditures as a Percent of GDP

1960	26.0%
1970	29.7%
1980	31.5%
1990	33.1%
INCREASE:	**25%**

Social Security and Medicare Payments as a Percent of GDP

1960	2.3%
1970	3.7%
1980	5.7%
1990	6.5%
INCREASE:	**60%**

Gross Federal Debt
as a Percentage of GDP

1960 ....57.4%

1970 ....38.6%

1980 ....34.4%

1990 ....58.7%

1997 (PROJECTED) 74.8%

INCREASE: ....**30+%**

Population (U.S.)

1960 179,323,175

1970 203,302,031

1980 226,542,203

1990 248,709,873

INCREASE: **35%**

Elderly population (U.S.)

1960..16,675,000

1970..20,107,000

1980..25,704,000

1990..31,241,831

INCREASE: **50%**

Sources

Beck, Melinda, et. al. "Counting Every Penny." *Newsweek*, 27 January 1992.

Calleo, David P. *The Bankrupting of America*. New York: William Morrow and Company, Inc., 1992.

Gray, Robert T., and Joan Szabo. "Social Security: Hard Choices Ahead." *Nation's Business*, April 1990.

Maalabre, Alfred L. *Beyond Our Means*. New York: Random House, 1987.

Office of the President. *1993 Federal Budget (proposed)*. Washington, D.C.: U.S. Government Printing Office, 1992.

Martz, Larry, and Rich Thomas. "Fixing Social Security." *Newsweek*, 7 May 1990.

Mudge, Robert S., ed., "Social Security and Retirement." *The Congressional Quarterly*, 1983.

Munnell, Alice Haydock. *The Effect of Social Security on Personal Saving*. Cambridge: Ballinger Publishing Co., 1974.

Pechman, J., et al. *Social Security: Perspectives for Reform*. Washington, D.C.: The Brookings Institution, 1968.

Samuelson, Robert J. "Pampering the Elderly." *Newsweek*, 26 November 1990.

U.S. Department of Commerce, Bureau of Census. *1990 Census of Population and Housing*. Washington, D.C: U.S. Government Printing Office, 1991.

Weaver, Carolyn. *The Crisis in Social Security: Economic and Political Origins*.

defense spending

from ancient times to the present day, human societies have

separated themselves into tribes, cities, states, or nations, and then

waged war upon their neighbors. The related needs to wage war and

to protect citizens from attack have been both a primary considera-

tion in the structure of societies and the primary goal of governments.

Even the very definition of manhood has often been synonymous with

Plato wrote, "In

truth for everyone

there exists by nature

at all times an

undeclared war

among all cities."

that of the warrior. The political entity came into being because of the need for common defense in the competition for resources. The word "polis" or politic appears to be derived from an Indo-European term used to designate a high place or citadel to which the residents of an area could retreat when threatened with attack. The Greek philosopher Plato wrote, "In truth for everyone there exists by nature at all times an undeclared war among all cities."

The American founding fathers understood this classic tendency toward war. Alexander Hamilton feared that this would be the American experience as well, unless the separate states were joined together in an extended commercial republic. If this linking did not occur, he felt the American colonies would become, like the Greek city states, a "collection of little, jealous, clashing, tumultuous commonwealths, wretched nurseries of unceasing discord."

Military institutions tend to strengthen and expand under the command of strong central governments; often, individual liberty is curtailed or destroyed in the process. This was demonstrated clearly during the rise of the U.S.S.R. The Second Amendment to the U.S. Constitution, assuring "the right of the citizen to keep and bear arms," was intended to guard against this tendency of citizen militias to transform into professional armies under the control of repressive regimes. Varying interpretations of this amendment are central to the gun-control argument currently raging in the U.S.

The degree to which the modern state owes its solidarity, its sense of identity, and even its existence to the threat and experience of war cannot be overestimated. The industrial revolution, population growth, and the technology explosion have all served to enlarge and entrench the military presence in American society. There seems to be no end to its increase, even in peacetime, and no limit but the limits of taxation. The rise of what President Eisenhower dubbed the military-industrial complex has been widely supported as a healthy stimulus to the economy and a guarantee of American preeminence in the world.

In 1957, the Soviet Union put its Sputnik satellite into orbit. This was the first in a series of Soviet victories in the space race, which became a peacetime replacement for war. By the early 1960s, the military establishment was characterized by nuclear deterrence, an emphasis on high-tech weaponry, and the race to dominate space. The Cold War was in full swing. By the end of the 1970s, the U.S. and the

By the end of the
1970s, the U.S. and
the Soviet Union had
the nuclear capability
to destroy the planet
several times over,
and an American had
walked on the moon.

Soviet Union had the nuclear capability to destroy the planet several times over, and an American had walked on the moon. The U.S. was winning the space race. At the close of the 1980s, the U.S.S.R. collapsed, taking with it the only major challenge to the superpower status of the U.S. The U.S. won the Cold War.

In recent years, the national purpose has begun to shift from defense to more consumer-oriented uses of technology. The antiwar movement that heated up during the Vietnam conflict questioned the notion that the Pentagon or any state authority should be the sole source of the nation's imagination. Small companies, co-opting the computer technology developed by defense and aerospace research and development, began to appear and flourish. Steve Wozniak, the founder of Apple Computer, is the son of a Lockheed aerospace engineer. Beginning in the 1970s and continuing throughout the 1980s, the entrepreneurial, consumer-based personal computer industry exploded.

Military spending as a percentage of gross national product (GNP) is now at about 5%, compared to 41% at the end of World War II. Even at the height of the Reagan buildup in 1985 military spending reached only about 6.4% of GNP. During these years, repeated reports of cost overruns and other irregularities in the weapons procurement process created considerable public distaste for the apparent corruption within the military-industrial complex. In addition to these concerns, the growing budget deficit and the collapse of the Soviet Union have made cuts in defense spending both acceptable and appropriate within most sectors of public opinion.

The political and economic consequences of a post-Cold-War defense build-down may be painful. The leading producers of military hardware, which include some of our largest corporations, count on U.S. Department of Defense (DoD) contracts for a substantial portion of their incomes. The communities that have developed and prospered around these corporations or military installations often oppose cuts that could mean the end of their livelihood. In California, where large-scale layoffs have already begun in defense-related industries, recession has hit hard. Unemployment rates are among the highest in the country, and many former aerospace engineers report that their services are not needed by the new breed of "lean and mean" corporations. The traditionally lax approach to the bottom line in the military procurement business, where cost has not been a major consideration, does not fit very well with the growing competitiveness of the global marketplace.

Those in favor of maintaining the status quo relative to weapons procurement contend that, even in the post-Cold-War era, U.S. resources are constantly being called upon to lead "peacekeeping" operations around the world. Our volatile world shows no sign of adopting the ideal of peaceful commercialism. Regional and ethnic conflicts, such as the one taking place in the former Yugoslavia, flare up constantly. The recent Los Angeles riots and the bombing of the World Trade Center in New York City alerted Americans that we are not immune to conflict and terrorism.

National Defense Outlays

(CONSTANT 1982 DOLLARS, IN BILLIONS)

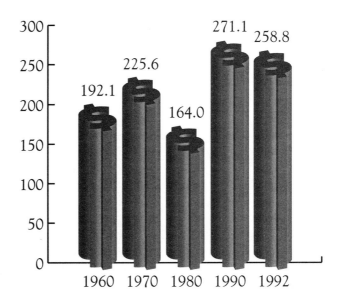

torn by the issues

The increased
defense spending
during the Reagan
administration was
directed towards
research and
development (R&D)
and weapons
procurement rather
than increases in
enlisted manpower.

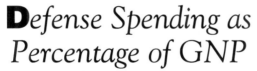

Defense Spending as Percentage of GNP

(CONSTANT 1982 DOLLARS, IN BILLIONS)

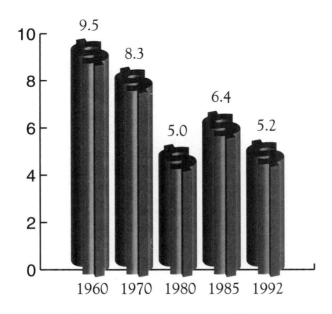

Between 1970 and 1991, there was a decrease in manpower of approximately 50% in the Army and 15% in the other branches of the armed forces. The increased defense spending during the Reagan administration was directed towards research and development (R&D) and weapons procurement rather than increases in enlisted manpower.

Timeline

1676

Nathaniel Bacon leads planters against an autocratic British governor, burning Jamestown in the colony of Virginia. Bacon dies, and twenty-three followers are executed.

1765

After oppressive taxes are levied on British goods sold in the colonies, nine colonies adopt the Declaration of Rights, opposing taxation without representation.

1773

British cargo is thrown overboard into Boston Harbor; the Boston Tea Party protests duties on tea.

1774

The First Continental Congress protests British oppression, calling for civil disobedience.

1775

Patrick Henry addresses the Virginia Convention, saying "Give me liberty or give me death."

A group of volunteer citizens organize as militia and besiege the British army in Boston. They are recognized by the Congress as the New England Armies. A committee is appointed to draft "rules and regulations for the government of the army." The Congress votes to raise ten additional rifle companies as a reinforcement. The next day, George Washington is appointed commander in chief of the "Continental forces to be raised for the defense of liberty." The Continental Army is our first national military organization.

The Marine Corps is founded as a special elite service within the Continental Army.

torn by the issues

The modern

democratic republic is

born in the aftermath

of the French and

American

Revolutions.

1776

The Declaration of Independence is approved on July 4th.

The Continental Army fights the American Revolution, ultimately defeating the armies of the king of England. The war costs $400 million to $680 million (in 1967 dollars) and equals 104% of GNP at its peak.

France and Spain assist the Continental Army with money and arms.

After the war, the size of the Army is reduced to about 700 men. This nucleus is periodically expanded in the 1780s and 1790s to meet threats from Indians and the French.

1789

The French Revolution is fought with a citizen militia fighting against the professional armies of the king of France.

The modern democratic republic is born in the aftermath of the French and American Revolutions. The formal alliance between the U.S. and France during the Revolutionary War is the last such alliance until the establishment of the North Atlantic Treaty Organization (NATO) in 1947.

The War Department is formed by Congress.

1794

Western Pennsylvania farmers protest the liquor tax of 1791. The "Whiskey Rebellion" is suppressed by 15,000 militiamen. Alexander Hamilton uses the incident to establish the authority of the new federal government to enforce federal laws by armed force.

1796

President George Washington's farewell address warns against permanent alliances with foreign powers, a big public debt, a large military establishment, and the devices of a "small, artful, enterprising minority" to control or change government.

1798

The U.S. Department of the Navy is created as a separate branch of the military.

1800s

It is held by many free-market economists in the nineteenth century that unless universal disarmament is achieved, military establishments would cripple market-based economies, because the war machine requires huge quantities of tax revenue for support and produces no product that can be bought by consumers.

1860–65

The Civil War costs $8.5 million (in 1967 dollars) or 74% of GNP at its peak.

1898

The U.S. declares war on Spain. Cuba is blockaded to help the Cuban independence movement. The U.S. occupies Puerto Rico. Spain finally cedes the Philippines, Puerto Rico, and Guam to the U.S. and approves the independence of Cuba.

1903

Orville Wright completes the first successful flight in a mechanically propelled, heavier-than-air airplane.

1912

The U.S. sends marines to Nicaragua, which is in default of loans from the U.S. and Europe.

1913

The U.S. blockades Mexico in support of the revolution against Spanish rule.

1914

The U.S. declares neutrality in the European war.

1915

A British ship, the *Lusitania*, is sunk by a German submarine, killing 128 Americans. President Wilson asks Congress for an increase in military funding.

1916

General Pershing enters Mexico. The U.S. establishes a military government in the Dominican Republic.

1917

As a result of increased attacks by German submarines, the U.S. declares war against Germany. The Conscription Law is passed in May, and the first U.S. troops arrive in Europe in June.

1918

Over one million troops are in Europe by July. The war ends in November.

1914–18

World War I costs $100 billion (in 1967 dollars) or 43% of GNP at its peak.

1919

The first transatlantic flight is completed by a U.S. Navy seaplane.

1920

The first "red scare" occurs in America. Some 2700 communists, anarchists, and other radicals are arrested.

Congress rejects membership in the League of Nations. Strong isolationist sentiment in the U.S. favors avoidance of foreign entanglements.

1921

The Limitation of Armaments Conference meets to curtail naval construction, outlaw poison gas, and restrict submarine attacks on merchant ships.

defense spending

In 1939, Albert

Einstein, a pacifist,

alerts President

Franklin D.

Roosevelt to the

possibilities of an

atom bomb.

1926

Dr. Robert Goddard demonstrates the first liquid fuel rocket, which travels 184 feet in 2.5 seconds.

Charles Lindbergh completes the first non-stop flight across the Atlantic.

1935–1939

Congress passes neutrality laws in 1935, 1936, 1937, and 1939. The U.S. maintains no military bases in other countries.

1939

Albert Einstein, a pacifist, alerts President Franklin D. Roosevelt to the possibilities of an atom bomb.

On September 8th, a Limited National Emergency is declared, a result of German aggression in Europe. President Roosevelt asks for a defense budget hike.

The nation has no armaments industry. In general, most people view the maintenance of a large army as politically and economically unwise.

Approximately 340,000 men are serving in the armed forces.

1940

After the German victories in the spring offensive culminate in the fall of France and the near destruction of the British army, the U.S. government decides the country is at risk and its defenses must be strengthened.

The first peacetime Military Conscription Act is passed.

"The Manhattan Project" is established to develop the atomic bomb. It is authorized by President Roosevelt without knowledge of or approval by Congress or the public. Keeping this dangerous technology out of the hands of the Germans was the overriding consideration justifying the secrecy.

New procedures for dealing with arms contractors are approved. Instead of requesting bids, contracts are negotiated. Generous federal assistance is given to hasten the buildup. Plants are built, tax breaks are granted, and contracts amended to shelter private companies against risk of losses due to error, poor judgment, or performance failures. Using private industry as the major producer of weapons is expected to have the obvious benefits of greater efficiency in production and swifter adaptation to changing technology.

1941

The U.S. armed forces number 1.8 million members.

Japan bombs the American fleet at Pearl Harbor, Hawaii, on December 7, killing 2300 people.

America declares war on Germany and Japan.

1942

The first nuclear chain reaction is achieved in Chicago.

1945

Germany surrenders on May 7.

President Harry S. Truman takes office after Roosevelt's death in April. He grants the military discretion in the use of the atomic bomb. The military command makes the decision to drop the first bomb on August 6, on Hiroshima. 71,000 people die instantly. Many thousands more die slowly from radiation poisoning. A second bomb is dropped on Nagasaki on August 9, killing 100,000 people. Japan surrenders on August 15.

The nuclear age is born.

President Truman records in his diary: "We have discovered the most terrible bomb in the history of the world, the most terrible thing ever discovered."

Later, in a radio address to the nation, Truman proclaims: "This is the greatest thing in history."

Twelve million people are serving in the armed forces.

In 1945, President Truman records in his diary: "We have discovered the most terrible bomb in the history of the world, the most terrible thing ever discovered."

1940–45

World War II costs $816.3 billion (in 1967 dollars). At the peak of spending in 1944, the cost is 41% of GNP.

1946

Three million people are serving in the armed forces. The post-war build-down begins. Many economists predict post-war recession or depression. However, the economy remains healthy.

Post-war Germany and Japan receive massive U.S. assistance in rebuilding their economies under the Marshall Plan. Truman declares the Truman Doctrine, a policy of containment of communist aggression, whereby assistance is offered to any country threatened by communism from within or outside of its borders. The Cold War begins.

German rocket scientists emigrate to the U.S. Wernher von Braun, who built rockets for Hitler, takes over America's ballistic missile and moon-shot programs.

Many other German scientists are hired to help develop the American defense and aerospace industries.

1947

The North Atlantic Treaty Organization (NATO) is formed. This is America's first alliance with another country for the purpose of mutual defense since the alliance with France during the Revolutionary War.

The U.S. Department of Defense (DoD) is created.

The U.S. Air Force is established as a separate branch of the armed forces.

1950s

The Korean conflict costs $69.3 billion or 15% of GNP at its peak.

About 3.7 million people are serving in the armed forces. America's military posture is based on nuclear deterrence and large troop deployments abroad. Enlistment declines after the conclusion of the conflict and remains at about 2.5 million people through the decade.

1953

President Dwight D. Eisenhower states that he believes an economy of war transforms an economy of growth and development into an economy of waste.

President Eisenhower announces that the U.S. has given France $60 million to assist with the war in Indochina.

1954

More aid to France for the war in Indochina is announced.

The longest war in U.S. history begins with the economic and technical assistance given to France for the Indochinese conflict. This war is fought with conventional weapons. Both sides fear the introduction of nuclear weapons.

The *Nautilus*, the first atomic-powered submarine, is launched at Groton, Connecticut.

It is reported that three quarters of the cost of France's war in Indochina is being met by the U.S.

1955

The U.S. agrees to help train the South Vietnamese army.

1957

The Soviet Union puts the world's first artificial satellite, Sputnik I, into earth orbit. (Sputnik is translated as "traveling companion.") Its two radio transmitters mark the first time in history that man-made radio signals are sent from space to earth.

This achievement startles America. It has been assumed that the Soviet Union is technologically backward. The space race is launched. Space is seen as the final frontier, and both superpowers struggle for dominance. This struggle parallels the Cold War. Space is viewed by many as the battleground of the future.

1959

The first atomic-powered merchant ship and the first U.S. ballistic missile submarine are launched.

1961

As he departs from the presidency, Eisenhower warns against the growth of what he dubs "the military-industrial complex":

> A vital element in keeping the peace is our military establishment. Our arms must be mighty, ready for instant action, so that no potential aggressor may be tempted to risk his own destruction....

> Until the latest of our world conflicts, the U.S. had no armaments industry. American makers of plow-shares could, with time and as required, make swords as well. But now we can no longer risk emergency improvisation of national defense; we have been compelled to create a permanent armaments industry of vast proportions.... We annually spend on military security more than the net income of all United States corporations.

> This conjunction of an immense military establish-ment and a large arms industry is new in the American experience.... We recognize the imperative need for this development. Yet we must not fail to comprehend its grave implications.... In the councils of government, we must guard against the acquisition of unwarranted influence... by the military-industrial complex. The potential for the disastrous rise of mis-placed power exists and will persist.

> We must never let the weight of this combination endanger our liberties or democratic processes. We should take nothing for granted. Only an alert and knowledgeable citizenry can compel the proper meshing of the huge industrial and military machin-ery of defense with our peaceful methods and goals, so that security and liberty may prosper together....

torn by the issues

1962

President John F. Kennedy announces that U.S. advisors in South Vietnam will fire if fired upon.

A Soviet offensive missile buildup is discovered in Cuba. The crisis is resolved after the U.S. orders naval and air blockades of further deliveries, and Russia agrees to dismantle the existing missile bases in Cuba.

1964

The effort to halt communist encroachment in Vietnam escalates into a major conflict. This involvement spanned the administrations of five presidents and led to severe domestic discontent in the late 1960s.

1968–73

The Vietnam War costs $148.8 billion or 14% of GNP at its peak.

During these years, antiwar sentiment grows in the U.S. Draft evasion and conscientious objection to military service become important issues in American culture.

The military draft ends after the Paris Peace Agreement is signed in 1973. After the Vietnam War is concluded, some doubt develops about the will of the U.S. to fight and win another war. The returning veterans, for the first time in American history, are not universally regarded as heroes. They are characterized by many as unwitting victims of misguided policy. This phenomenon is dubbed "the Vietnam syndrome."

The personal computer industry is born. Many companies in areas like California's Silicon Valley, formerly supported by defense and aerospace contracts, shift the application of their technologies to consumer-oriented products.

Ernest Fitzgerald, a civilian engineer and cost expert for the DoD, is fired after testifying to a congressional committee about hidden cost overruns for the C-5A cargo plane. He is reinstated, after an extended legal battle, and he launches a fight for the protection of "whistle-blowers."

Between 1968 and 1973, antiwar sentiment grows in the U.S. Draft evasion and conscientious objection to military service become important issues in American culture.

1972

The sixth and last manned lunar landing affirms the U.S. is winning the space race.

A ban on oil exports to the U.S. is imposed by Arab oil-producing countries. After creating economic turmoil in the U.S. for about six months, it is lifted. Americans become aware that U.S. energy supplies are largely under the control of potentially hostile Arab countries.

1976

A Senate subcommittee reveals that $22 million in bribes to foreign officials were made by Lockheed Aircraft Corp. to facilitate the sale of its planes. Lockheed admits payments in Japan, Turkey, Italy, and Holland.

A Government Accounting Office report states that since 1969, the initial planning estimates submitted by the DoD have turned out to be approximately 50% below the actual cost of major systems. The review fails to find one example of the DoD accurately estimating the cost of any major weapon system.

1981–1982

Defense appropriations are increased as President Ronald Reagan seeks to match the reported Soviet buildup of nuclear weapons. President Reagan believes that the economic pressure on the U.S.S.R to match the U.S. buildup will ultimately bankrupt the Soviet Union.

1983

Investigation into DoD procurement practices produces the following table of the cost of various items purchased for use by the armed services.

In 1985, President Reagan appoints the Packard Commission to study waste, inefficiency, and fraud in the defense contract process.

DoD vs. Commercial Procurement Costs

Tool	Retail Hardware Price	Contractor's Price
Hammer	$7.66	$435.00
Wrench, end box, 1 set	$4.99	$768.00
Pliers, slip joint	$.77	$430.00
Pliers, vise grip,	$21.58	$486.00
Wrench, socket set, 3/8"	$12.88	$545.00
Bar extension	$1.99	$430.00
Socket, 1/2"	$1.49	$456.00
Screwdriver, Phillips, 1 set	$1.69	$258.00
Screwdriver, offset	$2.79	$225.00
Crimping tool	$3.96	$729.00
Wrenches	$4.88	$1150.00
Wrenches	$1.57	$234.00
Drill set	$1.69	$599.00
Hex driver	$3.99	$469.00
Feeler gauge	$4.27	$436.00
Circuit tester	$3.39	$489.00
Tool box	$11.67	$652.00
Total	**$91.26**	**$8791.00**

In another report to Congress, a pair of pliers, worth $7.50 at retail, is reported to have been sold to the government for $748.00. This testimony forced Boeing to revise their contract as follows:

defense spending

Most public opinion

polls show that the

majority of the

American public,

while angered by

corrupt procurement

practices, are

supportive of a strong

military stance.

Revised Cost of Pliers

	ORIGINAL CONTRACT	REVISED PRICE
All tools *(including pliers reduced to $80 each)*	$528,536	$433,545
Proposal Preparation	$28,964	$30,648
Support Equipment Management	0	$93,307
Total	**$557,500**	**$557,500**

Note that the total amount of the contract remained the same, and it was approved and paid.

1985

President Reagan appoints the Packard Commission to study waste, inefficiency, and fraud in the defense contract process. The Packard Commission report states that "the defense acquisition system has basic problems that must be corrected. All too many of our weapon systems cost too much, take too long to develop, and, by the time they are fielded, incorporate obsolete technology."

The Packard Commission's proposed solution is to install self-policing mechanisms in the corporations that receive defense contracts and to appoint military officers to oversee this self-policing plan.

1986

Most public opinion polls show that the majority of the American public, while angered by corrupt procurement practices, are supportive of a strong military stance.

Congress imposes reductions in growth rates of defense appropriations as the federal deficit climbs to unprecedented levels. Cuts in discretionary programs are considered the only politically viable option.

President Reagan and Soviet Premier Mikhail Gorbachov reach a state of detente, or eased tensions, as Soviet society is opened up by Gorbachov's reforms. The U.S. and the U.S.S.R reach a tentative agreement to ban medium-range missiles.

torn by the issues

1987

An agreement is signed calling for the dismantling of all 1752 U.S. and 859 Soviet medium-range missiles.

1988

As a result of a secret Federal Bureau of Investigation (FBI) probe, a grand jury issues 245 subpoenas to a variety of corporate and Pentagon officials. The charges cover a wide range of offenses, including fraud, bribery, kickbacks, and cost overruns. Most of the corporations under investigation had willingly agreed to the Packard Commission's self-policing guidelines. None had filed reports of their own or anyone else's violation of the Packard Commission's procurement guidelines.

1989

Mikhail Gorbachov's liberalization of Soviet society and the ultimate failure of the repressive socialist economy result in the collapse of the Soviet Union at the end of the 1980s. The U.S. wins the Cold War.

Rockwell International, Inc. is fined $5.5 million for criminal fraud against the U.S. Air Force on a satellite contract.

1990

In its effort to expand its control of Mideast oil deposits, Iraq invades Kuwait.

Northrop Corporation, the builder of the stealth bomber, pleads guilty to thirty-four felonies and pays a $17 million fine for misrepresenting test results on nuclear cruise missiles and fighter jets.

1991

The U.S. leads a multinational force to expel Iraq from Kuwait. The war is over within a few days, and the U.S. status as the last remaining superpower is firmly established. The "Vietnam syndrome" is pronounced dead.

President Bush approves closure of thirty-four domestic military installations, and forty-eight others are realigned.

The Gulf War sets a precedent. In the future, external military intervention in regional conflicts will probably occur under international, not national or bilateral, auspices.

defense spending

In 1993, only one in

five age-eligible men

enter the military. By

1995, the ratio may

be down to about one

in ten.

The Gulf War sets a precedent. In the future, external military intervention in regional conflicts will probably occur under international, not national or bilateral, auspices. This was the choice of the U.S in the Gulf, for the following reasons:

- For financial support, in light of the U.S. budget deficit problems.

- To provide legitimacy, domestic and international, in the wake of antiwar sentiment. International coalitions, carrying the weight of world opinion, support and advance the goals of quick and decisive resolution of conflict, thus reducing both casualties and collateral damage (destruction of civilian buildings like homes, schools, and hospitals).

- To secure more efficiently such logistical support as bases, overflight rights, and the like.

1992

Since the Gulf War, American armed forces have been deployed in more than twenty different operations, few of which had traditional military objectives. Some examples are:

- Operation Provide Comfort and Operation Southern Watch to aid the Kurds in Iraq.

- Operation Sea Angel to aid flood victims in Bangladesh.

- The rescue of civilians in the Philippines and Italy after volcano eruptions.

- Drug interdiction along the U.S. border and in Latin America.

- The restoration of order after the Los Angeles riots.

- Disaster relief efforts following hurricanes in Florida and Hawaii.

- Spearheading relief efforts in Somalia.

torn by the issues

1993

A clear conception of the place of the military in American society survived from the early days of World War II right up to the beginning of the Vietnam War. According to this view, service in the military was a rite of passage for most American males. Eight out of ten eligible men served in World War II. From the Korean War to the early 1960s, about half of age-eligible men served. Four out of ten served in Vietnam. Now, only one in five age-eligible men enter the military. By 1995, the ratio may be down to about one in ten. This reflects not only the changing cultural attitude toward military service, but also the changing of the military from a manpower-intensive army to a technology-intensive force. There is less emphasis on ground forces and more on "smart" weapons that require less manpower and cause less collateral, civilian damage.

So-called "ethnic cleansing" in the former Yugoslavia and increased hostilities in Somalia threaten to demand more response from the U.S. as the power behind the United Nations. This movement toward multinational forces will likely gain momentum. Some are predicting the formation of a genuine international army with its own recruitment and promotional systems. It is not inconceivable that some regional powers could configure their militaries largely to serve the purpose of assisting the U.S. in quickly and decisively resolving regional conflicts. The political and economic consequences are matters of continuing debate.

Defense Contracts

The three main types of defense contracts are:

• The competitive bid contract, which ordinarily would be awarded to that company offering to provide the hardware at the lowest cost.

The need for secrecy

to protect national

security and the

demand for openess

that is essential in a

democracy are

conflicting elements

in our society.

- The negotiated contract, in which DoD officials discuss and reach agreement with a private company concerning materials or services and their costs.

- The cost-plus contract, in which the DoD guarantees the private company repayment of all costs involved in producing hardware or service, plus a stipulated amount or percentage of costs as profit.

All three methods of procurement have resulted in repeated reports of scandalous cost overruns. The competitive bid contract, while resulting in a lower initial estimate for a weapons system, can be altered at any time after the initial signing for any reason. The negotiated contract, which came into use at the time of the WW II buildup, was necessary to provide a rapid response to the German aggression. The costs are higher initially, because there is a sole-source provider and the need is immediate. As in a bidded contract, the contract can be altered at any time for any reason. The cost-plus contract is the most costly. The contractor can add an almost unlimited amount of hidden costs and hidden profits at any time for any reason. When questioned, all the players involved in this system say that it can't be changed without weakening our defense position.

Public outrage at this waste of taxpayer dollars is sometimes characterized as an unpatriotic attempt to discredit efforts to maintain a strong military posture. However, public opinion polls reveal a public generally in favor of a strong military stance, but opposed to the waste of their money in criminal profiteering.

Government defenders of the procurement system say that R&D overhead costs have to be distributed over the cost of all parts of a system, which will sometimes result in inflated costs for some of these parts. Media misinformation is then cited as causing the public's outrage. Still, the public questions why ordinary civilian manufacturing techniques, which work so well in the private marketplace, are not brought to bear on the weapons-procurement process.

A well-publicized example of this debate is the issue of the $7,622 coffee pot. Defense apologists said that the item was designed for the C-5A aircraft which carried as many as 365 passengers. After Lockheed was embarrassed publicly, it lowered the price to $3,046, which was about what commercial airlines pay for large capacity coffee pots. It was later revealed by the press that the pot in question was a 10-cup model.

184

The Issue of Secrecy

The need for secrecy to protect national security and the demand for openess that is essential in a democracy are conflicting elements in our society. The Constitution guarantees, in Article I, Section 9, that "no money shall be drawn from the treasury but in consequence of appropriations made by law; and a regular statement of account of the receipts and expenditures of all public money shall be published from time to time." Nevertheless, a significant portion of the activities and the budgets of the government are permitted to remain secret.

The Manhattan Project, the secret program established to develop the atomic bomb during WWII, was the beginning of the secret military budget that has remained in place, and grown, ever since. Currently, the three principal secret agencies that can negotiate contracts are:

- The Central Intelligence Agency.
- The National Security Council.
- The National Reconnaissance Office.

This last agency is responsible for spy satellites. It is so secret that its name cannot be mentioned on the floor of Congress or in any unclassified government document. Neither Congress nor the public are allowed to know about the content or cost of programs funded within these agencies.

These sections of the national budget are referred to as the "black budget." Three programs that are funded by this part of the defense budget were recently declassified to the extent that they could be considered by congressional committee as to their cost and usefulness. They are:

The Stealth Bomber

With its radar-absorbing skin, these planes will dodge enemy air defenses, drop nuclear bombs, and seek out and destroy enemy command posts. They are the most expensive weapons ever built, at an estimated cost of $820 million per plane. The Pentagon has ordered seventy-five for a total of $61.5 billion. They are so expensive that they probably will not be used unless full-scale nuclear war erupts.

The National Reconnaissance Office is responsible for spy satellites. It is so secret that its name cannot be mentioned on the floor of Congress or in any unclassified government document.

Since the

administration of

George Washington,

presidents have

warned against the

power inherent in the

military

establishment.

MILSTAR (Military Strategic Tactical and Relay System)

This is a space satellite program that would essentially be a space-based military brain in the event of nuclear war. It is capable of operating throughout a hypothetical six-month-long nuclear war, even though it is estimated that full-scale nuclear war would destroy most cities and military facilities almost immediately.

ACM
(Advanced Cruise Missile)

This is a $7-billion dollar, nuclear-tipped missile equipped with radar-evading Stealth technology. There have been reports that this weapon has not yet proven successful in tests. Its testing record and its budget have been totally secret for ten years. In 1989, Les Aspin, the Chairman of the House Armed Services Committee, reported to Congress that the ACM is "a procurement disaster…the worst the committee has looked at. Why? Because of classification, the reasons will have to remain sketchy, almost nonexistent."

Funding for the black budget reached $36 billion during the mid-1980s, but has since declined to about $30 billion due to the relaxation of the Soviet threat. The issue of secrecy continues to plague American society. In general, citizens understand the necessity for national security, but see such secrecy as a threat to the American ideal of an open society.

The Pros & Cons

Since the administration of George Washington, presidents have warned against the power inherent in the military establishment. It was this danger that prompted the founding fathers to place a civilian, the president, as commander in chief of the armed forces. Nevertheless the military establishment has grown beyond what anyone would have predicted during the formation of the republic. It has become a major source of employment and has encouraged the growth of many thriving and affluent communities that have sprung up around defense-related facilities, both public and private. When cuts in defense spending are considered, a significant problem is the unwillingness of these communities to cooperate in their own demise. Understandably, they lobby energetically for the status quo when their community and personal livelihoods are threatened.

Military spending, as a percentage of GNP, has steadily declined during the course of American history. It reached 104% of GNP at the peak of the Revolutionary War, and now hovers at around 5% of GNP. It provides employment for approximately 3 million people, not including those who work in the private sector under DoD contracts. Our massive military establishment provides Americans with a sense of security that is rare in the world today. For these reasons, many insist that maintenance of the current level of military preparedness is appropriate and necessary.

Many citizens take an opposing view, believing that the resources used in creating the military establishment could be put to better use, either in the public or private sector. The lack of low-cost housing is cited, as is the need for environmental protection and clean-up, education, health-care needs, and the like.

If defense cutbacks resulted in reductions in taxation, as many are calling for, the private sector economy might grow and prosper as a result, thus taking up the slack with needed employment. The need to reduce the deficit by reducing all government spending, including military spending, is also seen by many as a primary consideration. However, in spite of these obvious benefits, the proposed reductions are a very small percentage of what is required to balance the budget. The reduction of runaway entitlements is seen by most observers as far more urgent. Unfortunately, curtailing entitlements is politically difficult. Defense cutbacks usually have wide public support outside of the defense community, and thus are easier to accomplish politically. They will undoubtedly continue in the foreseeable future, unless world events demand otherwise.

If defense cutbacks resulted in reductions in taxation, as many are calling for, the private sector economy might grow as a result, thus taking up the slack with needed employment.

defense spending

Sources

Beers, David. "The Crash of Blue Sky California." *Harper's,* July 1993.

Fitzgerald, A. Ernest. *The Pentagonists.* Boston: Houghton Mifflin Company, 1989.

Garrity, Patrick J. "Regional Powers and the Persian Gulf War." *The Washington Quarterly,* Summer 1993.

Hoffman, Mark S. *The World Almanac and Book of Facts.* New York: Pharos Books, 1993.

Lehman, Ronald F. "Arms Control and National Strategy." *The Washington Quarterly,* Summer 1993.

Mahnken, Thomas G. "America's Next War." *The Washington Quarterly,* Summer 1993.

Moskos, Charles. "From Citizen's Army to Social Laboratory." *The Wilson Quarterly,* Winter 1993.

Plano, Jack C., and Milton Greenberg. *The American Political Dictionary.* 8th edition. Fort Worth: Harcourt Brace Jovanovich College Publishers, 1990.

Rahe, Paul A. "The Martial Republics of Classical Greece." *The Wilson Quarterly,* Winter 1993.

Stiles, T.J., ed. *The Citizen's Handbook.* New York: Berkley Publishing Group, 1993.

Townshend, Charles. "Militarism and Modern Society." *The Wilson Quarterly,* Winter 1993.

U.S. Department of Commerce. *Statistical Abstract of the U.S., 1992.* Washington, D.C.: Bureau of the Census, 1992.

Weiner, Tim. *Blank Check* New York: Warner Books, Inc., 1990.

Wright, John W. *The Universal Almanac.* Kansas City, Kansas: Andrews and McMeel, 1993.

Society's accountability to the poor has been a subject

of heated debate throughout history. When social welfare laws

began to emerge in the U.S. in the early nineteenth century, they

were designed to prevent the needy from becoming chronically

poor. Those who were able-bodied but refused to work were regarded

as criminals and were often jailed, placed in workhouses or private homes

The focus of reform

has usually been skill

development to

enable welfare

recipients to become

self-sufficient.

as indentured servants, or banished from the community. Often the children of impoverished widows were removed from their homes and placed in public or private orphanages or with families who were financially able to care for them. The laws made it very difficult to receive public assistance. The intention was to insure that only those who were physically or mentally unable to work or who were willing to accept the stigma of pauperism would seek public assistance. Family, friends, and private charities provided most of the assistance to the needy.

In the early twentieth century, the first law designed primarily to support dependent children was established in the U.S. This law was originally known as a widow's pension because it provided for assistance to be given to women whose husbands had died. The intent of the law was to keep families together and to allow women to remain at home with their children despite a lack of income. Laws providing public assistance to needy blind, elderly, and permanently disabled individuals were established shortly thereafter.

In the 1930s, federal responsibility for assistance increased with the advent of the Social Security and Aid to Dependent Children programs. Enrollment increased as growing numbers of individuals fell below poverty level. Many began to urge reforms in order to prevent the development of a culture of poverty. The focus of reform has usually been skill development to enable welfare recipients to become self-sufficient. Job training, education, job counseling, and child care programs, some of which continue today, were established to achieve this goal. Many people have been helped out of the culture of poverty and into self-sufficiency through these programs. There are four basic categories of federal and state welfare assistance: aid to families with dependent children, old age assistance, aid to the blind, and aid to the permanently and totally disabled. Most states also have a general assistance program to help those who are in need but do not fit into the other four categories.

Despite these attempts to address the problem, poverty becomes more and more entrenched. The causes are complex and the cures are difficult. Some feel that the welfare programs actually cause poverty and should be abolished, with the truly needy being provided for by family, friends and private charities, as in other eras. Others feel that this would result in disastrous consequences for a huge portion of our

torn by the issues

population, who are poor because of economic, cultural, and racial circumstances beyond their control. Poverty seems to be inherent in all the industrialized economies of the world.

As the costs of social welfare programs rise and the burden to taxpayers grows, all can agree that the creation of an efficient, humane system that instills a sense of personal responsibility in its beneficiaries is critical.

AFDC Funding Growth as Compared to Population Growth

(IN MILLIONS)
1955-1987

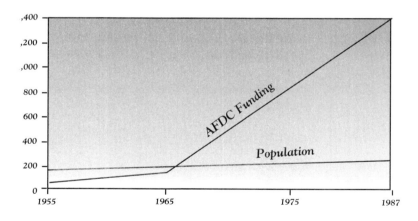

Roosevelt believes

that OAA will be

absorbed into Social

Security and that

AFDC will wither

away when the

country becomes

prosperous again.

Timeline

1700s–1800s

The intent of welfare policies is to control pauperism. Paupers are perceived as moral degenerates who live lives of drunkenness, corruption, and evil. They are considered criminals and outcasts. The poor who are willing and able to work are not considered paupers. The poor are therefore helped to become economically self-sufficient in order to lead them away from pauperism. Assistance is often refused or given under very harsh conditions in order to discourage individuals applying for benefits. There is a strong social stigma attached to the acceptance of public welfare assistance.

Relief administration is carried out at the local level. Municipal and county governments decide who should receive benefits, what kind, how much, and under what conditions.

1911

The first program assisting children of poverty is enacted. The program is originally designed to support widows and their children. Relief for the blind is also established at this time.

1920

The Old Age Assistance (OAA) program is established.

1935

President Franklin Delano Roosevelt introduces the Social Security Act. Title IV of the Act establishes the federal and state programs for Aid to Families with Dependent Children (known as ADC and later AFDC).

Roosevelt also appropriates money for the blind, the permanently and totally disabled, and the elderly. Roosevelt believes that OAA will be absorbed into Social Security and that AFDC will wither away when the country becomes prosperous again.

torn by the issues

1930s

Death of the husband/father is the primary cause of AFDC enrollment.

1940s

Abandonment by the husband/father is increasingly becoming the cause of AFDC enrollment.

1946

The national School Lunch Act is created with the ideals of promoting the health of American children and encouraging the use of domestic farm products. It is an early form of farm subsidy. The Act allows children to receive free or reduced-price lunches at school. Children are eligible for free lunches if their family income is below 130% of poverty. Children can receive reduced-price lunches if their family income is 130% to 185% of poverty.

1950

The U.S. Congress passes the Notice to Law Enforcement Officials Amendment in response to the rising number of AFDC recipients. This amendment creates a federal law requiring that when aid is to be given to a deserted or abandoned child, prompt notice must be given to law enforcement officials so that the father may be sought for support payments.

1951

The U.S. Congress amends the Social Security Act to allow disclosure of the welfare rolls under certain conditions. Originally, the Act provided that information of this type was confidential and restricted and could not be used for political or other purposes.

1955

About thirty American children per thousand are receiving AFDC assistance.

In 1963, President

Lyndon B. Johnson

begins the "War on

Poverty." He hopes

to eradicate poverty

in the U.S.

1960

About 2.4 million Americans receive AFDC assistance. Between 1960 and 1967, the AFDC program expenditures increase by 73%, despite low unemployment rates in the U.S.

1962

Public Welfare Amendments authorize the Community Work and Training Program (CWTP). The program provides AFDC enrollees with public service jobs that do not displace other workers. States can accept or deny enrollment of adult AFDC recipients based on work potential. Between October 1962 and June 1968, CWTP workers receive $195 million in earned wages. By the time the program is terminated in 1968, it involves as many as 27,000 participants.

1963

President Lyndon B. Johnson begins the "War on Poverty." He hopes to eradicate poverty in the U.S.

1964

The Economic Opportunity Act allows states to develop job training programs. The work experience program spends $300 million, with participation at a high of 72,000 persons in 1967. The program is now defunct. It is not known what effect the program had on the employment status of welfare recipients.

1965

Medicaid, a program designed to provide medical assistance to low-income individuals, becomes federal law.

1965–1970

Welfare enrollment rises from 4.3 million to 8.5 million during this five-year period.

1966

The School Breakfast Program is developed under the Child Nutrition Act.

torn by the issues

Welfare recipients

often discover they

can get more money

from welfare than

they can earn from

a job.

Free or reduced-price breakfasts are provided in eligible school and child care centers.

The Special Milk Program is also created as a part of this act. It is designed to encourage children to drink milk and help support U.S. dairy farmers. Any children who do not participate in other federally supported nutrition programs are eligible to participate.

The Summer Food Service Program is established. This program provides nutritious meals to children during the summer when school is not in session. To operate in a particular area, at least one half of the children must be from families with incomes at or below 185% of poverty.

1967

The Work Incentive (WIN) Program is enacted as a part of new Social Security amendments, in an attempt to help AFDC recipients to be less dependent on welfare. The program, which includes job training, counseling, and assistance in obtaining basic education and job skills, is developed in response to the 24% increase in families headed by women eligible for AFDC benefits. By 1971, it becomes apparent that most participants in the program are not finding jobs. Amendments are enacted in 1971, 1980, 1982, and 1984. In October 1990, the WIN program ends and is supplanted by the JOBS program.

From 1967 to 1972, the number of AFDC recipients rises by over 75%.

1968

The Child Care Food Program is established as a part of the National School Lunch Act. It provides eligible schools and child care centers with free lunches. The program is exempt from budget cuts.

A report commissioned by the Johnson administration and completed in 1968 notes that many welfare recipients want to get jobs and are not in need of "work ethic" rehabilitation; however, they often discover they can get more money from welfare than they can earn from a job. The report suggests abolishing the present welfare system, substituting a guaranteed annual income of $2,400, and building into that guarantee a set of incentives that would make it more profitable to work.

1969

President Nixon proposes the Family Assistance Plan. According to the plan, a family of four in which both parents are unemployed would receive a guaranteed income of $2,320 per year including food stamps. (In 1990 dollars, that would be about $7000). Nixon hopes to abolish AFDC. The Senate rejects the plan on the grounds that it does not encourage work over welfare.

California governor Ronald Reagan commissions a task force in an attempt to stop the growth of welfare enrollment in California, which is increasing at the rate of 40,000 AFDC recipients a month.

Welfare enrollment in the U.S. rises to 6.7 million in 1969.

1970

Nearly eighty-five children per thousand in the U.S. receive AFDC benefits.

About one in fourteen Americans is receiving welfare.

The U.S. Secretary of Health, Education, and Welfare tells Congress that "the present welfare system has been a failure."

About 25.5 million people or 13% of the U.S. population, are living below the poverty level of $3,968 annual income for a family of four.

1971

Governor Ronald Reagan presents his California welfare plan that will theoretically exclude ineligible individuals. In May, California AFDC enrollment includes 1,285,742 people. One year after the plan is put into effect, enrollment includes 1,270,970 people.

1972

Public assistance expenditures including medical care total $1.5 billion per month, approximately $18 billion per year.

In 1977, the Food
Stamp Act provides
monthly vouchers to
low-income families
for food purchase.

The Supplemental Food for Women, Infants, and Children (WIC) program is established as an amendment to the Child Nutrition Act of 1966. The program is designed to promote the health and nutrition of low-income pregnant women, women who are breast feeding, and children under age five. WIC provides food, nutritional education, and access to health services. All women with children are eligible for WIC benefits if their incomes are below 185% of the poverty level. About one in every five newborns in the U.S. receives WIC benefits.

1973

The Comprehensive Employment and Training Act (CETA) combines several federal employment and training programs. The Act is in effect for about ten years.

1975

11.3 million Americans receive AFDC benefits.

1977

The Food Stamp Act authorizes seven urban and seven rural workfare pilot projects that are operational between 1979 and 1980. The food stamp program is administered by the Department of Agriculture. The program provides monthly vouchers to low-income families for food purchase. The net income of the family must be at or below 100% of poverty.

President Jimmy Carter announces his President's Program for Better Jobs and Income. The program outlines a plan whereby the deserving poor will receive a substantial guaranteed income. Those who are able to work will receive a lower guaranteed income, but will be guaranteed a job. If the enrollee is unable to find a private sector job, a public or private sector job will be provided. The program fails to pass through the legislature.

1980

Congress establishes a system by which states will be held accountable for errors in food stamp issuance.

1981

Amendments to the Food Stamp Act grant authority to states to establish workfare programs for food stamp participants. Noncompliance with the program may result in the loss of food stamp eligibility.

1982

The Job Training Partnership Act replaces the Comprehensive Employment and Training Act. It is an attempt to lessen CETA's emphasis on public service jobs and create a new emphasis on jobs in the private sector. Job search and child care assistance are provided. The majority of AFDC mothers find jobs upon leaving the program, with an average wage of about $4.40 an hour, $1 above the minimum wage.

1983

The Temporary Emergency Food Assistance Program Act is established to provide for distribution of surplus agricultural products to the needy. The foods available for monthly distribution include cheese, butter, non-fat milk, honey, flour, corn meal, and rice. Each state is allocated food products based on the number of persons unemployed or living below poverty level.

1984

A federal General Accounting Office report shows that errors made in determining food stamp eligibility and in calculating participant benefits cost the federal government about $1 billion.

The Deficit Reduction Act requires that eligibility verification systems be established in welfare programs, and that the IRS provide income records to welfare program administrators.

1986

AFDC expenditures total nearly $18 billion, and AFDC payments are received by 3.8 million U.S. families.

1987

The federal government spends $834.4 billion on all social welfare expenditures, a $51.7 billion increase from 1986.

About 5.5 million families with children have annual incomes below the poverty line.

Food stamps are received by 6.3 million households in the U.S.

Despite the existence of and participation in the food stamp program, nearly 20 million Americans are undernourished and /or chronically hungry.

Every month about 7.4 million children are enrolled in AFDC programs.

The Stewart B. McKinney Homeless Assistance Act authorizes more than $1 billion to be spent yearly in emergency relief to homeless individuals. Congress appropriates $400.5 million for the act in 1989 and $596.1 million in 1990. The McKinney Act includes five programs that assist homeless people in finding both transitional and permanent housing.

1988

President Reagan signs the Family Support Act into federal law. The plan establishes state education and training programs, child care and medical benefits for two-parent families in need, and stronger child support enforcement.

Of all AFDC adult recipients, 89% are women.

Of 8.8 million women raising children alone, 2.8 million have incomes below the poverty level.

Sixy percent of AFDC families have been receiving assistance for three years or less. The median length of time for each AFDC case is twenty-five months, two months less than in 1986. Twenty-five percent have been receiving assistance for over five years.

Six percent of AFDC women and 11% of AFDC men are employed.

In 1991, President

George Bush

formulates the Home-

ownership and

Opportunity for

People Everywhere

(HOPE) plan.

About 40% of all adult AFDC women are registered in work programs. Male registration is 61%.

About 21% of all households with children five to eighteen years old receive free or reduced price lunches under the National School Lunch Program. Almost half of all households headed by women had children who received free or reduced price lunches.

1990

The Job Opportunities and Basic Skills Training (JOBS) Program replaces the WIN program of 1967. JOBS works in conjunction with the Family Support Act to promote self-sufficiency of AFDC recipients. The program provides education, training, employment, child care, and other supportive services. Program objectives are:

- To target resources toward those individuals hardest to serve, particularly women with young children and individuals who are likely to need extended welfare.

- To provide job training and work experience.

- To maximize use of existing resources.

- To allow states program flexibility.

- To target funds primarily towards services rather than administration.

About 4.4 million households receive assistance from the Department of Housing and Urban Development, up from 3.1 million in 1980.

1991

Federal expenditures for the Head Start Program increase by $400 million since 1990. Job Training Partnership expenditures increase by $143 million, and expenditures for the WIC Program increase by $224 million.

President George Bush formulates the Home-ownership and Opportunity for People Everywhere (HOPE) plan. The purpose is to expand opportunities for low- to moderate-income families to manage their rental properties, to own their own homes eventual-

torn by the issues

In 1991, The Weed

and Seed Program

budget supports a

four-year pilot project

called Moving to

Opportunity.

ly, and to provide other housing services. The Bush administration proposes that $2.15 billion be spent for HOPE grants between 1991 and 1993.

President Bush proposes the Weed and Seed Program, an initiative designed to help rejuvenate communities and neighborhoods. The program is designed to take advantage of economic revitalization and job incentive programs and to offer more comprehensive social services. The program intends to give states the option to increase to $10,000 the assets limit of families who are already on the AFDC rolls. Currently when family assets exceed $1,000, the family is no longer eligible for AFDC. The assets limit for new families applying for AFDC benefits would remain at $1,000 in an effort to keep enrollment from rising.

The Weed and Seed Program budget supports a four year pilot project called Moving to Opportunity. Counseling and other types of assistance will be provided to 1500 low-income families who wish to move from high-poverty neighborhoods to mixed-income areas. Studies on previous programs have shown that two thirds of the individuals who participated in the program had jobs within five years.

The Weed and Seed program also permits individuals who live in public housing to have savings accounts held for them that they can receive once they leave public housing. The savings account is based on their earnings and could be used as a down payment under the home ownership voucher program.

1992

The JOBS Program is appropriated $1 billion.

Other current programs are:

- Job Corps, an employment and training program serving severely economically disadvantaged youths between sixteen and twenty-one. The intent of the program is to prepare these individuals for employment or entrance into educational institutions.

- Child Support Enforcement Program, which is intended to locate absent parents, establish paternity, establish child support obligations, and enforce child support orders.

- Targeted Jobs Tax Credits, a program offering tax incentives to employers who hire targeted individuals such as handicapped people, AFDC recipients, ex-offenders, and disadvantaged youths, etc.

- The Summer Youth Employment and Training Program, providing disadvantaged youths with job training and educational services during the summer.

- Sections 8 and 202 of the U.S. Housing Act. This legislation appropriates government funds to pay the difference between fair market rent and a rental amount the tenant can pay, usually through contractual arrangements with landlords.

- The Low Income Home Energy Assistance Program, which assists low-income households with energy costs. Some states grant AFDC recipients automatic eligibility.

AFDC

It is assumed by many states that if a man is living in the household, even if he is not the father of the dependent children, he shares responsibility for the family, and the family thus loses eligibility for AFDC assistance. State laws vary on this issue.

Some states do not reduce benefits unless the man is continuously present in the home.

The AFDC program is the largest, costliest, and most controversial cash assistance program. Its fundamental goals are to meet the immediate financial needs of needy families with children, help parents become self-sufficient through job training, and assist parents in their job search.

Unlike the earlier aid program for widows with dependent children, AFDC is designed to support children of divorced, never-married, and abandoned women.

*F*ederal (Medicaid)

contributions have

risen from $2.5

billion in 1970 to

$23 billion in 1986,

a nearly tenfold

increase.

Households with both able-bodied parents present in the home are not eligible for AFDC, so fathers often leave the home so the mother can establish eligibility. With the intent of preserving family stability, Congress changed eligibility requirements to include two-parent homes if a parent has recent work history and is considered temporarily unemployed.

Female applicants whose children have been abandoned by their father are required to cooperate with law enforcement officials in the prosecution of the father for non-support. Welfare authorities make unannounced inspections of recipients' homes at irregular hours to determine if the father is present, or if there is evidence of fraud or child abuse.

Medicaid

Medicaid is a state and federally funded medical assistance program for low-income individuals and families. The federal government contributes 50% to 77% of the funds. Many states have some method of cost sharing, in which recipients pay a small deductible for medical care and the state and federal funds cover the remaining costs. The program provides medical assistance to those already eligible to receive assistance under AFDC or Supplemental Security Income (SSI).

Medicaid is an optional program for states and U.S. territories. States and territories formulate their own restrictions. The U.S. Bureau of Census reports that two fifths of the nation's poor are ineligible for benefits according to state standards.

In 1969, Medicaid was estimated to cost between $400 and $1,200 per year per family. Federal contributions have risen from $2.5 billion in 1970 to $23 billion in 1986, a nearly tenfold increase. In 1987, over 19.5 million people received Medicaid benefits.

Some view welfare

as a means by which

an individual who has

not had the same

educational and

financial

opportunities as

others will be given a

new start.

More Welfare Facts

- The number of AFDC recipients rose from 3 million in an average month in 1960, to 4.3 million in 1965, to 8.5 million in 1970, to 11.3 million in 1975. About 11.9 million adults and children received AFDC benefits in 1988 and about 12.4 million received assistance in 1989.

- The cost of AFDC tripled between 1960 and 1970, and the number of recipients nearly tripled.

- The largest category of poor people in America is children.

- Over 30% of all children received assistance at some time between 1983 and 1986.

- In May 1990, the unemployment rate for white males over twenty years old was 4.2%. For black males over twenty, the unemployment rate was 9.1%.

- In 1964, 19.2% of the population lived below the poverty level. In 1989, 22.1% was living below the poverty level.

- Currently, about 17% of the child population in the U.S. is living below the poverty level. In Canada, the percentage is 9.6%; in Great Britain, it's 10.7%; and in Germany, it's 8.2%.

Welfare Pro & Con

Pro

- Society has a moral obligation to provide a minimum subsistence level for those who are unable to provide for themselves. Many believe that one fundamental duty of a society is to provide for the well-being of its members, especially those who for any reason are unable to care for themselves.

- Welfare gives underprivileged individuals an equal chance to succeed in society. Some view welfare as a means by which an individual who has not had the same educational and financial opportunities as others due to difficult life circumstances will be given a new start and an equal chance to succeed without the obstacles of hunger, poverty and homelessness.

- The possibility of economic disaster, poverty, hunger or homelessness disallows freedom for all members of society. These conditions must be abolished in a society that is dedicated to freedom, and a welfare system is a means of abolition.

- Poverty is a catalyst for many societal problems including crime, sickness, hunger, and homelessness. These conditions have an adverse affect on society as a whole. Therefore, welfare is a necessary evil.

- The economically insecure are victims of a societal system that is often cruel. Unemployment, unaffordable health care costs, unaffordable education costs, unaffordable housing costs, and other demands of modern life create victims who are unable to control or improve their circumstances. Welfare is a means by which this victimization can be alleviated.

- It is psychologically healthier for individuals to receive help through government programs in an anonymous way than to ask for private charity. Anonymity lessens the social stigma attached to receiving relief benefits.

- Welfare assists children who would not otherwise be provided for or who would not be able to remain with their families. Underprivileged children are victims of circumstances they are not able to change. Society has an obligation to assist children so that they may have equal opportunity to lead productive lives. Children should be able to remain with their parents despite the fact that the family is financially unstable, as the family is an important societal institution that deserves to be preserved.

Welfare assists children who would not otherwise be provided for or who would not be able to remain with their families. Underprivileged children are victims of circumstances they are not able to change.

Government

programs are unable

to assess each case

properly, and fraud,

overcompensation,

and other problems

are unavoidable.

Con

- The government has no right to give the tax dollars of working people to those who are unable or unwilling to work. Many view welfare as a system of compulsory giving in which their tax dollars are given to others without their consent.

- The qualities of initiative and ambition are destroyed by a system in which individuals can get something for nothing. Welfare programs are damaging to the work ethic and to the feeling of self-esteem associated with supporting oneself. A system of guaranteed income destroys the incentive to work and earn a living, as well as the recipient's self esteem.

- The welfare system supports a "poverty is the best policy" mentality by maintaining a system in which individuals who support themselves will have to support others, and those who do not support themselves will be supported by others.

- The welfare system creates a false sense of security among the needy by appearing to promise that all needs will be fulfilled by the government. This may not always be the case, and this perception should not be encouraged.

- The welfare system is impersonal, bureaucratic, inefficient, and wasteful. Government programs are unable to assess each case properly, and fraud, overcompensation, and other problems are unavoidable. In addition, public welfare administration is much more costly than the administration of private charities.

- The welfare system is unmanageable and will continue to grow uncontrollably. Despite attempts to decrease unemployment and resurrect a stable economy, welfare enrollments and costs will continue to rise, because of the attraction of getting "something for nothing."

- Welfare programs are difficult to remove because of the extreme dependence that they create among recipients. This is detrimental to society.

Some Suggestions for Reform

Create Workfare Programs

Massachusetts, California, New York are some of the states that have instituted such programs. Welfare recipients in these states are expected to work at public service jobs or in private sector jobs that are sometimes subsidized by the government. This helps to defray the cost of their benefits and gives them a sense of personal responsibility. Critics argue that workfare will produce no significant results, and is just another reform mirage. Some unions are against workfare programs because they believe jobs will be taken from union workers. Workfare is seen as an imperfect solution, but better than nothing. State welfare administrators are constantly trying to refine these programs to make them more effective and efficient.

Strengthen Non-Cash Assistance Programs

Some advocates of welfare reform believe that strengthening job training, work experience, employment services, and educational programs will help welfare recipients acquire the skills needed to become self-sufficient. Critics of these programs claim they are already proven to be inefficient and unsuccessful in reducing welfare enrollment. They believe that even if allotted more funding, these programs will fail to bring about significant change in the number of long-term welfare recipients.

Extend Healthcare and Food Stamp Benefits

Many recipients realize that if they start to work they will no longer be eligible for many of the benefits they receive through welfare, particularly basic health care and food stamps. If these programs are extended to people who are starting to work, and kept available until

They believe these

problems are inherent

in a system that

allows people to get

something for

nothing.

the recipient is financially stable, then there will more incentive to work. Critics of these proposals believe this approach would not provide an incentive to work. They feel also that recipients of extended health care and food stamp benefits would become just as dependent on these services as they were when they were not working. In addition, these program extensions would be extremely costly and uncontrollable.

Expand the Earned Income Tax Credit

Advocates of this plan feel that tax credits should be extended to families attempting to go off welfare. According to this plan, families would receive a refundable tax credit of 14% of the first $5,714 to $9,000 of earned income. Above $9,000, the credit would be reduced by $0.10 for each dollar of earned income up to $17,000. Critics see this plan as too complicated and difficult to administer.

Narrow Eligibilty

This would ensure that only those who are truly in need would receive benefits. Critics claim that under present eligibility standards, many people whose incomes are below poverty level are already ineligible, and this would only exclude more of the truly needy from receiving assistance.

Abolish the Current System Entirely

Some believe this is the only way to solve the current welfare problem. Responsibility would then fall on friends, family, and private charity. Supporters of this view generally believe that there is no way to ameliorate the problems associated with welfare. They believe these problems are inherent in a system that allows people to get something for nothing. Critics of this view believe that the government has a responsibility to provide for those unable to provide for themselves. They believe that private charities are unable to provide this assistance on a consistent basis, particularly in light of the fast-growing popula-

Advocates of capping

believe that the

current system

encourages women to

continue to have

more children to

receive additional

benefits.

tion. In addition, they feel that the need for individuals to beg for charity would be even more psychologically damaging than the public programs and that this would be detrimental to society as a whole.

Cap Welfare Benefits

Advocates of this proposal believe that the current system encourages women to continue to have more children to receive additional benefits. Critics of this plan view it as an intrusion on individual freedom, but suggestions along these lines are being heard from community leaders who see the rising number of illegitimate births as ominous for their own community's health and stability.

Increase Cash Assistance

Proponents feel that increasing cash assistance would promote self-sufficiency, because recipients could focus on learning new skills, without worry about poverty, homelessness, or sickness. Critics feel this would only promote more dependency, and increase an already-heavy tax burden.

Sources

Anderson, Martin. *The Political Economy of Welfare Reform in the United States.* Stanford, CA: Hoover Institution Press, 1978.

Bender, David L. *The Welfare State: Opposing Viewpoints.* St. Paul, Minnesota: Greenhaven Press, 1982.

Berkowitz, Edward. *America's Welfare State: From Roosevelt to Reagan.* Baltimore: Johns Hopkins University Press, 1991.

Binford, Shari, et al., eds. *Social Welfare: Help or Hindrance?* Wylie, TX: Information Plus, 1990.

Gottschalk, Peter. "AFDC Dependence Across Generations." *American Economic Review,* May 1990.

Gueron, Judith. *Reforming Welfare with Work*. New York: Priority Press Publications, 1987.

Handler, Joel F. *Reforming the Poor*. New York: Basic Books, 1972.

Handler, Joel, and Ellen Jane Hollingsworth. *The Deserving Poor*. Chicago: Markham Publishing Co., 1971.

Hoffman, Mark S., ed. *1989 World Almanac and Book of Facts*. New York: Pharos Books, 1989.

Johnson, Otto, ed. *The 1992 Information Please Almanac*. Boston: Houghton Mifflin Company, 1992.

Office of the President. *1993 Federal Budget (proposed)*. Washington, D.C.: U.S. Government Printing Office, 1992.

Moffitt, Robert. "Work Incentives in the AFDC System: An Analysis of the 1981 Reforms." *American Economic Review*, May 1986.

Pechman, Joseph A., ed. *Welfare Policy After Welfare Reform: Fulfilling America's Promise*. Ithaca, NY: Cornell University Press, 1992.

Rovner, Julie. "Welfare Reforms Get Backing from Ways and Means." *Congressional Weekly Report*, 27 June 1992.

Sampson, Timothy J. *A Handbook for Friend and Foe*. Philadelphia: United Church Press, 1972.

Stoesz, Davis, and Howard J. Karger. *Reconstructing the American Welfare State*. Lahnham, Maryland: Rowan and Littlefield Publishers, 1992.

"Welfare Dependence Within and Across Generations." *Science Magazine*, 29 January 1988.

energy

in the years since the dawning of the Industrial Revolution, the world, and the United States in particular, have developed an insatiable and constantly escalating appetite for energy. The very survival of civilization as we know it depends on a continuing supply of enormous amounts of fuel for energy. The development and production of energy has become the paramount human endeavor.

The need for huge, immediate, and dependable supplies of energy is only one aspect of the current energy issue. There is also a growing awareness of the relationship between the production of energy fuels and the state of the environment. The production of energy and the disposal of harmful by-products create logistical problems related to the maintenance of a viable planetary habitat.

Irresponsible operation of fuel production and energy-generating facilities can result in lower air and water quality, destruction of arable land, endangerment of animal and plant species, and a general reduction in the level of human health. A consensus has yet to be reached on how to balance cultural convenience and economic growth with overall quality of life on the planet.

Finite reserves of fossil fuels and the effects of unpredictable world trade practices on fuel availability are additional aspects of the energy issue. The fuel-dependent economies of the United States and other developed nations of the world demand a stable worldwide fuel market. Obviously, a fuel crisis precipitates an economic crisis.

The petroleum industry is the single largest business on earth. Petroleum is no longer merely a luxurious convenience for better illumination, as it was in the days of John D. Rockefeller. The energy produced from petroleum is now intimately tied to survival issues as diverse as transportation, heating, refrigeration, and medicine. If the energy available from the use of petroleum were to vanish suddenly, so would modern civilization.

Conservation is a major factor in considering the viability of energy supplies. Conservation principles can be effectively applied to energy usage, energy storage, and product design. For maximum effectiveness, conservation needs to be practiced not only by government and private industry but also by individual households. Choices of what products to own and use and when to use them can be made on an individual basis, usually with no loss of comfort or well-being. Production and packaging efficiency could carry increasing weight in determining consumer choices, and this would impact on the marketplace.

The issues of energy and fuel production have, as with so many other issues, become highly politicized, sometimes to the detriment of the common good. Significant questions are:

Should government

policy include

military intervention

in areas outside

national boundaries

to protect national oil

interests?

- Does the free-market law of supply and demand provide sufficient motivation to develop the ways and means to achieve energy stability?
- Does government intervention, via regulation and research funding, solve problems or just create new problems?
- Can the U.S. government depend on oil, auto, or utility lobbies to formulate responsible and dependable energy policy?
- Should government policy include military intervention in areas outside national boundaries to protect national oil interests?
- Should the attention of both government and private industry be directed toward development of sustainable energy production via alternative, non-fossil fuels?

Timeline

2000 B.C.

The people of Glamorganshire, Wales, use coal in their funeral pyres.

1100 B.C.

The Chinese use coal for cooking and heating. They also obtain petroleum from shallow, hand-dug wells and geologically-occurring natural gas.

Coal is mentioned in the writings of Aristotle and by King Solomon in the Book of Proverbs.

A.D. 1306

Upon noting the injurious effects of coal pollution on the people's health, King Edward I of England issues a proclamation declaring its use punishable by death.

1542

Explorer Juan Cabrillo repairs his ship with asphalt found on the California coast.

1600

Jesuit priests observe Native Americans scooping up oil from natural seepages to use for fuel and medicine.

1679

Coal is discovered in what is now Illinois by a French priest, Father Louis Hennepin. Various Native American tribes had previous knowledge of its existence, most notably the Pueblo tribes, who used it in pottery.

1750

Coal mining operations begin near Richmond, Virginia, after a large deposit is discovered there. By this date, many oil seepages have been found in New York, Pennsylvania, and Virginia. Oil is also discovered accidentally while drilling salt brine wells.

1759

Coal mining begins in western Pennsylvania.

1791

Anthracite coal, the highest quality coal, is discovered in eastern Pennsylvania.

1824

Citizens of Fredonia, New York are the first to use commercially available natural gas for illumination.

1834

Vermont blacksmith Thomas Davenport builds the first electric motor.

1841

The city of Philadelphia begins to use coal gas for street illumination.

1849

Samuel M. Kier of Pittsburgh, Pennsylvania begins bottling petroleum and selling it for medicine.

1850

James Young of England discovers a process for extracting oil from oil-bearing shale. As this oil becomes known for its superior illumination qualities, it begins to replace whale oil, which is more expensive.

1854

Abraham Gesner of Nova Scotia, Canada, patents an improved illuminating oil derived from coal.

1859

Edwin L. Drake strikes oil in Titusville, Pennsylvania, at sixty-nine and a half feet; this is the first well drilled specifically for petroleum. The well produces thirty barrels a day that is stored in open ditches and transported in second-hand whiskey barrels. By this year, there are sixty-four plants in the United States producing oil from coal and shale.

1861

Samuel Andrews begins the first kerosene production facility in Cleveland, Ohio. Kerosene is a product made from crude oil that produces gasoline as a by-product. Gasoline is considered an unusable waste product during these years and is dumped into rivers.

Lacking the capital to fund the building of a commercial refinery, Andrews successfully appeals to fellow church-goer John D. Rockefeller.

Rockefeller becomes the major force behind the development of the American oil industry in the next half-century. He builds his empire on kerosene, which is the best and cheapest source of illumination in the world until the advent of the electric lamp. Rockefeller observes that the unregulated petroleum industry of the period is the cause of wide fluctuations in crude oil prices and sets out to stabilize prices by gaining controlling interest in American oil production. His company, Standard Oil, formed in 1870, is among the first recognized trusts, or monopolies, of the era.

1862

Colonel George Shoemaker is arrested in Philadelphia for attempting to sell a few wagonloads of anthracite coal. Coal is thought by many to be useless during this period, and its sale is considered fraudulent.

1865

In Pennsylvania, Samuel Van Syckel builds the first oil pipeline to transport oil from Pithole City to the nearest railhead.

1873

Oil fields in the Baku region of Russia are opened to development. Swedish businessmen Ludwig and Robert Nobel, brothers of Alfred Nobel, who established the Nobel prize, enter the oil business in the Baku fields.

1874

Captain J.J. Vandergrift completes the first oil trunkline from the Pennsylvania oilfields to Pittsburgh, severely undermining the railroad monopoly of oil transportation.

1878

The first sea-going oil tankers begin transporting crude to foreign markets.

The first hydropower plant is completed at Niagara Falls, New York.

1879

On October 21, Thomas Edison begins testing the first incandescent electric lamp.

1881

Jacques d'Arsonval of France proposes using temperature differentials to operate a heat engine to generate electricity. This theory is applied to the development of ocean thermal energy conversion plants.

1882

Thomas Edison throws the switch starting the first commercial power plant in Manhattan.

John D. Rockefeller and associates form Standard Oil Trust.

1883

Pittsburgh, Pennsylvania becomes the first major city to use commercially available natural gas as heating and lighting fuel.

1900

Eighteen million of Edison's incandescent bulbs are in American households. The shift to electricity for illumination causes a decline in kerosene use. Petroleum refining focuses upon gasoline for the rapidly growing automobile industry and fuel oil for heating and cooking.

1901

The Spindletop well just south of Beaumont, Texas, produces 75,000 barrels a day. This ushers East Texas into the petroleum industry and leads to the establishment of Sun, Texaco, and Gulf as national oil producers.

1904

The town of Larderello, Italy, generates the first electricity from geothermal steam.

1905

Albert Einstein suggests that mass and energy can be converted into each other: $E=mc^2$. This is the first step in the development of nuclear energy technology.

1906

Theodore Roosevelt's administration brings suit against Standard Oil under the Sherman Anti-Trust Act of 1890.

1907

The first drive-in gasoline station opens in St. Louis, Missouri.

1908

Oil is discovered in Persia (Iran).

1910

Half a million automobiles are on American roads.

1911

Oil is produced in Egypt for the first time.

The U.S. Supreme Court hands down its decision in *United States v. Standard Oil*, ruling that Standard Oil's trust is not in the public interest and will be dissolved within six months. In the resultant breakup of Standard Oil into smaller companies, Standard Oil of New Jersey later became Exxon, Standard Oil of New York later became Mobil, Standard Oil of California later became Chevron, Standard Oil of Ohio later became Sohio, Standard Oil of Indiana later became Amoco, Continental Oil later became Conoco, and Atlantic later became Arco and eventually Sun.

1913

Oil is produced in Iran for the first time.

Amoco opens new refineries using William Burton's revolutionary "thermal cracking" process, yielding double the amount of gasoline per barrel than conventional processes.

1914

Both the American and British navies complete conversion of fleets from coal to oil.

1915

Due to increased automobile use and the effect of electric utilities development, gasoline production outstrips kerosene production.

1916

There are 3.6 million automobiles on American roads.

The United States supplies 80% of the Allied petroleum during World War I.

1924

The Teapot Dome scandal erupts as a result of illegal oil leasing agreements between Sinclair Oil and Warren Harding's Secretary of the Interior, Albert Fall. The credibility of both the Harding and Coolidge administrations is severely damaged.

1927

Oil is produced in Iraq for the first time.

1929

There are more than 23 million automobiles on American roads.

Georges Claude builds the first ocean thermal energy conversion plant off the coast of Cuba.

1930

Twenty-nine years after the famous Spindletop gusher, Columbus "Dad" Joiner discovers the Black Giant field in East Texas. This field ultimately proves to be ten miles by forty-five miles in area, 140,000 acres altogether.

1931

The first cyclotron (atom-smasher) is built by E. O. Lawrence in the United States.

1932

Oil is discovered in Bahrain.

1936

Oil is produced in Saudi Arabia for the first time.

Boulder Dam, later renamed Hoover Dam, is completed at a total cost of $385 million.

1938

The uranium atom is split by Otto Hahn and Fritz Strassmann in Germany.

1941

Japan invades southern Indochina, causing the U.S., Britain, and the Netherlands to embargo oil to Japan. In response, Japan bombs the U.S. Navy base at Pearl Harbor. The U.S. enters World War II.

1942

The first successful nuclear reaction is achieved, on December 2, at the University of Chicago.

1942–1945

Gasoline and fuel oil are rationed in the U.S. as a result of scarcity brought on by World War II.

The U.S. supplies 90% of the oil used by the allies during World War II.

1945

The first atomic bomb is detonated on July 16, in Alamogordo, New Mexico. The U.S. drops the atom bomb on Hiroshima and Nagasaki in Japan, bringing an end to the war.

torn by the issues

1947

The Atomic Energy Commission (AEC), created by Harry Truman in 1946, takes control of the development of atomic energy from the U.S. Army.

Construction begins on the Trans-Arabian Pipeline (Tapline), a 1040-mile route across Saudi Arabia, Jordan, and Israel. This will replace the 7200-mile route from the Persian Gulf to the Suez Canal.

1951

A nuclear reactor that produces heat by burning uranium-235 powers a steam turbine to produce electricity.

Mohammed Mossadegh nationalizes Iranian oil, causing the first postwar oil crisis.

1953

The first breeder reactor is announced by the Atomic Energy Commission.

1954

The U.S.S. *Nautilus*, the first nuclear-powered submarine, is launched.

1955

The first commercially produced electricity from atomic power is made available in the state of New York.

1956

The Egyptian army closes the Suez Canal, precipitating the second postwar oil crisis.

Oil is discovered in Algeria and Nigeria.

1958

A geothermal electric energy plant begins operating on New Zealand's North Island.

1960

The Organization of Petroleum Exporting Countries (OPEC) is founded in Baghdad. Its five member countries—Saudi Arabia, Venezuela, Kuwait, Iraq, and Iran—control over 80% of the world's crude oil exports.

The first American geothermal electricity facility goes into service in California.

1967

The Clean Air Act passes the U.S. Senate.

On June 5th, Israel pre-empts Egyptian and Syrian military build-up near their borders, starting the Six-Day War. Nasser closes the Suez Canal, precipitating the third postwar oil crisis.

1968

As a result of the increasing pollution problems in New York City due to using coal in the production of electricity, the state of New York converts its utilities entirely to oil.

Oil is discovered in Alaska.

1969

During well-drilling off the coast of Southern California, near Santa Barbara, oil bubbles up through an undetected fissure and spills an estimated 6000 barrels of oil into the ocean and onto thirty miles of local beaches. In the wake of public outcry, the Nixon Administration imposes a moratorium on offshore drilling in the area.

1973

Egypt and Syria simultaneously attack Israel on October 6th, the holiest of Jewish holidays (Yom Kippur), and embargo exports of crude oil, precipitating the fourth postwar oil crisis. By December, crude oil prices have risen from $2.90 per barrel to $11.65 per barrel. Shortly thereafter, Congress approves the Alaskan pipeline.

In 1974, the

International Energy

Agency is founded to

harmonize energy

policy between the

U.S. and Western

Europe.

1974

The International Energy Agency is founded to harmonize energy policy between the U.S. and Western Europe. The French refuse to join. French Foreign Minister Michel Jobert calls the agency an "instrument of war."

The Nuclear Regulatory Commission (NRC) is formed. Its function is to license and regulate nuclear reactors and to assume many of the functions of the AEC, which is dissolved the following year.

1975

Automobile fuel efficiency standards are established in the U.S.

1979

An accident takes place at the Three Mile Island nuclear facility in Pennsylvania. Operator error, insufficient emergency controls, and equipment failure are cited as the causes. Although there are no deaths or injuries attributed to the accident it is considered a near-disaster. Investigations during the aftermath lead to sweeping reorganization of the NRC.

1975–1980

Funding for research and development of renewable sources of energy rises from less than $100 million to over $700 million.

1980

Iraq wages war against Iran.

1979–1981

Panic generated by Iranian hostility to American oil interests sends oil prices from $13 to $34 per barrel. This is the fifth postwar oil crisis.

1981

There are seventy-four nuclear power generating plants operating in the United States. Government grants for an additional seventy-six plants have been approved.

1983

OPEC cuts oil prices to $29 per barrel.

1985

Ninety-five nuclear power generating plants are in operation. Thirty additional units have been approved.

Oil prices drop to $10 per barrel for domestic oil and $6 per barrel for imported as a result of OPEC quota fluctuations and the subsequent oil glut.

1986

A nuclear accident at the Chernobyl nuclear plant in the U.S.S.R. involves radioactive releases.

As in the Three Mile Island incident, operator error was a major factor in the accident. The enormous harm done to the environment and the populace is greatly compounded by the political manipulations of the secretive governmental regime.

There are thirty-one deaths resulting from the Chernobyl accident and 600,000 people are classified as "significantly exposed" to radiation. These people will be monitored for the rest of their lives to determine the effect of the accident.

1989

The *Exxon Valdez* tanker runs aground off the coast of Alaska, spilling 240,000 barrels of oil into Prince William Sound.

Funding for renewable energy research and development reaches an eight-year low.

1990

Saddam Hussein invades Kuwait, precipitating the sixth postwar oil crisis. An embargo imposed against Iraq and Kuwait effectively removes 4.3 million barrels of crude oil per day from the world market. Prices shoot to $40 per barrel. Both the U.S and OPEC increase production.

Legislation in Congress strengthens the Clean Air Act by requiring gasoline reformulation to reduce pollutants from automobiles. This legislation requires reduction of levels of hydrocarbon and sulfur emissions from other sources as well.

1991

NATO drives Iraq out of Kuwait. Saddam Hussein sets Kuwaiti oil fields afire.

1992

The U.S. has 111 nuclear power generating plants fully operational, with eight additional units under construction. These plants account for 20.6% of electricity production. Coal accounts for 55%, petroleum for 4% or 5%, hydropower for 10%, and natural gas for 9% of U.S. electricity.

Conventional Energy Sources

Fossil Fuels

Fuels derived from fossilized prehistoric plant and animal remains include coal, natural gas, and petroleum. Use of these fuels varies widely by region, climate, and socioeconomic class, but all three are primary sources for our energy needs.

Coal has been used as a source of heat, electricity, and in earlier days, fuel for ships and locomotives. It has been mined and used extensively in the U.S. since the mid-eighteenth century and has been a major factor in the rise of the U.S. as an international industrial power. In its bituminous form, coal is still the least expensive fossil fuel on the American market today. U.S. consumption has risen 22% over the past decade.

Bituminous coal accounts for most of the reserves east of the Mississippi, with the only known reserves of anthracite coal in eastern Pennsylvania. Bituminous, sub-bituminous, and lignite coal reserves are found in slightly larger quantities west of the Mississippi.

Although coal is the least expensive of available fossil fuels, other costs, both capital and environmental, are associated with its use. Bituminous and other soft coals account for most of the total coal use in the U.S., and they typically do not burn as clean as the harder and slower-burning anthracite variety. Much of the soft coal used in energy production contains large quantities of sulfur, which is released into the air during combustion. When combined with atmospheric moisture, this sulfur becomes sulfuric acid, the main contributor to the acid rain problem of recent decades. Unfortunately, the only known remedy to control sulfur emissions is the costly installation and maintenance of "scrubber" equipment that removes the sulfur from the emissions prior to release into the environment. This procedure leaves residual sulfur and various other particulate wastes that are difficult to dispose of safely. Strip-mining coal also disturbs large areas of land, destroys natural habitat, and leaves the area vulnerable to loss of topsoil through erosion. The policy of the U.S. government has been to partially subsidize the reclamation of these areas at taxpayer expense.

The Chinese were the first to use naturally occurring methane gas. Today they are the leading users of biologically derived methane, produced mainly from agricultural wastes.

Although naturally occurring methane gas has recently developed into a major commodity in the American economy, until after the second World War it was treated primarily as a useless byproduct of petroleum production and burned off on drilling sites. In the postwar energy boom, the use of natural gas expanded rapidly. In the western U.S., where there are large reserves, it is still the major source of heating and cooking fuel.

Although natural gas produces some pollutants, principally in the form of carbon dioxide and carbon monoxide, it burns much cleaner than coal and petroleum. The newer technologies can boost conversion efficiencies, cutting air pollutants from natural gas by 90% to 99%, and carbon dioxide emissions from 30% to 65%. Natural gas accounted for 27% of overall U.S. energy production in 1990.

Geologists now believe that natural gas is more abundant than petroleum and is dispersed more widely around the world, making possible its expanded use as a bridge fuel to a renewable, sustainable fuel economy.

Petroleum is perhaps the most crucially important fuel source of the 20th century, largely because of its use in transportation. Since the introduction of the automobile at the turn of the century, gasoline use has risen steadily. It now accounts for 64% of all petroleum products used in the U.S. in 1990. (Petroleum products accounted for 23% of domestic energy use for that year).

Petroleum, unfortunately, is a nonrenewable resource, at least within reasonable time frames. Most of the remaining accessible reserves are outside American boundaries, much of it beneath the soil of nations hostile to American interests.

The petroleum industry is undoubtedly the world's biggest business, not only in itself, but also as it affects all other businesses and governments. The power of any government over other governments is directly proportional to the amount of oil that country holds in reserve to use or market abroad, as the most recent oil crisis in Kuwait bears witness. How else could a country smaller than most American states cause the military might of the western world to come together in its defense?

Chemical refining of crude oil also produces a variety of plastics for use in products including kitchen utensils, clothing, agricultural chemicals for fertilization and pest control, lubricants, and a host of seemingly indispensable household cleaners and toiletries. Indeed, the average consumer would be hardpressed to locate a product that does not depend upon petroleum for its production or distribution.

The deficiencies of petroleum as a primary energy source for the U.S. are twofold. First, U.S. reserves are insufficient to meet demands, rendering the U.S. dependent upon foreign sources. The advent of

On December 2,

1942, under the

direction of Enrico

Fermi, the first

controlled chain

reaction was created

in a reactor secretly

built underneath

Stagg Athletic Field at

the University of

Chicago.

OPEC and its control of crude oil prices leaves the U.S. in the unenviable position of being unable to stabilize its own economy. Secondly, the considerable environmental degradation associated with combustion is at odds with the increasing public demand for a cleaner environment. The costs of ensuring human health and well-being are more frequently being factored into the costs of energy production. The costs will be shared by producer and consumer alike.

Nuclear Power

During the course of World War II, a group of renowned physicists from around the world were commissioned by the U.S. government to unlock the secrets of obtaining energy through the process of nuclear fission. On December 2, 1942, under the direction of Enrico Fermi, the first controlled chain reaction was created in a reactor secretly built underneath Stagg Athletic Field at the University of Chicago. These efforts were intended to produce a weapon of such magnitude that one or two would be sufficient to turn the tide in the war. The U.S. was successful in that effort, and the first atomic bombs were dropped on Hiroshima and Nagasaki in 1945.

After the war, scientists began to search for a way to harness nuclear energy for domestic use. In 1951, the first nuclear reactor was used to create electricity. Nuclear generated electricity became commercially available for the first time in New York in 1955. Since that time, the United States has added 110 nuclear facilities to its power generating capacity. Nuclear power now generates more than 20% of the electricity used in this country.

The fuel used in the nuclear fission process is uranium-235, a highly refined substance derived from raw uranium. Although the production of electricity by nuclear fission creates very little pollution of the conventional type produced by combustion, it does produce large amounts of the highly toxic byproduct plutonium-239 as well as other radioactive substances. Plutonium is an extremely unstable element used to produce nuclear warheads. Due to the lengthy half-life of plutonium-239 (24,000 years), it is dangerous to human life for a quarter of a million years or 12,000 human generations. A hardly visible amount is lethal to a human being. As little as 130,000,000th of an ounce can cause cancer. One evenly distributed pound could kill everyone in the U.S. There are 20,000 tons of irradiated fuels awaiting disposal by the U.S. government, in addition to what has been produced by private utilities and industry. Where and how to dispose of them has not yet been determined. Plutonium-239 is highly sought after by third-world countries interested in building a nuclear capability. Large amounts of this substance for sale on the world market is a cause for great concern.

Estimates for cleaning up the U.S. weapons plants alone run to more than $300 billion with schedules that stretch into the middle of the next century. According to the U.S. Office of Technology Assessment, many sites may never be returned to a condition suitable for human life.

Perhaps the greatest concern regarding nuclear energy is the threat of accident. According to the accident registry at the Oak Ridge National Laboratory there were 284 major radiation accidents worldwide between 1944 and 1986. Accidents that may have occurred in the Soviet Union during that period were kept secret.

The accident risk for the water-cooled reactors used in the U.S. has never been scientifically established. Although several large-scale government tests on nuclear reactors have been made since the 1960s, the results of these tests were not made public until after the Freedom of Information Act was passed in 1974. These reports showed that most of the safety recommendations were made on the basis of experimentally unverified theory and arbitrary assumptions. Testing for worst-case scenarios was too dangerous and too costly, and some tests were not performed to avoid sharing potentially unpleasant results with the public.

The 1979 Three Mile Island loss-of-coolant accident in Pennsylvania and the 1986 Chernobyl disaster in the U.S.S.R. both revealed a lack of technical knowledge by operators, and an inability of the respective governments to act decisively and cooperatively in the public interest. There were no deaths directly attributable to the Three Mile Island accident; however, the number two reactor had to be sealed off and is still inoperable. Metropolitan Edison indicated to the public that the reactor was in cold shutdown shortly after the accident. It was actually still hot (in degrees and radioactivity) over a year later.

Due the lengthy half-life of plutonium-239 (24,000 years), it is dangerous to human life for a quarter of a million years or 12,000 human generations.

Over 40,000

exajoules (EJ) of

sunlight fall on the

landmass of the U.S.

each year, equivalent

to 500 times the

current U.S. energy

consumption.

In Chernobyl, thirty-one people died during the disaster, twenty-four were severely disabled, and over 600,000 were "significantly exposed" to high-level radiation. About 130,000 were permanently relocated, and thousands of square kilometers of arable land were rendered useless for generations. Many of the implicated government workers were tried, convicted, and imprisoned.

Alternative Energy Sources

Solar Power

Over 40,000 exajoules (EJ) of sunlight fall on the landmass of the U.S. each year, equivalent to 500 times the current U.S. energy consumption. One exajoule is the equivalent of four days of U.S. energy use, twenty-six days of U.S. gasoline use, 170 million barrels of oil, 60 million tons of dried hardwood, or 45 million tons of coal. The earth receives as much energy from sunlight in twenty days as is stored in the entire world reserves of coal, petroleum, and natural gas. In 1991, the U.S. recovered 0.08 EJ of solar energy for commercial consumption, in comparison with 89 EJ total consumption for that year. In order to recover a greater amount of solar energy, more research and development will be required. Funding for solar research has increased 68% since 1989.

Solar energy can be used in a number of ways. Most government funding for solar research is directed towards the development of high-volume commercial electricity generation. However, many people are experimenting with solar power on an individual basis, and the technology is expanding. Solar power can also be used to heat buildings and water, including systems for collecting, storing, and transferring heat. Solar energy can be used to convert sunlight into thermal concentrating systems. This produces steam, which will turn electric power turbines. Solar-generated electricity can also be used, through electrolysis, to produce hydrogen, which can be used as fuel.

The primary drawback of solar power is the need for large areas of land surface to make a significant amount of energy commercially available. Another lesser concern is the toxic waste hazards inherent in the production of photovoltaic cells. They are made of silica, which is dangerous to human lungs.

Wind

Wind energy has the potential to supply as much as 20% of total U.S. energy consumption over the long term. One estimate indicates about 3000 EJ, or 40 times the current annual energy consumption, are dissipated in winds annually. Even with the most severe land restrictions, the windiest areas of the U.S. could supply from 18% to 53% of the electricity consumed in 1990.

Electricity is generated by wind via propeller-driven turbines ranging in size from those that produce 0.25 to 50 kilowatts to an intermediate size producing 50 to 500 kilowatts. Some larger turbines have been built and tested by the U.S. Department of Energy, but these were only partially developed due to high cost and technical problems.

The biggest problem to be overcome in the development of a viable wind-power generating system is acquiring suitable sites for the wind farms, as these generating facilities are called. Weather patterns with suitable wind speed and daily duration periods are not always available, nor are topographic conditions always suitable. Terrain may be mountainous, swampy, or otherwise unusable. Furthermore, the potential areas may not be sufficiently developed and populated to make use of the energy, presenting the problem of transmitting the power to another area, perhaps hundreds of miles away.

Although wind-generated power does not produce any toxic wastes, it does have at least one environmental drawback. It presents a certain danger to some types of birds, most notably eagles and raptors. These are considered endangered species. During a three-year period at the California Altamont Pass wind farm, more than a hundred of these predatory birds were killed or injured by spinning props or electrocution.

Although wind-generated power can probably be used only as a supplemental power source to other generating methods, research and development groups continue to progress in improving the possibilities for its use.

Biomass

Until the latter part of the last century, burning wood, dried plants, plant oils, animal dung, and animal fat met most heating, lighting, cooking, and transportation fuel needs. Firewood still supplies cooking and heating fuel for many rural populations. Wood burning declined in the U.S. until the 1960s, but has since grown to equal about 4% of total energy consumption for 1990.

The future use of biomass will probably not take the form of direct combustion. It will rather be the production of liquid fuels such as ethanol (grain alcohol) and methanol (wood alcohol) via plant material fermentation. These liquid fuels have the environmental advantage of producing less pollution than their fossil fuel counterparts, and the economic advantages of being renewable and independent of the caprice of foreign regimes. The research, development, and subsequent use of ethanol as an automobile fuel occurred as a direct result of the petroleum crises of the early 1970s.

Corn and wood have been the materials used most in the production of liquid fuels. Corn produces a high-quality ethanol, and wood yields a high quality methanol. Fuels produced from crops have the disadvantage of depleting the soil, as they require an annual cycle of planting and harvesting. Corn farming results in approximately two bushels of topsoil depletion for every bushel of corn. This is not the case for wood and wood wastes, as some types of trees will regenerate from roots after they have been harvested. The disadvantage for wood lies in transportation and storage.

Other biomass-to-fuel materials include dried aquatic materials, crop residues, solid municipal wastes, solid industrial wastes, and methane occurring in landfills. As of 1990, there were 117 methane power plants operating in conjunction with landfills in U.S. The technology exists to make use of products such as wastepaper, grass clippings and wood wastes to produce methane at a retail cost of from $1.30 to $1.60 per gallon, or approximately the projected cost of gasoline for the late 1990s.

The environmental concerns associated with the use of biomass in producing energy are greater and more varied than with wind or solar alternatives. This is because biomass requires material combustion, which always produces some airborne pollution. Biomass-fueled power

torn by the issues

It is estimated that

sufficient high-power

natural steam exists

in the United States

to generate 35% to

40% of U.S. needs

for 30 years.

plants produce less sulfur dioxide and toxic metals than coal-fired plants, but such plants produce particulate emissions that must be controlled with devices like the cyclone precipitator. Direct combustion of wood and solid wastes are even greater polluters. While many researchers are continuing to develop biomass fuel production methods, most agree that biomass fuels will be best used, if at all, as transitional fuels bridging the gap between fossil fuels and noncombustion technologies.

Geothermal

Humankind has made use of geothermal energy throughout the ages. The ancient Greeks and Romans soaked in hot baths supplied by natural hot springs. Even today, public bathing facilities using naturally occurring hot water are in use in Japan, Europe, and Iceland. Only during the last century, however, has geothermal energy been exploited for commercial production of electricity. The town of Larderello, Italy, first produced electricity from natural steam in 1904. New Zealanders followed suit in 1958, and the first American plant went into service in California in 1960. Today, more than 3000 megawatts of geothermal electric energy are produced, mostly from The Geysers in Northern California.

Heat beneath the earth's crust originates primarily from the decay of radioactive elements such as uranium and thorium. Due to the insulating nature of the crust, this heat dissipates slowly. It is this heat that produces the molten rock and gases that give rise to volcanic activity. By drilling through the earth's crust, steam fields can be located and used to turn electricity-producing turbines. Where dry hot rock is found, water can be pumped into fissures to create the steam. Electricity and direct heat use of geothermal energy account for 0.2% of primary energy consumed in the U.S.

Although geothermal energy can be said to be a renewable resource, the amount of time needed to regenerate the heat in a depleted steam bed may preclude widespread use. The steam power plants at The Geysers in Northern California have declined in power output by 25% since 1987, due to a drop in steam pressure caused by overproduction. Even in high pressure reservoirs, the efficiency conversion factor is quite low—10% to 15%—compared to more than 30% for conventional steam turbines. Even so, it is estimated that sufficient high-

Hydropower has been

a mainstay of

American energy

production since the

eighteenth century,

when it was used

extensively in the

operation of flour and

lumber mills and,

most notably, in the

textile industry.

power natural steam exists in the United States to generate 35% to 40% of U.S. needs for thirty years.

Other uses of geothermal power include direct-use methods for space heating buildings, greenhouses, and fish farm tanks. The most commonly used geothermal technology currently in use is in the oil recovery field. This process pumps warm water from thermal wells into oil wells to reduce oil viscosity. If large-scale operations are economically sound, hot water can even be used to drive thermal-absorption chillers to cool buildings.

Along the northern coast of the Gulf of Mexico, in Texas, Louisiana, and Mississippi, there is another source of untapped energy. Geopressured brines, a hybrid of geothermally heated water and fossil fuel gasses, contain three potentially useful forms of energy: heat, hydraulic pressure, and dissolved natural gas in concentrations of up to 100 standard cubic feet per barrel of brine. These fields are currently being investigated by private energy consortiums.

The primary environmental concern for geothermal steam-produced electricity is the release of toxic gases, minerals, and metals that have been dissolved in geothermal reservoirs. In closed systems this is not a problem, but open systems require scrubbers and solid waste disposal measures. The most promising method of waste disposal currently under study is reinjection of the wastes back into the porous strata of the well. This process also helps prevent land subsidence, or sinking, but care must be taken that the wastes be reintroduced well below fresh water aquifers to prevent their contamination.

Hydropower

Hydropower has been a mainstay of American energy production since the eighteenth century, when it was used extensively in the operation of flour and lumber mills and, most notably, in the textile industry to run spinning jennies, shuttles, and looms.

The first hydropower plant was completed at Niagara Falls, New York in 1878. This form of energy production now supplies 10% to 12% of U.S. energy demand and 20% of world demand. Hydroelectric dams, such as the famous Hoover Dam in northern Arizona, are the typical hydropower facilities of the twentieth century. Whatever the fuel source for generating electricity (with the exception of solar), the process is essentially the same: the fuel powers large turbines to turn generators. At the Hoover Dam, water is collected behind the 726-foot-high dam wall and dropped from the intake towers through large-diameter penstocks to the generating turbines at the base of the dam. The generally accepted rule for determining the generating power of a dam is one gallon of water per second falling one hundred feet can generate one kilowatt of electrical power. Smaller facilities do not produce as much power but they can sometimes avoid the creation of a reservoir, thus reducing the ecological impact.

Hydropower is seasonal and production is based on the amount of snowfall precipitated at higher elevations. For this reason, hydropower cannot be relied on to produce a steady flow of electricity year-round and therefore cannot be used as a primary source of electricity. It is a cheap source of supplemental power, however, with the advantage that production can be easily be turned on and off.

Ocean thermal energy conversion (OTEC) is an energy-producing method that shows promise in several areas. These systems use the temperature differential that exists between the ocean surface and temperatures below one kilometer to create energy. These systems require large-diameter pipes one kilometer or more in length to transfer cold water existing at great depths to the plant's engines. In one scenario, these plants would be installed on unmoored ships which could graze the oceans for the best thermal gradients. The electricity generated could be used to produce hydrogen, a liquid fuel used in internal combustion engines which could then be transported to the nearest port for consumption.

Tidal and wave power have also been researched as possible alternative sources of energy. Due to the geological placement of tidal patterns, tidal power has thus far proved impractical for development. Of the 3 million megawatts dissipated in tides worldwide, only 2% can realistically be captured, given current technology.

Hydropower from large dams presents a number of environmental problems. Reservoirs inundate large areas of forest, farmlands, and wildlife and human habitats, while carrying sediments that can suffocate downstream waterways. The higher water temperature and lower dissolved oxygen content flowing out of reservoirs can alter the balance needed to support various forms of plant and animal life. Reservoirs can cause large fluctuations in downstream water flow, block fish migration, and destroy spawning grounds.

In 1990, almost

50% of U.S. daily

petroleum demand

was supplied by

imported oil (8

million barrels).

Energy Facts

- U.S. overall energy use totaled 81.4 quadrillion British thermal units (BTU) in 1990, a 10% increase since 1981. Of the total, 29.2 quad were consumed for residential cooking and heating, 30.2 quad were consumed by industry, 22.1 quad were consumed for transportation, and 29.6 quad were consumed by electric utilities. One quadrillion BTU (quad) is the equivalent to energy generated by 45 million tons of coal, or 170 million barrels of crude oil, or 4 average days of U.S. energy consumption.

- Approximately 60% of the U.S. total coal produced in 1990 was strip mined.

- The cost of coal used by electric utilities averaged $30.43 per ton in 1990, making it the least expensive energy fuel available.

- Coal emits some 40% more carbon dioxide than oil and 100% more carbon dioxide than natural gas.

- Coal accounted for the largest percentage (33%) of overall U.S. energy production in 1990.

- Natural gas accounted for 27% of overall U.S. energy production in 1990.

- Petroleum accounted for 23% of overall U.S. energy production in 1990.

- Nuclear power accounted for 9%, hydro-electric power for 4%, and natural gas liquids for 3% of overall U.S. energy production in 1990.

- Alternative energy sources such as solar, geothermal, wind, and waste-product fuel accounted for 0.2% of overall U.S. energy production in 1990.

- In 1990, almost 50% of U.S. daily petroleum demand was supplied by imported oil (8 million barrels).

- Of the total 8 million barrels per day of petroleum imported into the U.S., 4.3 million were OPEC imports.

- The United States has 26.3 billion barrels of crude oil in proven reserves, plus an additional 35.6 million barrels of crude oil-equivalent in the form of natural gas and natural gas liquids.

torn by the issues

- At present rates of consumption, proven U.S. oil reserves will last 10 years, and known world oil reserves will last 40 years.

- The United States nuclear power generating capacity has doubled since 1981.

- Since 1981, domestic production of uranium has declined by 77% and importation has risen by 73%.

- A 1988 Harris poll indicated that 61% of Americans were opposed to the construction of additional nuclear-powered utilities, while 30% were in favor.

Sources of U.S. Energy Production in 1990

(In Quadrillion British Thermal Units)

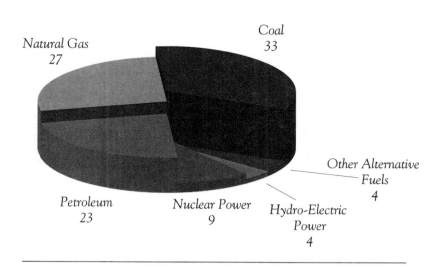

Natural Gas 27 · Coal 33 · Petroleum 23 · Nuclear Power 9 · Hydro-Electric Power 4 · Other Alternative Fuels 4

Sources

Brower, Michael. *Cool Energy: Renewable Solutions to Environmental Problems*. Cambridge: MIT Press, 1992.

Brown, Lester R., Project Director. *State of the World: A Worldwatch Institute Report on Progress Toward a Sustainable Society*. New York: W.W. Norton and Company, 1992.

The Budget of the United States, FY 1993. Office of Management and Budget, Office of the President, Washington, D.C., 1992.

Complex Cleanup: The Environmental Legacy of Nuclear Weapons Production. Washington, D.C.: Congress of the United States, Office of Technology Assessment, 1991.

The Energy Information Administration. *The Motor Gasoline Industry: Past, Present and Future*. Washington, D.C.: Dept of Energy, 1991.

1990 Energy Facts; Supplement to the Annual Energy Outlook. Washington, D.C.: Department of Energy, 1992.

Fanning, Leonard M. *Men, Money, and Oil: The Story of an Industry*. Cleveland: The World Publishing Company, 1966.

Jones, Morris J., ed. *The 1957 World Book Encyclopedia*. Chicago: Field Enterprises, Inc., 1957.

Medvedev, Zhores A. *The Legacy of Chernobyl*. New York: W.W. Norton & Co.,1990.

Solsberg, Carl. *Oil Power: The Rise and Imminent Fall of an American Empire*. New York: The New American Library, 1976.

Stephens, Mark. *Three Mile Island*. New York: Random House, 1980.

Webb, Richard E. *The Accident Hazards of Nuclear Power Plants*. Worcester: The University of Massachusetts Press, 1976.

Yergin, Daniel. *The Prize: The Epic Quest for Oil, Money, and Power*. New York: Touchstone, 1992.

animal rights

the issue of animal rights is argued in the courts, in the

media, in the streets, and in the wilderness. Battle lines are drawn

between those who feel it is a moral imperative to end the needless

suffering of all animals, and those who view animals primarily as a

means to enrich the lives of humans. The battle is fought on two

fronts. In the laboratories, where the use of animals in testing and experimentation is a long-accepted method for research, some are questioning the morality of this use, and the cruelty involved. In the wild, where the use of animals for human needs has rarely been questioned, the recent upsurge in species extinction has environmentalists up in arms.

From biblical times, there have been laws governing the treatment of animals. All fifty states have laws against cruelty to animals. The laws are enforced by local and state police departments as well as sheriff's departments. Some states also have provisions that allow humane societies to designate a person or persons to enforce the anti-cruelty laws. The U.S. Department of Agriculture (USDA) enforces animal protection laws primarily through three offices. The USDA Regulatory Enforcement and Animal Care office enforces the Animal Welfare Act, the Federal Veterinarian's office enforces both the Twenty-Eight Hour Law and the Horse Protection Act, and the Food Safety Inspection Service enforces the Humane Slaughter Act.

Animals have no legal rights because they are not legal persons. They are considered private property if domesticated, and public or state property if stray or wild. A criminal act against an animal is legally considered an act against the owner or against society in general. Animal rights groups would like to see the laws changed to give animals legal standing. Animals could then enjoy the benefits of legal action instituted on their behalf.

Common provisions of anti-cruelty laws throughout the U.S. show that people generally believe animals have the right to a life free of cruel treatment; that domestic or captive animals should be provided food, water, and shelter; that animals should not be abandoned or poisoned. Most states, however, exclude scientific experimentation from their laws if the work is being done by professionals in an authorized facility that provides humane treatment of the animal without unnecessary suffering.

Pro Animal Rights

Animal rights advocates see animals as living beings with intelligence, needs, wants, memories, and the ability to feel pleasure and pain. They feel that animals must therefore be treated as we would treat ourselves. If animals experience suffering and the awareness of suffering, it is our moral duty to avoid inflicting suffering on them and to alleviate their suffering whenever possible. Animal rights activists believe in an animal's right to life and in an animal's right to live as its inherent nature dictates. For example, the killer whale, a social animal that has evolved in the open ocean, is denied its right to live as its nature dictates when it is taken into captivity and kept alone in a swimming pool.

Animal rights advocates see animals as living beings with intelligence, needs, wants, memories, and the ability to feel pleasure and pain.

Anti Animal Rights

Opponents of animal rights believe that animals are here for our use. Animals, because they lack language and rationality, are little more than biomachines; they are a means to an end, and that end is man. Those against animal rights justify using animals for the good of humanity. As a food source, for clothing, for companionship, for entertainment, and perhaps most importantly for the development of scientific knowledge, animals are a very valuable resource for humans.

Priests in ancient

Egypt, who are

responsible for the

care of sacred

animals, learn how to

treat various maladies

through animal

autopsies.

Timeline

10,000 B.C.

The dog is domesticated.

9,000 B.C.

Sheep and goats are domesticated in Persia and Afghanistan as the agricultural revolution begins.

3500–1000 B.C.

Lions are hunted to extinction in Bronze Age Greece. Priests in ancient Egypt, who are responsible for the care of sacred animals, learn how to treat various maladies through animal autopsies. This leads to more effective treatment of humans.

350 B.C.–A.D. 200

Aristotle begins the study of living creatures (biology) and develops a classification system for animals that remains unchanged until 1735. A natural philosopher, Erisistratus of Alexandria, uses animals to study bodily functions. A little later, Galen, a Roman physician, proves through experiments on apes and pigs that veins carry blood rather than air. In the following centuries many physiological theories are proved by using animals as testing subjects.

1100s

Bears and beavers become extinct in Britain.

1400s

Europeans begin whaling off the eastern coast of North America. The number of humpback whales in the North Atlantic is estimated in the hundreds of thousands. By 1900 there are less than 4000 remaining.

1641

The world's first animal anti-cruelty legislation is passed by the Puritans of the Massachusetts Bay Colony in their legal code, "The Body of Liberties." Liberty 92 states, "No man shall exercise any Tyranny or Cruelty towards any brute Creature which is usually kept for man's use." Liberty 93 requires proper rest, food and water be provided for any cattle being led or driven "to a place that is far off" that might result in making the animals "weary, or hungry, or fall sick, or lame." This is the first legislation protecting animals during transport.

1822

New York makes excessive beating of a horse by a cartman punishable under common law as a misdemeanor.

1828

New York becomes the first state to enact animal anti-cruelty legislation, in a law that states, "Every person who shall maliciously kill, maim, or wound any horse, ox, or other cattle, or sheep belonging to another, or shall maliciously and cruelly beat or torture any such animal, whether belonging to himself or another, shall, upon conviction, be adjudged guilty of a misdemeanor."

During the next ten years, three more states pass similar anti-cruelty laws: Massachusetts in 1835, and Wisconsin and Connecticut in 1838. The penalty in Massachusetts is a fine up to $100 and up to one year in prison.

1858

Charles R. Darwin and Alfred R. Wallace announce their theory of evolution by natural selection, i.e., all species of animals or plants develop from earlier forms, by hereditary transmission of slight variations in successive generations, and natural selection determines which forms survive.

1859

Charles R. Darwin publishes *On the Origin of Species*. A part of his theory, often cited by opponents of wildlife conservation regulation, states that extinction is part of a natural process. From observations of the natural world, Darwin determined that animals must evolve by making adaptations to their environment or face extinction. Those animals that have enough genetic flexibility to adjust are naturally selected for a continued existence. This process is sometimes referred to as the survival of the fittest.

Most of the species that have appeared over the last 650 million years are now extinct. The greatly accelerated rate of extinctions over the past 400 years is due to the human population boom and the resulting man-made changes in the environment.

1866

The American Society for the Prevention of Cruelty to Animals (ASPCA) is founded by Henry Bergh in New York. He drafts new anti-cruelty legislation that year and again in 1867. The revision to the 1828 law, passed on April 12, 1866, is aimed at preventing the abandonment of lame horses and mules and for a "more effectual prevention of cruelty to animals" in general. It stands today as a model for the anti-cruelty laws of forty-one other states and the District of Columbia.

1867

The revision to the 1866 anti-cruelty law is more specific about possible abuses and includes "any living creature" (not just horses, cattle, and oxen), prohibits animal fights, requires licensing for dogs used in drawing vehicles for business purposes, and demands proper treatment of impounded animals, as well as giving an agent of the ASPCA the power to arrest any person violating the anti-cruelty law.

1868

The Massachusetts Society for the Prevention of Cruelty to Animals (MSPCA) is founded.

In 1897, the Roman

Catholic Church

describes its position

on animals by

stating that they

have no rights.

1873

The Twenty-Eight Hour Law is passed by Congress to insure that humane standards are met while transporting livestock. Published reports of inhumane treatment, including gross overcrowding, deprivation of food and water, and brutal mishandling of the animals leads to the enactment of this law. One report found that cattle shipped on steamers between Indianola, Texas, and New Orleans, Louisiana, were kept below deck in overcrowded conditions without food or water for up to five days. On one trip, forty out of one hundred and fifty head of cattle died. Another report, from the Chicago Livestock Reporter, found that transported cattle often arrived at their destination with broken legs and horns, bruises, sores, great weight loss, or dead.

The law is subsequently repealed, but in 1906, a new Twenty-Eight Hour Law is enacted, limiting the number of hours livestock can be kept in boxcars before they must be unloaded for food, water, and rest. By 1908, 410 violations of the law are recorded, amounting to fines of over $60,000. By 1976, less than 100 violations are reported and in 1988, there are none.

1889

The National Zoo, a part of the Smithsonian Institution, opens. One of its purposes is to attempt to preserve the Plains Bison, an animal whose population was severely reduced by the settling of the American West.

1897

In *The Catholic Dictionary*, the Roman Catholic Church describes its position on animals by stating that they have no rights. In fact, it is "lawful to put them to death, or to inflict pain on them for any good or reasonable end . . . even for the purposes of recreation."

1900

There are less than 4000 humpback whales left in the North Atlantic.

In 1947, Everglades

National Park is

opened in Florida. It

is the first national

park designed

specifically to

protect wildlife.

The Lacey Act is passed, making it a federal offense to transport wildlife killed in violation of state laws across state lines. This law is needed to halt the large-scale killing of birds for their feathers. In Florida, hunters had reduced the egret population from tens of thousands to less than 300 birds. Flamingos, herons, ibises, and songbirds also suffered great losses due to the feather trade. The Act is later amended to prohibit the importation of wildlife killed, captured, or exported illegally from another country.

1903

Theodore Roosevelt establishes the first national wildlife refuge in the country, on Pelican Island, Florida, in part to begin the conservation of animal species favored for hunting. In the 1920s, Roosevelt is also one of the few westerners to successfully hunt and kill the rare and endangered giant panda in the mountainous region of Szechwan China.

1913

The Wilson Tariff Act, passed in 1913, bans the importation of wild bird plumes, which are used for women's hats.

1914

North America's only native parrot, the Carolina parakeet, becomes extinct.

1918

Canada, Great Britain and the U.S. sign the Migratory Bird Treaty Act to prohibit the killing of non-game migratory birds.

1940

The Bald Eagle Protection Act is passed in an effort to ward off extinction, making it illegal to kill a bald eagle. Ranchers, with concerns over protecting their livestock, managers of fisheries worried about damage to their stocks, hunters killing the animal for sport, and collectors who value the feathers and talons of eagles continue to hunt the animal.

1947

Everglades National Park is opened in Florida. It is the first national park designed specifically to protect wildlife.

1951

The American Welfare Institute is founded. Its goal is the advancement of the rights of all animals, especially the welfare of research animals.

1954

The Humane Society of the United States is founded, forming after a split with the American Humane Association because of AHA's refusal to fight legislation that would require pounds and shelters to release animals for research.

1958

The Federal Humane Slaughter Act is signed into law by President Eisenhower, to be effective June 30, 1960. The law provides for an end to the unnecessary suffering of animals during slaughter. The specific target is to halt the practice of shackling and hoisting conscious animals and to discontinue the practice of stunning animals with a sledge-hammer. It is hoped that this law will result in better conditions for the workers carrying out the slaughter. The Hormel company finds less turnover of personnel after more humane methods are introduced. Improved products and profits for the industry and other benefits for producers and consumers are also reported.

The humane methods described in the law include "a single blow or gunshot or an electrical, chemical or other means that is rapid and effective" that renders the animal instantly insensible to pain. For ritual slaughter for religious faiths, the animal must suffer loss of consciousness by simultaneous and instantaneous severance of the carotid artery.

In 1958, the Federal Humane Slaughter Act is signed into law…to halt the practice of shackling and hoisting conscious animals and to discontinue the practice of stunning animals with a sledge-hammer.

1962

The Bald Eagle Protection Act is amended to include the golden eagle.

1966

Congress passes the Endangered Species Preservation Act, to be administered by the Fish and Wildlife Service of the Department of the Interior and the National Marine Fisheries Service of the Department of Commerce. The Act imposes federal penalties for the export or import, the destruction of habitat, and the hunting and trapping of an endangered species. Now known as the Endangered Species Act, the act was strengthened in 1969 and again in 1973. In 1978, an amendment to the act included endangered subspecies.

Congress passes the Animal Welfare Act. Originally designed to prevent the theft of dogs and cats by requiring researchers to buy animals only from licensed dealers, the act has undergone several revisions that shift the focus to safeguarding the welfare of laboratory animals. The law is enforced by the Department of Agriculture.

1970

The National Environmental Policy Act (NEPA) becomes law, furthering the movement toward protecting natural ecosystems and the species that are part of the ecosystem.

1972

The Marine Mammal Protection Act becomes U.S. Law. The law protects marine mammals (whales, dolphins, and seals) from being hunted, captured, harassed, or killed, and from attempts to hunt, harass, capture, or kill in U.S. waters or by U.S. citizens abroad. Exceptions include taking marine mammals for scientific research, for public display in aquariums, and for the hunting needs of Native Americans and Eskimos.

Sea birds and birds of prey were added to the Migratory Bird Treaty Act. The Secretary of the Interior can make exceptions to the act, and the Interior Department now lists sixty-five species of birds that are available for hunting during defined seasons.

1975

Animal Liberation, by Australian Peter Singer, is published. The response to the book stimulates the animal rights movement. This book coins the term "speciesism" to describe the assumption that humans are superior to non-human animals and are therefore justified in using and exploiting animals.

1976

The Southern Bald Eagle is placed on the Endangered Species list.

1978

The Humane Methods of Slaughter Act of 1978 amends the 1958 act to allow federal inspectors to prevent inhumane practices by withholding certification until cruel methods are corrected. It also prohibits the importation of any meat slaughtered using inhumane methods.

1981

Chinese scientists succeed in cloning a fish. This accomplishment has profound implications in the field of species protection, and for human life in general.

1985

The Health Research Extension Act is passed. It establishes procedures to be followed by researchers to ensure humane treatment of animals used for scientific research.

1986

A worldwide ban on commercial whaling begins, instituted by the International Whaling Commission (IWC). The IWC is an association of countries formed in 1946 by treaty to manage whale populations and to set whaling quotas. Limited exceptions to the

The advancement of

medical science is due

largely to the

knowledge gained

through

experimentation and

research on animals.

ban include the hunting of bowhead whales by the Inuit people. Not all countries engaged in commercial whaling heed the ban.

1988

Sweden passes a law prohibiting cruel factory livestock and poultry practices, such as veal crates, battery cages for hens, and the tethering of pregnant sows.

Animal Use in Research, Testing & Education

The advancement of medical science is due largely to the knowledge gained through experimentation and research on animals. Surgical techniques, including open-heart surgery, brain surgery, organ transplants, and microsurgery to re-attach limbs, were all first developed using animal subjects. Vaccines against polio, mumps, and smallpox were first tested and proved effective on animals. Treatments for diabetes, heart disease, cancer, and alcoholism were advanced through animal testing. Medical scientists believe that the use of animals in research is necessary if they are to find a cure for AIDS.

Nearly every medical procedure and every medicine was developed, either directly or indirectly, through animal research and made safe for humans through animal testing. Studies on the blood of the Rhesus monkey led to a procedure for avoiding a fatal blood disease affecting many newborn human babies. The armadillo is the only other animal besides humans to contract leprosy. Studying this animal may lead to an understanding of, and possibly a vaccine for, the disease. The cure for hepatitis may be found through studies of the woodchuck, which carries a hepatitis virus that may be identical to the one found in humans.

The use of animals in science is well-regulated by the federal government. Since the 1890s, there have been formal guidelines in this country that establish standards for the humane treatment and care of research animals. These guidelines set the standards for handling, transportation, housing (including the size of cages to be used), veterinary care, feeding, and the use of pain-relieving drugs. Nevertheless, animal rights advocates feel concern about the pain and suffering laboratory animals experience, in spite of the importance of the research.

More Facts About the Use of Animals

- Each year, an estimated 17 to 22 million animals are used in research, testing, and education. Rats and mice bred for research make up 85% of the animals used. In 1988, an estimated 180,000 dogs were used in experimentation; between 40,000 and 50,000 of these dogs were bred specifically for research.

- The remaining approximately 135,000 came from pounds and animal shelters.

- That same year, about 52,000 cats, 554,000 rabbits, and 50,000 to 60,000 non-human primates were used. The overall total of animals used in research, testing, and education is on the decline, down from 38 million in 1968.

- In 1973, the Department of Defense was prohibited by Congress from using live dogs in experiments to develop chemical and biological weapons. The Department of Defense was also prohibited from shooting dogs and using them as subjects for experimental gunshot wound treatments.

- In 1948, Minnesota became the first state to require pounds and shelters to release animals for research purposes. Similar release laws are in effect in Iowa, South Dakota, Utah, Oklahoma, and the District of Columbia. Eight states allow the release of impounded animals for research purposes but do not require it. In 1983, it became illegal to recycle former pets for research in Massachusetts laboratories. It is now illegal in thirteen states to sell pound animals to laboratories.

- Ten million dogs are killed each year by pounds and shelters. For every dog released for research, one hundred are killed in pounds and shelters.

Only 1% of the research animals obtained by laboratories are used to test cosmetics.

- The Federal Food and Drug Administration (FDA) requires that any chemical compound considered promising for the treatment of human disease must first be tested on animals.

- Animal experiments were directly involved in two thirds of the research projects that led to Nobel prizes in medicine or physiology.

- Only 1% of the research animals obtained by laboratories are used to test cosmetics.

- The 1988 Animal Welfare Enforcement Report by the Department of Agriculture states that 94% of all laboratory animals are not exposed to painful procedures or are given drugs to relieve any pain caused by a procedure.

- The budget for the enforcement of the Animal Welfare Act for Fiscal Year 1990 was $7.567 million. Enforcement of the act is the responsibility of the Animal and Plant Health Inspection Service. In 1990, there were sixty-three inspectors, responsible for overseeing 1296 laboratories and 4415 animal dealers, as well as several other entities regulated by the Act.

- In 1973, California passed a law prohibiting high school and elementary school students from conducting painful or intrusive experiments on live vertebrates. Since then, Florida, Maine, New York, Massachusetts, Pennsylvania, Illinois, and New Hampshire have passed similar legislation. California and New Jersey also have laws making the dissection of dead animals by high school or elementary school students optional and prohibiting any penalty based on their decisions.

- Membership in the animal rights organization called People for the Ethical Treatment of Animals grew from 8000 members in 1985 to 250,000 in 1990.

- There are presently 7000 animal protection groups in the U.S. The combined membership is about 10 million with a total budget of $50 million.

- At least seventy-one criminal acts against animal research facilities have been reported since 1985. The Animal Liberation Front, a radical animal rights organization, has claimed responsibility for many of these acts.

torn by the issues

The number of
animals needed for
educational purposes
could be drastically
reduced through the
use of computer
simulation.

- A survey of 126 medical schools revealed that 76 schools reported losing over $4 million and 33,000 labor-hours from break-ins, vandalism, demonstrations, and delays in construction in the past 5 years. Also reported were 3800 incidents of harassment of staff and faculty, including bomb and death threats.

Alternatives

The concept of using alternatives to animals in research was proposed in 1959 in a book entitled *The Principles of Humane Experimental Technique*, by R. L. Burch and W. M. S. Russell. The main points are known as "the three Rs"—reduction, replacement, and refinement. Reduction is the principle of reducing the number of animals used in experimentation, especially by not duplicating experiments. Replacement is the attempt to use non-animal subjects in research whenever possible and to use invertebrate animals, like the horseshoe crab, in place of vertebrate animals, especially companion and domesticated animal species. Refinement is the idea of refining experiments and testing methods to cause as little pain and suffering for the animals as possible. These principles are now widely accepted as the basic tenets to be followed to prevent large-scale suffering of animals in research laboratories.

Reforming the existing system of using live animals in research could be accomplished through further application of existing alternative methods. The number of animals needed for educational purposes could be drastically reduced through the use of computer simulation. Although animal experimentation is still needed to write the software and to prove the validity of the program, once in place, computer simulation would take the place of live animals in studying such areas as animal physiology. A computer can now simulate the organization of the entire cardiovascular system, including the interacting functions of the heart, lungs, kidney, and brain. Computers are also employed to establish comprehensive data banks containing results of experiments previously performed. By developing an information network, scientists and educators can share their information and further reduce the number of animals used.

There are two methods of testing the toxicology of a substance that animal rights advocates would like to see discontinued: the Draize test and the LD50 test. The Draize test measures the irritant qualities in substances to be used in cosmetics and household products. The irritating substance is put into the eye of a rabbit and any lesions are noted and evaluated. The test has been criticized for poor reproducibility and poor ability to project results for humans, as well as being unnecessarily cruel. An alternative is the substitution of chicken embryos for the live rabbits.

The LD50 (LD means lethal dose) test is a way of judging the toxicity of a substance. The test shows the amount of a substance that, when administered in a single dose to a group of animals, will result in the death of 50% of the group within fourteen days. It is used widely to test the ingredients of insecticides, pesticides, drugs, food additives, and household products. Critics say the test shows only the short term results of large doses and therefore is unreliable in indicating a product is safe for humans. In addition, using only ten animals instead of one hundred would furnish the same information and prevent millions of animals from being needlessly killed. In an article written in 1976, "Modern Toxicology: New Concepts in Safety Evaluation," Frederick Sperling states, "It is no longer sufficient to count bodies and from such an account develop an index of toxicity.... The LD50 is in fact only marginally informative, toxicologically inadequate, and misleading."

Animal welfare organizations often claim alternative methods of testing are better and less expensive than tests using live animals. A methodology being developed for toxicity testing called "in vitro" testing (literally, "in glass"; the term is used generally to describe experiments done in test tubes) uses the cells of the animals rather than the whole animal. Cultures of cells, organs, and tissues often can replace the use of mice, rats, rabbits, and other animals. Instrumentation is being developed that studies "micro areas"; for example, one solitary blood cell may be examined for any abnormalities rather than autopsying the animal.

The limitation of in vitro testing is that there is no way to study the reaction, behavior, or recovery of the organism as an entity. Using live animals in research allows scientists to study lifecycles and generations of the animal, to study complete systems, and to study and control such variables as genetics and environmental factors.

torn by the issues

Intensive Farming

The growth of the population and subsequent growth of cities led to an increased need for mass production of foods, including farm-raised animal foods such as eggs, chickens, pork products, milk, and beef products. World War II increased the demand for food production, so farmers, with the help of pharmaceutical companies and feed companies, developed methods that would produce more food at a lower cost. The use of mechanized systems to feed and pluck chickens, drugs to combat disease caused by overcrowding and poor ventilation, and drugs to stimulate growth (vitamins A and D and growth hormones), manure removal systems, and automatic lighting systems all began in the 1940s and 1950s to meet the need for increased production to satisfy the growing market. In the twenty-year period, between 1955 and 1975, the number of birds in an average egg factory rose from 20,000 to 80,000 laying hens.

The living conditions of animals raised in intensive farming environments are often criticized as cruel and inhumane. The practices of crating veal calves and feeding them an entirely liquid diet (advertised as "milkfed veal"), keeping laying hens in battery cages, tethering pregnant sows, and force-feeding geese to enlarge their livers for foie gras, are among the intensive farming techniques that have come under fire from animal rights groups.

Crating of veal calves involves taking the newborn calf away from its mother, sometimes as soon as one day after birth, and keeping it in a wooden stall so limited in size that the calf cannot walk or turn around. This keeps the muscles soft and results in very tender meat. The calf is kept on a liquid diet of very limited protein to create a pale meat.

The battery cage for laying hens may be as small as eight inches by sixteen inches. Up to five hens are packed into the cage, and with so little room to move that their feathers may be literally stripped off from friction. The wire cages are stacked four or five high in long lines. Some laying sheds contain as many as 70,000 birds. When a hen's egg production rate falls off, she is killed.

Sows are tethered or chained in a small cement pen. The pregnant sows are not given enough slack on the tether to stand or turn around. When ready to give birth, the sow is transferred to a crate that further restricts her movement to prevent crushing her litter. Often, rather than risking the chance of contamination during natural birth, the sows are subjected to a sanitary Cesarean section.

In Europe, in 1976, eighteen countries ratified the European Convention for the Protection of Animals Kept for Farming Purposes, which prohibits these practices. The convention also provides that animals kept for farming purposes must be allowed adequate care, feeding, accommodations, and enough freedom of movement and exercise to avoid pain, injury, or suffering. They charge that it is cruel and inhumane to keep an animal from being able to move freely (or at least to lie down and turn around), or to be caged for its entire life and deprived of natural sunlight, or to be raised exclusively on a liquid diet.

Another complaint against the intensive stock farming systems is that drugs used to maintain the health and encourage the growth of farm animals are dangerous to humans who consume these animals. Bovine growth hormone (BGH), is currently controversial. The drug was developed to increase the amount of milk produced by dairy cows. Although a senior scientist at the FDA reported that adequate studies have not yet been done on the effect of BGH on humans, some side effects have been reported in the cows. There has been an increase in metabolic disease (possibly due to the highly concentrated diet needed to maintain an increased rate of milk production). Also reported are increased susceptibility to disease and enlargement of internal organs.

Facts About Intensive Farming

- Eighty different drugs are currently used by milk producers. The average amount of milk produced by a dairy cow in 1930 was twelve pounds per day; in 1989 the amount was thirty-nine pounds per day. Full-scale use of BGH could increase milk production to forty-nine pounds per day.

- Because of milk surpluses, over 1.5 million cows have been slaughtered or exported. In 1985, 14,000 dairy farmers were paid by the U.S. government to kill their cows and retire from dairy farming.

- The number of farms decreased from 6 million in 1940 to 2.7 million in 1980.

- Farm animals produce over 2 billion tons of manure each year. In a typical laying house, 60,000 hens will produce 82 tons of manure each week. To reduce feed costs, some farmers recycle animal excrement into food for their animals. It is legal in at least 12 states to transport and sell recycled wastes as animal feed.

- Between 1974 and 1976, the Department of Agriculture found illegally high levels of drugs and pesticides in 14% of all meat and poultry inspected. Federal inspectors condemn about 140,000 tons of poultry annually, due to damage or disease.

- On an intensive farm, one person can take care of 20,000 hens.

Hunting

- Hunting in America is a $10-billion-per-year industry.

- There are at least 17 million hunters in the U.S., 6% of whom are women.

- Hunters outnumber wildlife conservation officers by about 9000 to 1.

- Thirty-two states have enacted laws that protect hunters from harassment.

- These laws make it illegal to interfere with hunting, fishing, or trapping activities. There has been an increasing number of incidents of animal rights activists disrupting hunts and harassing hunters.

- Estimates of 1991 kills include 50 million mourning doves, 28 million quail, 22 million squirrels, 102,000 elk, 1000 wolves, and 750 bison. An estimated 170 million animals were hunted and killed.

- "Canned hunts" is a term used to describe a facility that offers an artificial hunting environment where the animal being hunted has no chance of escape. In the U.S. there are more than 4000 game shooting preserves and big game ranches offering canned hunts, many illegally offering endangered species as the prey.

- A hunter will pay up to $5,000 for guide service to illegally shoot the protected grizzly bear. On a small island in Texas, hunters may stalk farm-raised lions for a fee of $3500 per animal. There are about 60 species of exotic animals being raised on 370 different Texas ranches for the sole purpose of being released and hunted in a closed environment. Hunting fees range from $5000 for a zebra, $3000 for a gazelle, $2500 for a bison, and $300 for a turkey.

- In 1990, the Animal Damage Control (ADC) program administered by the USDA spent $29.4 million in federal funds and $15 million in state funds to kill birds and mammals considered predators or pests. The ADC kills an average of 76,000 coyotes each year. Hunters and trappers are responsible for killing 350,000 annually. The Department of Animal Regulation in the City of Los Angeles received 700 complaints regarding coyotes in 1991 and made 160 kills.

- Deer populations in many areas in the U.S. are growing to the degree that they are considered pests, and hunting seasons allow controlled numbers to be hunted to keep the population numbers under control. Those in favor of these laws insist that without this control, the deer starve to death, cause widespread crop destruction, and are a traffic hazard.

- The steel-jaw leg-hold trap, which is designed to clamp tightly on an animal's leg, is outlawed in seventy countries but it is legal in the U.S. Repeated attempts at introducing federal legislation banning the traps have been made since 1957, but so far no bill has reached the floor of Congress for a vote. A study by the humane society estimated that 23% of the animals found in these traps were unintended victims; many domesticated dogs and cats, bald and golden eagles, hawks, deer, calves, lambs, and goats have been accidentally trapped. The leg-hold trap is banned in Florida, New Jersey, and Rhode Island, and many other states regulate the maximum size of a trap and limit its use to water settings. The use of cage traps is urged by animal rights activists as a more humane alternative. The animal is caught unharmed and non-target animals may be released.

Zoos

- About 250 million people visit zoos all over the world each year.

- Major changes have taken place in response to criticisms of the practice of holding animals in captivity in cages. In some of the larger zoos, like San Diego's "Wildlife Park," animals roam freely in landscaped areas modeled after their natural habitats. In Chicago's Brookfield Zoo, there are three geographically distinct rain forests (Asian, African, and South American). A growing understanding of natural behavior, reproduction habits, and nutritional needs has allowed zookeepers to make the lives of captive animals more comfortable.

- Zoos help to keep endangered species from extinction through the development of captive breeding programs and programs for reintroduction to native habitats. Some of the most endangered animals now being captively bred in the U.S. include the California condor, the lowland gorilla, the African bush elephant, the snow leopard, the black rhinoceros, and the white tiger.

- Although some zoos have been guilty of acquiring exotic and endangered animals on the black market, the CITES treaty, which nearly half the world's nations have signed, has helped to drastically reduce the business of selling rare and endangered animals to zoos. By the mid-1980s, animals bred in captivity accounted for 90% of the mammals and 75% of the birds acquired by zoos.

- Orca, also known as the killer whale, can live up to one hundred years in the wild. In captivity, life expectancy is five years.

Orca, also known as the killer whale, can live up to one hundred years in the wild. In captivity life expectancy is five years.

Pets

- Over 50% of all households in America have some kind of pet, the most popular being dogs and cats. The dog business is a $7-billion-per-year industry.

- About 20 million unwanted pets are killed each year in pounds and shelters. Most of these are dogs and cats.

- A "puppy mill" is a place of intensive breeding for dogs to be sold to pet stores. There are 5000 of these operations in the U.S. Criticized for their often shockingly inhumane conditions, the puppy mills lose about 50% of the puppies before they can be sold.

- Close to 12% of the total number of dogs born each year are killed by animal control people.

- Dog racing has been outlawed in thirty-one states. Dog fighting is illegal in every state; in forty-two states it is a felony.

- Genetic diseases are increasing in purebred dogs. In 1987, of 2.4 million puppies eligible to be registered by the American Kennel Club (AKC), 86% were from breeds with serious genetic defects. These diseases include blindness, hip dysplasia, and hemophilia.

The Endangered & the Extinct

- An endangered animal is a species or subspecies that has been so reduced in its population as to be in serious jeopardy of becoming extinct. Humanity's contribution to the decline of a species takes three forms: exploitation through hunting, destruction of habitat (deforestation, destruction of wetlands, urban sprawl, etc.), and pollution of an ecosystem. There are presently 1.4 million classified species of plants and animals, representing perhaps 10% of all species on earth. There may be as many as 30 million species of insects alone. It is impossible to determine the total number of species that have recently become extinct, but it is known that the current rate of species disappearance is reliably considered comparable to the mass extinction of dinosaurs 65 million years ago.

- Animal rights advocates feel that human survival may depend on a commitment to preserving a healthy and vital ecosystem. An ecological system is an interconnected web of life. For example, if a species of bird is killed off, the population of insects on which it fed multiplies. This increase may destroy crops, or carry disease to humans or other animals.

- When the red wolf was eliminated from the American southwest, the opportunistic and more adaptable coyote took its place, posing a greater threat to livestock than did the red wolf. The introduction of the mongoose in Hawaii to eradicate the rat population unexpectedly resulted in the loss of indigenous bird species, on whose eggs the mongoose voraciously fed. The reduced number of birds meant a lower rate of pollination of the exotic flowering trees, which in turn became endangered or extinct. The mongoose population flourished and is now considered a pest.

- Hunting for food, profit, protection of domestic stock, or sport, has been responsible for the disappearance of many species in America. The valuable fur of the sea mink, cousin to the American mink, led early American settlers to hunt this animal to extinction by 1888. The eastern elk, wanted for its meat and its teeth, was gone by 1877. The passenger pigeon, once so numerous that a single flock was estimated to contain 2 billion birds, disappeared from the wild by 1889. The last passenger pigeon died at the Cincinnati Zoo in 1914.

- Habitat destruction has been the primary cause of extinction for many animals, especially birds, snakes and insects. Of the sixty-eight species of birds found only in Hawaii when Europeans first came to the islands, forty-one species have been driven to extinction or near extinction. This is primarily from deforestation and the introduction of non-native plants and animals.

- Pesticides and herbicides used in agriculture have had a major impact on animal populations in the U.S. The peregrine falcon became extinct in the eastern U.S. due in large part to the effects of DDT, a chlorinated hydrocarbon used as a pesticide. (A small number continued to exist in Canada, and have since been re-introduced into the U.S.). The plight of the peregrine falcon, as well as the brown pelican and osprey, led to restriction of the use of DDT and related chemical pesticides. It was feared that if these chemicals were killing these specific animals, they were probably affecting the entire food chain, including humans.

- Lead poisoning killed 5000 Canadian geese in a single waterfowl hunting marsh in Wisconsin in 1981. The lead they consumed was from the pellets of shotgun shells used to hunt the geese.

- About 2000 of 11,000 species of birds and mammals of the world are presently endangered.

- In the Adirondack region of upstate New York, at least 250 lakes have no fish due to the effects of acid rain.

- The number of bison in North America at the time of European settlement is estimated at 75 million. The American bison was hunted to extinction in the eastern U.S. by 1830. At the turn of the century, the bison became protected, their numbers down to 500 individuals. Today there are 25,000 to 30,000 American bison living in parks, reserves, and on private ranches.

- In 1979 the U.S. government estimated that the importation of live endangered animals was a $100 million business. A rare South American macaw or Asian cockatoo may be sold in the U.S. for as much as $8,000. Spix's macaw, from Brazil, sold for as much as $40,000 to collectors in the mid-1980's. As of 1992, one male Spix macaw was reported left in the wild.

- CITES (the Convention of International Trade in Endangered Species of Wild Fauna and Flora) is a worldwide treaty established in 1973 to completely prohibit the international trade of the 600 most-endangered species and products derived from them. The treaty also specifies that "any living specimen will be so transported and cared for so as to minimize the risk of injury, damage to health or cruel treatment." The restrictions against transporting live animals were an attempt to stop practices that resulted in mortality rates of more than 50% in shipments of live birds. Between 1980 and 1986, about 260,000 birds arrived dead at ports of entry in the U.S. Sixty-one nations signed the convention. It has since been ratified by 106 nations.

- After commercial whaling had seriously reduced the populations of humpback and blue whales, they were finally extended protection in 1966. Protected since 1947, the California gray whale is the only species to have made a significant comeback following protection. Its numbers have climbed to an estimated 19,000 to 22,000 individuals, recovering from near extinction. Nine other species of whales are now endangered.

- The heart of a blue whale weighs 1000 pounds. A full-grown adult can reach 150 tons and stretch to a length of over one hundred feet. It is the largest animal ever to have lived on the planet. Hunted until considered commercially extinct, the blue whale is now protected.

- The bald eagle, the U.S. national symbol, was reduced to 1% of its original population in the lower forty-eight states. This was mainly due to loss of habitat, although hunting and the weakening of their eggshells from effects of pesticides contributed to the population decline. From a low of fewer than 700 individuals in the 1960s, the bald eagle's numbers have increased to several thousand.

Sources

Animal Welfare Institute. *Animals and Their Legal Rights: A Survey of American Laws from 1641 to 1990*. Washington, D.C.: Animal Welfare Institute, 1991.

Beirmann, Karl. "Why Animal Experimentation Should Continue." *The Humanist*, July-August 1990.

Breo, Dennis L. "Animal Rights vs. Research? A Question of the Nation's Scientific Literacy." *The Journal of the American Medical Association*, 21 November 1990.

Burton, John, ed. *The Atlas of Endangered Species*. New York: Quatro Publishing, 1991.

Erlich, Paul, and Anne Erlich. *Extinction: The Causes and Consequences of the Disappearance of Species*. New York: Random House, 1981.

Fox, Dr. Michael W. *Inhumane Society: The American Way of Exploiting Animals*. New York: St. Martin's Press, 1990.

Mason, Jim, and Peter Singer. *Animal Factories*. New York: Crown Publishers, Random House, 1980.

Morris, Desmond. *The Animal Contract*. New York: Warner Books, 1990.

National Academy of Sciences. *Science, Medicine and Animals*. Washington, D.C., National Academy Press, 1991.

Pardes, Herbert, et al. "Physicians and the Animal Rights Movement." *New England Journal of Medicine*, June 1991.

Quammen, David. "To Live and Die in L.A." *Outside*, June 1992.

Regan, Tom. *The Case for Animal Rights*. Berkeley: University of California Press, 1983.

Ritzo, Harriet. "Toward a More Peaceable Kingdom." *Technology Review*, April 1992.

Rollin, Bernard E. *Animal Rights and Human Morality*. Buffalo, N.Y.: Prometheus Books, 1981.

Shook, Larry. *The Puppy Report*, New York: Lyons and Buford, 1992.

Stokes, Bill. "The Guns of Autumn." *Chicago Tribune*, 13 October 1991.

Tester, Keith. *Animals and Society: The Humanity of Animal Rights*. London: Routledge, 1991.

infrastructure

infrastructure

infrastructure originally referred to permanent facilities

required primarily for purposes of national security, such as mili-

tary bases, seaports, airstrips. The definition of infrastructure has

broadened to include almost every physical support system of mod-

ern industrial society, public or private. Infrastructure grows with

technological advances and is now an intricate, delicate web of supporting elements including roads, sewers, national transportation grids, communication systems, media, housing, education, computer networks, and most recently the fiber-optic "information superhighway."

For almost two centuries, broad public support for infrastructure development has been coupled with a difference of opinion about how to pay for it. Before 1850, private interests in America could not command sufficient capital for major infrastructure development. Some public investment, in the form of money, land grants, tax exemptions, and the like, was seen as a necessary investment in future prosperity. State and local governments played the dominant role with no coherent national plan guiding their efforts. Rivalries between companies, states, and regions rendered discussion of a national plan virtually impossible.

The triumph of privately run railroads in the mid-1800s led many to feel that increased public sponsorship was both unnecessary and unwise. A growing availability of private capital resulted in a series of state constitutional amendments prohibiting state investment in internal improvements. However, the states and the federal government continued to support these projects, directly or indirectly, as they always had. Even the railroads had received generous state and federal assistance, usually accompanied by outrageous political corruption.

The notion of increasing employment through federal spending on public works surfaced in the 1930s, when unemployment levels rose to 25% during the Great Depression. Before that time, public works were built with a combination of public and private money solely to further economic prosperity. Public works construction subsequently evolved in the twentieth century under the domination of federal patronage and planning. Highways and other projects have been built as an investment in future prosperity, to provide services to the population, and to create jobs in bad economic times. These projects can also support and advance political purposes. The term "pork-barrel politics" was coined to describe the tendency of politicians to bring federal projects, and the resulting economic stimulus, to their home communities, regardless of the actual need or propriety of the project.

Rising inflation in the 1970s, compounded by energy price jumps after the Arab oil embargo of 1973-74, cut sharply into federal

torn by the issues

With lower federal

spending, there is an

increased willingness to

return to the mixed-

enterprise that

characterized the

building of

infrastructure in the

early years of our

history.

purchasing power. Rising interest rates discouraged state and local borrowing. Consumers cut energy consumption, and gas tax revenues fell. By the mid-1970s, federal infrastructure spending had slowed dramatically. With lower federal spending, there is an increased willingness to return to the mixed-enterprise that characterized the building of infrastructure in the early years of our history.

Timeline

1700s

President George Washington and his treasury secretary, Alexander Hamilton, are early supporters of a federal role in what are called internal improvements, chiefly road- and canal-building. Opponents of federal involvement with internal improvements fear the potential for corruption inherent in central governments, but the clear need to build roads and canals and the insufficient accumulation of private capital to build them overcome these concerns. A limited state role in supporting such projects is generally acceptable.

1791

Pennsylvania begins its first state road program, chartering the Pennsylvania and Lancaster Turnpike Company. This private company completes its road in three years and starts to earn a profit, sparking a turnpike boom in other states.

1793

The growing populations in urban centers place increasing strain on water delivery systems, as well as other infrastructure support systems. In Philadelphia, outbreaks of yellow fever, probably caused by contaminated water supplies, take 4000 lives.

1798

Philadelphia reports the loss of 3500 more lives to yellow fever. The city is the first to support public improvements in its water delivery systems.

1799–1801

Two steam engines are built to pump water from Philadelphia's Schuylkill River to a reservoir for distribution through wooden mains. The engines consume huge quantities of coal and blow up repeatedly.

1800

Thomas Jefferson and his secretary of the treasury, Albert Gallatin, take tentative steps toward planning road projects and lending federal support to state and private builders. Most Americans recognize that links between the coast and the interior are essential for economic and political reasons. As Jefferson states, "No other single operation within the power of government can more effectively tend to strengthen and perpetuate the union, which secures external independence, domestic peace, and internal liberty."

1807

New York has sixty-seven state-chartered turnpike companies. Connecticut has chartered fifty.

1808

Gallatin presents his "Report on Roads and Canals." This proposal for a national transportation system includes a coastal waterway, a turnpike from Maine to Georgia, connections between rivers, and roads to New Orleans, St. Louis, and Detroit. Connections are planned between the Hudson River and the Great Lakes. Gallatin argues that only the federal government could accumulate the necessary capital.

torn by the issues

Heated public debate ensues about the propriety of using public funds for these kinds of projects. Opponents claim there is no constitutional authority to construct roads. Supporters reply that the constitutional authority is inherent in the injunction to "promote the general welfare."

Congress decides to build a national road from Cumberland, Maryland to Wheeling, West Virginia (from the Potomac River to the Ohio River) during Jefferson's term. Again strong opposition is voiced on constitutional grounds.

This expression of lofty constitutional scruples is often only a thin veneer covering regional jealousies. Pennsylvania blocks construction of the planned road for years, until a part is rerouted through Pennsylvania. (Regional infighting for desired projects is the same pork-barrel phenomenon so well-known today.)

1812

The War of 1812 stalls action on road-building projects, but Britain's success at blocking trade along the East Coast during this war makes Gallatin's proposals more attractive.

1817

U.S. Congressmen John Calhoun and Henry Clay propose higher import tariffs to support American manufacturing and also to fund a system of canals and highways.

The Congress passes this legislation, but President James Madison vetoes it as unconstitutional.

Governor De Witt Clinton of New York begins construction of the Erie Canal. Its many detractors derisively dub it "Clinton's Ditch." However, the canal, built in eight years at a cost of $7 million, pays for itself in nine years, cutting shipping time from Buffalo to New York City from 20 days to 8. The canal opens up the midwest, and New York leapfrogs Boston and Philadelphia to become the premier East Coast city in the span of a few decades. It is so successful and so profitable that it instigates widespread canal-building activity throughout the country.

Opponents (to the use of public funds) claim there is no constitutional authority to construct roads. Supporters reply that the constitutional authority is inherent in the injunction to "promote the general welfare."

1822

Philadelphia's Schuylkill River is dammed, and water wheels replace the malfunctioning steam engines. Most other cities have privately built water systems, but quality and quantity are undependable, frustrating municipal efforts to clean streets and fight fires.

President James Monroe vetoes another internal improvement bill.

1824

The U.S. Congress appropriates $75,000 to improve the Mississippi and Ohio Rivers for better use as trade routes.

1827

The Baltimore and Ohio Railroad is chartered by the state of Maryland.

1830

Thirteen miles of track is completed with a $500,000 investment from the state of Maryland. Local hometown booster funds become important sources of railroad capital as the connection between railroads and local prosperity becomes obvious.

President Jackson vetoes a bill for a Kentucky turnpike, effectively closing the discussion of a federal role in internal improvements. President Jackson boasts in his farewell address that he has "finally overthrown . . . this plan of expenditure for the purpose of corrupt influence."

1832

Manhattan experiences a cholera epidemic and a devastating fire.

1837

A municipally funded water system is begun in New York City with the construction of a dam on the Croton River, thirty miles north of the city; a stone bridge across the East River; a thirty-five-acre, 180-million-gallon reservoir in what is to become Central Park; and a 20-million-gallon reservoir on Murray Hill.

During the 1850s, horse-cars create enormous sanitation problems. Horses generate gallons of urine and about twenty pounds of solid waste per day.

1840s

Built with 70% private capital, there are 3200 miles of canal open across the nation.

Railroads are expanding rapidly. Approximately 3328 miles of track are complete. Railroads, though privately owned and operated, are aided by public subsidies.

While Jackson's 1830 veto eliminated on constitutional grounds the direct federal funding of these projects, grants of money and land to states or private companies are common. The U.S. Army Corps of Engineers commonly provides technical support, principally surveying services. Also, during this period, the U.S. is the prime recipient of foreign loans. Railroads, canals, mines, and factories are built with huge infusions of borrowed European capital.

American cities grow with new waves of immigration and industry. Growing populations strain the ability of corner pumps to provide adequate drinking water. Outbreaks of cholera and typhoid are frequent.

1850s

Water systems grow more widespread, extensive, and complete. Other municipal systems begin to emerge, providing gas for light and heat, telegraph lines, and early electrical networks.

Urban transportation is dominated by the privately owned omnibus, a long horse-drawn coach seating about twelve passengers. Street railway systems (horse-drawn) are introduced in New York City in 1837, but not until 1856 in Boston and 1858 in Philadelphia. Cities control the development of these systems by issuing franchises to private operators for specified routes.

Horse-cars create enormous sanitation problems. Horses generate gallons of urine and about twenty pounds of solid waste per day. Sewage had heretofore been a private responsibility, but the growing cities are experiencing serious problems with contamination of

By *the 1860s*

municipal debt per

capita more than

doubles as cities rush

to put infrastructure

in place.

groundwater. At one point, citizens of Boston are forbidden by law to take a bath without a doctor's order.

Sewers are the only long-term solution. The enormous cost and complexity of citywide sewer systems leave municipalities with no choice but to capitalize them, plan them, and build them themselves.

Hundred of turnpikes are built by private companies, many with tax exemptions or other forms of public subsidy, and approximately 8879 miles of railroad track are complete.

Sectional politics include a fierce struggle between the North and the South over the location of the eastern terminus of a transcontinental railroad. Many southerners oppose federal involvement in internal improvements, fearing the precedent would encourage federal interference in other matters, most notably the institution of slavery.

Large-scale bridge-building and landfilling begin.

The U.S. Congress appropriates $6 million to improve rivers and harbors.

1860s

The completed 30,636 miles of railroad track begin to connect to form a network, largely without planning on a national scale.

Municipal debt per capita more than doubles as cities rush to put infrastructure in place.

1869

The Union Pacific Railroad and the Central Pacific Railroad are connected at Promontory Point, Utah. These lines are subsidized with twenty-foot rights-of-way and generous federal land grants.

All told, the railroads receive about 130 million acres of public land, 9.5 % of all the land in the country.

1870s

By the time federal support for railroads slows down in the midst of political scandal, the nation, in its haphazard way, has built the

torn by the issues

national transportation network envisioned by Albert Gallatin in 1808.

1870–1920

Underground sewers, water-pumping systems, and paved streets had originated in Europe, but the technologies are embraced with enthusiasm in America, and they develop rapidly. The U.S. pioneers electric power and electric streetcars.

The largest cities have sewers by 1870; the smaller cities have them in place by 1890 to 1920. These are followed by water filtration systems, sewage treatment plants, parks, beautification projects, and street planning. Urban planning begins during this era, as it becomes critical to understand the linkages between these systems.

1880s

Approximately 100,000 horses and mules are pulling 18,000 horse cars over 3500 miles of track in American cities. These are later replaced by electric trolleys.

New York and Los Angeles build massive water delivery systems.

Municipal corruption is widespread. Pork-barrel politics is rampant.

1890s

After Lake Michigan and the Chicago River have become polluted and the existing water supply system proved inadequate, Chicago begins construction on the Ship and Sanitary Canal to reverse the flow of the Chicago River completely, in order to carry water down the Mississippi Basin. This requires excavating mountains of earth and rock. When the canal opens in 1920, typhoid deaths fall to 20, down from 2000 in 1891.

Outside of the cities, roads are constructed mostly by local governments and private citizens to serve the needs of a largely rural economy. A "good roads" movement is launched by bicyclists who push the state governments into increased subsidies for paved rural roads.

The Great

Depression

transforms

infrastructure

development.

President Herbert

Hoover, like Franklin

Roosevelt after him,

views big public

works projects as an

important weapon for

combating massive

unemployment.

An office is formed in the U.S. Department of Agriculture to gather information about roads. This agency propels the federal government into its leadership in highway affairs.

1900

New York City begins to build subways.

There are 8000 motor vehicles registered in the U.S.

1904

There are 204,000 miles of paved road in the U.S.

1916

The Federal Aid Road Act is designed to subsidize state road projects. It is the first continuing federal appropriation for roads.

1921

The numbered route system is planned by the federal government.

1926

The Air Commerce Act authorizes the Commerce Department to establish air navigation aids, and the aviation industry is further regulated and stabilized with the creation of the Civil Aeronautics Board.

Federal subsidies for mail delivery form the foundation for commercial air service.

1930s

The Great Depression transforms infrastructure development. President Herbert Hoover, like President Franklin Roosevelt after him, views big public works projects as an important weapon for combating massive unemployment.

Hoover launches such ambitious projects as Boulder Dam (later renamed Hoover Dam) on the Colorado River. He is opposed to the concept of government handouts and limits himself to self-liquidating projects that generate revenue.

Roosevelt goes further than Hoover. He considers these projects a legitimate way to relieve unemployment and develop the great regions of the country for the benefit of future Americans.

The Works Progress Administration (WPA), in existence from 1935 to 1943, builds 639,000 miles of paved roads, and 78,000 bridges. The federal government becomes involved in building schools, hospitals, other public buildings, water systems, sewer systems, electric power plants, flood control projects, and airports.

The WPA provides the main financial support for the Tennessee Valley Authority, the Grand Coulee Dam, the Bonneville Dam on the Columbia River, Fort Peck Dam in Missouri, New York's La Guardia Airport, Chicago's water filtration plant, flood control in Los Angeles, the Pennsylvania Turnpike, the Lincoln Tunnel and the Tri-Borough Bridge in New York, and many other projects.

Such projects firmly establish the link between federal employment programs and infrastructure.

In 1900, there are 8000 cars registered in the U.S.; by 1940, there are 32,453,233.

1940

New York City has 150 miles of subway lines in use.

There are 32,453,233 cars registered in the U.S.

1944

The Federal Aid Highway Act provides a huge increase in funding for roads. An interstate highway system is planned but not funded.

1956

President Dwight Eisenhower and the U.S. Congress authorize a 42,000-mile National System of Defense and Interstate Highways. It really has very little to do with defense concerns; it passes Congress only because it also contains funding for other roads, both urban and rural.

1960s

By the beginning of this decade, 3557 miles of toll roads are complete, after the success of the Pennsylvania Turnpike proves Americans will pay to use high-speed, limited-access roads.

The New Frontier

and the Great Society

bring a new surge of

federal activism. The

1960s and early

1970s are often

referred to as the

"golden age" of

infrastructure

building.

The New Frontier and the Great Society bring a new surge of federal activism. The 1960s and early 1970s are often referred to as the "golden age" of infrastructure building.

1965

There are a total of 2,075,000 miles of paved roads in the U.S. Infrastructure spending accounts for 5.5% of all federal outlays.

1967

The Silver Bridge across the Ohio River collapses, killing 46 people. As a result, the federal government mandates national inspection standards and training for bridge inspectors. (Today most bridges are inspected every two years.)

1968

The U.S. Department of Transportation is formed. As always, pork-barrel politics make infrastructure programs popular. The optimistic common perception that all problems, from poverty to traffic jams to pollution, can be solved by a federal program contributes to the rise of federal spending on infrastructure projects.

1970

The Urban Mass Transportation Act is passed. It is an attempt to reduce the use of the private auto in increasingly congested urban areas.

1972

The Water Pollution Control Act is passed, providing for the construction of water treatment plants.

Mid-1970s

The growth of federal infrastructure spending stops. This change in policy is caused by such economic factors as rising inflation, rising interest rates, energy price jumps, and decreases in gas tax revenues.

1980

There are 155,796,219 cars registered in the U.S.

1983

The Mianus River Bridge on Interstate 95 in Connecticut collapses. Three people are killed, and traffic is disrupted for months.

1988

The Congressional Budget Office concludes that the infrastructure has largely been built, and maintenance is all that is necessary.

There are 3,491,000 miles of paved roads in the U.S.

1990

Infrastructure spending accounts for 2.5% of all federal outlays, compared to 5.5% in 1965.

There are 190,228,000 vehicles registered in the U.S.

1991

The U.S. Department of Transportation reports that half the nation's 578,000 bridges are in need of repair or other improvements to meet safety requirements. Some are outdated because they are too narrow, but many are incapable of sustaining loads that current design standards demand.

1992

Downtown Chicago is flooded when construction workers accidentally punch a hole in a decaying tunnel built in 1909. Chicago's central business district is shut down for several days.

1993

Pittsburgh declares it would take $100 million dollars just to begin repairs on 120 of its bridges that are either too unsound to use or should carry only reduced loads.

Weather and traffic cause bridge failure, in that water corrodes or otherwise weakens structures, and the vibration of passing vehicles causes bridges to flex. Cracks then begin to destroy the bridge's integrity. This integrity can also be severely damaged by accidental collision of ships with support structures. About 5000 bridges have been closed due to structural damage. Every year, between 150 and 200 spans suffer partial or complete collapse.

In September, 1993, a railroad bridge near Atlanta, Georgia, collapses under the weight of a full Amtrak passenger train bound for Florida. Subsequent investigation reveals that the bridge supports had been struck by a barge shortly before the train passed over it. The collapse results in the loss of forty-seven lives.

Privatization

Many feel that the repair and expansion of America's highways, airports, and other key infrastructure elements are critical to America's future productivity growth. Building our part of the global information superhighway may be especially crucial to global competitiveness in the future. As public investment in infrastructure is stalled due to rising debt and other budgetary problems, it may be necessary to re-invent the funding methods for public works. With lower federal subsidies available, state and local officials have shown a renewed willingness to experiment with privatization.

Experiments in privatization are already underway. The California Department of Transportation has proposed a series of privately funded toll road and bridge schemes as a way to build needed arteries. A $2.5-billion high-speed rail link between two Florida cities, Orlando and Tampa, is a private venture, as is a scheme to build a fourteen-mile toll road connecting Dulles International Airport to other parts of the Washington, D.C. area.

In the 1992 presidential campaign, American voters expressed deep skepticism about the motives of politicians, public engineers and other public servants. Many advocates of privatization and user fees claim that these methods offer the best guide to creating what is really needed, repairing what really needs repairing, and abandoning those projects that are not really needed or wanted.

Cost-benefit analysis is a highly uncertain art. It is easily manipulated by proponents and opponents of various projects. Forecasting cost and use has been very wrong, time and time again. This creates terrible dilemmas for decision makers, both public and private.

Markets attempt to resolve these uncertainties by using an effective tool: failure. Markets quickly recognize failure. A company that loses its shirt on a project will not likely repeat its mistakes. In the public sector, failure is harder to define. Public officials have every incentive and opportunity to delay embarrassing recognition of costly mistakes. It is often in the best interests of the politicians to do so, because public works projects provide jobs and revenue for their particular communities.

In our history, the private sector has played a major role in the building of the infrastructure:

- The construction of the railroads, canals, and turnpikes in the nineteenth century was carried out largely by private firms, with public subsidies usually in the form of tax exemptions, land grants, and cash assistance.

- America's $260-billion telecommunications infrastructure of copper and fiber-optic cables, switching systems, and satellites was built largely through private investment. One form of public subsidy was the monopoly protection granted to AT&T.

- Electronic media, though publicly regulated, are privately owned. Private industry recently wired 50 million houses with cable TV.

- Every year, utility companies, which are largely owned by private investors, invest $10 to $15 billion in new plants and equipment.

- The planned information superhighway is predicted to cost $325 billion over the next decade, by some estimates. It will be financed mostly by private capital. Many feel that America's future competitiveness worldwide will depend on

Some strategies are

being proposed that

would charge peak-

time user fees on

major urban arteries,

so those traveling

during rush hours

would pay more.

these high-capacity networks that will carry voice, video, and data. This modern global communications network will be as important to the emerging information revolution as railroads, bridges, and canals were to the industrial revolution more than a century ago.

Hybrid public-private ventures usually involve government establishment of some rules of the game, such as environmental protection and monopoly restrictions, and the private sector works within that structure. Market principles and market information can be well used to select projects and to determine pricing. An increased willingness to experiment with user fees may open up opportunities to address other environment-related problems, such as waste management and recycling efforts.

Thanks to innovations in computer technology, it is predicted that the inconvenient slowdowns at toll booths can be alleviated or completely eliminated. Electronic toll collection is now in place on the Oklahoma Turnpike and in several other locations. Some major bridges and tunnels are now being outfitted with such technology. Cars will be equipped with credit card-like devices, and sensors overhead or embedded in the road surface will read them without the car having to slow down. The extinction of congestion-inducing toll booths removes a major barrier to establishment of user fees, and thus to privatization of many roads, tunnels, and bridges.

The virtues of market-based infrastructure development are not widely appreciated or understood. Tolls are regarded as another form of taxation and they are resisted as such, by both lawmakers and voters alike. Advocates of privatization scenarios maintain that user fees would represent the real cost for the use of a given service or facility, and they would effectively regulate demand. This can help to indicate where new infrastructure is not justified and ultimately save tax dollars. A pricing strategy that charges fees for the use of resources would let people freely sort out various tradeoffs for themselves. This could also result in a raising of consciousness, in some cases, as to the actual environmental cost of the building, maintenance, and use of infrastructure.

These user-fee scenarios would have to address the need that all citizens have for these facilities and services, regardless of their ability to pay. Some strategies are being proposed that would charge peak-time user fees on major urban arteries, so those traveling during rush hours would pay more. It is hoped that this would encourage people to adjust schedules when possible to ease congestion at these peak times. The wisdom of imposing user fees as a way to control rush-hour congestion is widely disputed. Rush-hour congestion occurs because most people must be on the job during the core hours of 8:00 A.M. to 5:00 P.M. They do not have a choice on this issue, and so to penalize these workers for their use of the roads at these times seems unfair to many. It is suggested that installing peak-time fee structures would significantly increase the cost of living for many people at all levels of income. This is not seen as a desirable solution, unless citizens perceive some pay-back in the form of lower taxes or markedly improved quality of life.

In spite of these disputes over pricing strategies, market approaches are gaining increased acceptance in light of our budget deficit problems. These privatization approaches do appear to have the advantage of flexibility, whether building new infrastructure or adapting existing facilities. Most feel that public-private joint ventures may adapt more rapidly to changing needs, more quickly abandon failed or unnecessary endeavors, and find the best way to use what we already have.

Sources

Dunker, Kenneth F., and Basile G. Rabbat. "Why America's Bridges are Crumbling." *Scientific American*, March 1993.

Ellis, James E. "Reinventing America: The Arteries of Commerce." *Business Week*, Special Issue, 1992.

Seely, Bruce, and Jonathan Gifford. "The Saga of American Infrastructure." *The Wilson Quarterly*, Winter 1993.

Small, Kenneth A. "Urban Traffic Congestion." *The Brookings Review*, Spring 1993.

Wright, John W., ed. *The Universal Almanac*, 1993. Kansas City, Kansas: Andrews and McMeel, 1993.

AIDS

aIDS (acquired immune deficiency syndrome) is a

worldwide health problem. The World Health Organization

(WHO) released a report in 1993 that 14 million people world-

wide are infected with the AIDS virus, and 20 million more will be

infected by the end of the decade. The Centers for Disease Control

(CDC) report 230,179 cases of AIDS over the past decade in the

In 1981, U.S.

doctors noticed

several similar cases

of previously healthy

homosexual men

being treated for

symptoms of

uncertain origin.

U.S. By the end of 1993, the CDC estimates between 390,000 and 480,000 U.S. cases of AIDS will be diagnosed, resulting in 285,000 to 340,000 deaths.

In 1981, U.S. doctors noticed several similar cases of previously healthy homosexual men being treated for symptoms of uncertain origin. These clusters of symptoms included night sweats, fevers, chronic diarrhea, weight loss, and swollen lymph nodes. These patients exhibited a continued depletion of the immune system, and eventually developed unusual and fatal infections. The most common infections were Kaposi's sarcoma, a rare form of skin cancer, and pneumocystis carinii pneumonia, a rare form of pneumonia. Scientists initially believed that this disease process was unique to homosexual men because the first several identified cases were found exclusively within this group. For this reason, the disease was initially called GRID (gay-related immune deficiency). In an attempt to explain the apparent confinement of the disease within the gay community, scientists hypothesized that the breakdown of the immune system might be related to the frequent recreational use of nitrites as sexual stimulants by many of the affected gay males or by the repeated infection with sexually transmitted diseases (STDs) not uncommon to individuals with numerous sexual partners. However, not all of the infected individuals had used nitrites or had experienced repeated bouts with STDs. These original theories were therefore abandoned.

When doctors began noting cases of AIDS in individuals other than homosexual men, the notion that the disease was gay-related was cast aside. Intravenous drug users, sexual partners of AIDS-infected individuals (heterosexual, bisexual, and homosexual), and recipients of blood transfusions and blood products were also contracting the disease. It became evident that the disease was transmitted through the bloodstream and not only through homosexual contact. The name of the disease was changed from GRID to AIDS, acquired immune deficiency syndrome.

In 1983, researchers in France and the United States isolated the virus which is believed to cause AIDS. The virus was named human immunodeficiency virus (HIV).

The original misconception that AIDS was a disease unique to male homosexuals created a wave of homophobia and heightened discrimination against the gay community. AIDS became known as "gay cancer" or the "gay disease." Today, it is known that the disease does not affect only male homosexuals. Anyone who has unprotected intercourse with, shares needles with, or is transfused with the blood of an AIDS-infected person, or is born to an AIDS-infected mother, is at risk of contracting the disease. The virus that causes AIDS remains latent in the body for a lengthy period of time after infection. Once the symptoms become apparent, the disease is fatal. Individuals infected with AIDS usually die within two to three years after the initial manifestation of symptoms. There is no known cure for AIDS at the present time.

The virus that causes AIDS remains latent in the body for a lengthy period of time after infection. Once the symptoms become apparent, the disease is fatal.

Timeline

1981

At Beth Israel Center in New York, two homosexual men die from cytomegalovirus (CMV), a virus of the herpes family that can cause blindness, pneumonia, esophagitis, and colitis.

Dr. Linda Laubenstein of the New York University School of Medicine diagnoses her sixth case in a year of Kaposi's sarcoma, a rare cancer characterized by purplish-brown skin lesions on the legs and torso. All of the cases are found among homosexual men.

Five homosexual men in Los Angeles are found to have a type of pneumocystis carinii pneumonia (PCP) that does not respond to drug therapy.

The Centers for Disease Control in Atlanta report 108 cases of Kaposi's sarcoma or other rare, opportunistic infections resulting in 43 deaths.

1982

The Centers for Disease Control reports show that 691 people in the U.S. have contracted the strange new disease characterized by unusual opportunistic infections, and 278 people have died as a result. The disorder is known as GRID, gay-related immuno-deficiency disorder, because, at this time, the cited cases are only among gay males. Later, it is discovered that hemophiliacs and other recipients of blood products, intravenous drug users, and both homosexual and heterosexual individuals with numerous sexual partners have contracted the disorder. The acronym GRID is abandoned because it becomes obvious that the disease is not unique to gay men. The epidemic disease becomes known as AIDS: acquired immune deficiency syndrome.

1983

The AIDS Medical Foundation is formed by Dr. Mathilde Krim to encourage AIDS research and treatment. The Centers for Disease Control report that the average time of AIDS dormancy (time before a person infected with AIDS begins to show signs of illness) is about 5.5 years.

Dr. Luc Montagnier of the Pasteur Institute in Paris discovers a virus which he believes causes AIDS. He names the virus lymphadenopathy-associated virus (LAV).

1984

The Centers for Disease Control report 3,000 cases of AIDS. The center also discovers and announces that AIDS can be transmitted from one person to another even before the infected person begins exhibiting symptoms of the disease.

At the National Cancer Institute in Bethesda, Maryland, Dr. Robert Gallo isolates a virus he believes causes AIDS similar to the virus discovered by Montagnier. Gallo names the virus HTLV-III.

Abbott Laboratories develops a test designed to indicate the presence of AIDS antibodies, which is then approved for use by the FDA.

1985

The FDA orders all blood banks to begin testing all donated blood for AIDS antibodies.

torn by the issues

The FDA approves the Western blot test, which is a more accurate test for AIDS.

American actor Rock Hudson receives AIDS treatment in France.

The American Foundation for AIDS Research (AmFAR) is formed by actress Elizabeth Taylor and Dr. Mathilde Krim.

1986

The Supreme Court, in *Bowers v. Hardwick*, rules that consensual homosexual sodomy (anal intercourse) is not a protected act of privacy according to the U.S. Constitution.

The International Committee on the Taxonomy of Viruses gives the name human immunodeficiency virus to the virus isolated by both Montagnier and Gallo.

The New York Supreme Court upholds New York City's policy allowing most children infected with HIV to attend public school.

The U.S. government proposes to ban all immigrants to the U.S. who are infected with HIV.

1987

The Supreme Court, in *School Board of Nassau County v. Arline*, rules that people with contagious diseases are entitled to the right of handicapped status under federal law.

The World Health Organization reports that there is no evidence that the AIDS-causing virus, HIV, can be spread through casual contact, including contact with the tears or saliva of an infected person.

U.S. Surgeon General C. Everett Koop reports that nearly 100 million people worldwide could die as a result of AIDS by the year 2000 if a cure or vaccine for the disease is not found. He notes that condoms are the most effective protection against the transmission of AIDS through sexual intercourse. In response, national newspapers and journals begin to accept condom advertisements, and some network television affiliates begin airing late-night condom advertising that directly relates to AIDS protection.

In 1987, The World Health Organization reports that there is no evidence that the AIDS-causing virus, HIV, can be spread through casual contact, including contact with the tears or saliva of an infected person.

The drug azidothymidine (AZT) is approved for commercial use by the FDA. AZT is the first drug approved for the treatment of AIDS in the U.S.

1988

A Center for Disease Control study shows that three of every 1000 students (0.3%) at twenty universities were carriers of HIV.

The three major television networks begin to air public service announcements encouraging the use of condoms to prevent the spread of AIDS through sexual contact.

1989

It is estimated that 2.5 million people in the western hemisphere have been infected with the AIDS virus and that 500,000 will be diagnosed with AIDS by 1992.

The FDA approves the drugs gancyclovir, which is used to treat viral infections, and erythropoietin, which was developed to treat AIDS-related anemia. The FDA also approves the Recombigen HIV-1 test for HIV infection.

The FDA approves fluconazole, a drug which inhibits fungal infections in AIDS patients.

Artist Keith Haring dies of AIDS.

1991

Earvin "Magic" Johnson, Los Angeles Lakers basketball player, announces that he has contracted HIV.

Rock singer Freddie Mercury dies of AIDS-related pneumonia.

1992

The FDA approves the use of the Murex test for detection of HIV infection. The test detects infection in ten minutes.

Former tennis pro Arthur Ashe announces that he has contracted HIV.

Actor Anthony Perkins dies of AIDS.

torn by the issues

HIV belongs to the

retrovirus family.

Retroviruses can live

in the body for an

extended period of

time without

manifesting any sign

of illness.

1993

Dancer Rudolph Nureyev dies of AIDS. Arthur Ashe dies of AIDS.

The World Health Organization releases a report showing that 14 million people are now infected with the AIDS virus and 20 million more will be infected by the end of the decade. This represents about 3 million new infections per year, or 60,000 a week.

The Human Immunodeficiency Virus

HIV belongs to the retrovirus family. Retroviruses can live in the body for an extended period of time without manifesting any sign of illness. They are often quite fragile and die quickly when exposed to disinfectants, heat, or alcohol. However, retroviruses in the body have a high rate of mutation and therefore frequently form new strains. Thus, development of effective vaccines against rapidly changing retroviruses is difficult. The body's immune system has difficulty overcoming these viruses.

When the first identifiable cases of AIDS were reported in the United States in 1981, doctors and scientists believed they had discovered a new disease characterized by the gradual failure of the body's immune system. When HIV was discovered to be the forerunner to AIDS, further investigation of worldwide health records revealed that it was present in Africa before the cases were reported in the U.S. HIV was found in stored blood serum from Zaire, Africa from as far back as 1959. Records of African individuals who had died from opportunistic infections before 1975 showed several cases that meet the current Centers for Disease Control (CDC) definition of AIDS.

HIV is classified as a lentivirus. Before the discovery of HIV, lentiviruses were known to infect only hoofed animals such as horses, cattle, and sheep.

HIV resides primarily in the cells of the body's immune system.

Especially affected are T4 helper cells. When healthy, the T4 cells locate foreign viral, fungal, and parasitic bodies in the bloodstream and then release chemicals that trigger the immune system to begin fighting the invaders. However, when infected with the HIV virus, the T4 cells eventually cease to perform their necessary functions. As a result, the immune system is weakened and the body becomes vulnerable to opportunistic infections. These infections are caused by fungi, parasites, viruses, and protozoa with which the body frequently comes in contact and is normally able to destroy. The virus progressively kills the T4 cells.

The reduction in the number of T4 cells is an indication of the onset of the disease. Depletion happens gradually, and is marked by continual symptoms of various illnesses, including unusual infections and disorders.

HIV also affects the T8 or suppressor T-cells that are responsible for halting the effects of the T4 cells once the body has fought off invading substances. The decline of T8 cells often causes the immune system to indiscriminately attack healthy cells that are necessary for the survival of the body. This condition is known as auto-immune response. HIV does not immediately destroy the immune system. It has an extensive incubation period during which no symptoms are apparent. This period normally lasts between four and eight years, but may extend for more than ten years. Although there are no obvious symptoms during the incubation period, it is possible for an infected person to transmit the disease to others.

Although the body produces proteins called antibodies to fight HIV, they are not effective against the virus. It is difficult for the body to fight off HIV because it mutates frequently and the immune system cannot produce the necessary antibodies quickly enough to combat it. HIV produces new virus particles and mutates at an extremely rapid pace.

The deaths of individuals with AIDS usually result from infections that occur following the failure of the immune system. Deaths that result directly from HIV most often involve brain damage.

There is still some uncertainty surrounding the role of HIV in AIDS. Some scientists believe that HIV is not solely responsible for

torn by the issues

causing AIDS. However, HIV is accepted as the cause of AIDS by most of the scientific community.

The most common early symptoms of AIDS and AIDS-related infections and disorders include:

- Swollen lymph glands in the neck, armpits, or elsewhere.
- Unexplained weight loss.
- Shortness of breath.
- Night sweats.
- Persistent and recurring fevers, headaches, cough and/or diarrhea.
- Extreme fatigue and tiredness.
- Unusual skin rashes.
- White patches inside the mouth.

These are also symptoms of many other disorders including the common cold, and the presence of one or even all of these symptoms does not necessarily indicate HIV infection.

With the progression of the virus, the immune system begins to break down. Organs and systems most often affected by AIDS-related infections are the lungs, skin, gastrointestinal tract, eyes, lymph nodes, and brain. Many of these infections are termed "opportunistic" because they occur only when the body's defense systems are weakened.

Some infections and disorders common to AIDS patients include:

- Pneumocystic carinii pneumonia (PCP)—a parasitic infection of the lungs characterized by difficulty in breathing, dry cough, and fever. It is the most common complication of AIDS and is often fatal.
- Tuberculosis (TB)—a highly communicable disease caused by tubercle bacteria which primarily affects the lungs.
- Aspergillosis—an infection caused by fungi which infects the lungs and the mucous membranes of the ear, nose, and throat. It may also cause meningitis and skin lesions.
- Cytomegalovirus (CMV)—a virus that is a member of the herpes family. AIDS patients often develop spots on the retina which may cause blindness.

- CMV may also cause pneumonia, esophagitis, and colitis.

- Candida albicans (thrush)—an infection caused by a yeast-like fungus which forms whitish, patchy growths along the mouth, throat, and/or esophagus. This is often one of the first signs of HIV infection. AIDS patients often experience painful growths so extensive that eating and swallowing become very difficult and sometimes even impossible.

- Crytosporidiosis—caused by a parasitic protozoan. The disorder is characterized by severe diarrhea which may become chronic and lead to malnutrition.

- Shigellosis—a condition caused by bacteria normally found in the intestines of humans, which results in severe diarrhea in individuals infected with HIV.

- Isosporiasis—a condition caused by a protozoan commonly found in the small intestine of humans which results in an inflammation of the intestines in individuals infected with HIV.

- Kaposi's sarcoma (KS)—a rare cancer characterized by painless purplish-brown skin lesions on the legs and torso. The cancer then progresses to the lymphatic system. This type of cancer is usually limited to older individuals, usually of certain African, Mediterranean, and Eastern European descent.

- Herpes simplex—an acute viral infection, characterized by the formation of groups of lesions on the skin or mucous membranes. These lesions tend to spread.

- Herpes zoster—caused by a herpes virus that results in shingles and chicken pox. The infection affects the roots of the peripheral nerves and is characterized by clusters of painful blisters that usually form along the nerve path of the face or neck.

- Hepatitis B—a viral inflammation of the liver.

- Meningitis—a bacterial infection which causes inflammation of the membranes enveloping the brain and spinal cord.

- Toxoplasmosis—a parasitic infection resulting in an inflammation of the brain.

- Cryptococcus infection—a yeastlike fungus that forms pockets of infection (abscesses) in the brain or lung and is often associated with meningitis.

Difficulties in thinking and concentrating may be a sign that the virus has entered the brain and/or nervous system. Once the brain has been affected, routine mental tasks may take longer than before the infection set in. Speech and movements may be slowed. Memory loss, tremors, epilepsy-like seizures, loss of vision, frequent mood changes, and symptoms of severe mental illness may also result from brain infection. Neurological symptoms are often misdiagnosed as clinical depression, a psychological disorder common to individuals with terminal diseases.

There is no known case of recovery from AIDS. Once the virus manifests itself in bodily symptoms, the disease is fatal. Once the disease is diagnosed, life expectancy for adults is two to three years. Medical treatment may prolong the life of HIV-infected individuals, but there is no known cure. HIV-infected newborns usually develop clinical symptoms of the disease within six months of birth; most die within two years.

There is no known case of recovery from AIDS. Once the virus manifests itself in bodily symptoms, the disease is fatal.

Transmission

HIV is transmitted through the bloodstream. For the virus to pass from one person to another, the blood, semen, or vaginal fluids of an infected person must contact the bloodstream of another person. Unlike other viruses and infections, the HIV virus does not enter the body through the lungs or digestive tract, and it cannot pass through unbroken outer skin. The most common ways the HIV virus is transmitted from one person to another are:

Sexual Intercourse

Exchange of bodily fluids, such as blood, semen, or vaginal fluids that can carry the virus, usually occurs during intercourse.

HIV is transmitted

through the

bloodstream. For the

virus to pass from one

person to another, the

blood, semen, or

vaginal fluids of an

infected person must

contact the

bloodstream of

another person.

Therefore, sexual intercourse is the most common means of transmission of the disease. Transmission of the virus is more likely to occur during anal intercourse than vaginal intercourse because HIV may directly infect cells in the rectum and colon. Also, wounds and tears of the skin are more likely during anal intercourse.

Intravenous Drug Use

Sharing hypodermic needles for illicit drug use is the second most common means of transmission in the U.S. When a person uses a needle, small amounts of blood remain in the needle and can be transferred to another who uses the same unsterilized needle. Disposable needles that are used only once and needles that have been properly sterilized before use, such as those used by health care workers, are completely safe.

Blood Transfusions

Transfer of blood or blood products through transfusion can also transmit HIV. However, there is a very low risk of HIV transmission because all donated blood is carefully screened. In 1985, the FDA ordered all licensed blood banks to begin testing of all donated blood for HIV antibodies. About 3% of all adult HIV infections have been linked to transfusion of blood or blood products. Donating blood presents no risk of contracting the virus.

HIV can also be transferred from infected mothers to their babies. Babies born to HIV-infected mothers frequently contract the virus because the blood of the mother and the baby are in close contact at birth. The unborn fetus of an infected woman may also receive the virus through the placenta during pregnancy. In addition, an HIV-infected woman may transmit the virus to her baby through her breast milk, although this is a very rare occurrence.

These modes of transmission account for about 85% of the cases of HIV-infected children in the U.S.

There have been no reported cases of AIDS transmission through such casual contact as coughing, sneezing, hand-shaking, hugging, or kissing. Mosquitoes do not transmit the virus. It is also very unlikely to contract AIDS through the exchange of saliva or through engaging in oral sex. Swallowing small amounts of infected saliva, semen, or vaginal fluids is extremely unlikely to result in the transmission of HIV, although the virus can theoretically be transferred through the mouth or genital membranes if there are lesions or injuries present in the mouths and/or genital areas of both people.

Through extensive studies, the Centers for Disease Control have established that the following groups may be at risk for contracting the AIDS virus:

- Intravenous (IV) drug users.
- Individuals (homosexual, bisexual, or heterosexual) who have or have had numerous sexual partners.
- Individuals with hemophilia or other blood clotting disorders.
- Individuals who have received blood transfusions or organ transplants before 1985.
- Babies born to and/or receiving breast milk from HIV-infected mothers.

Obviously, not all individuals falling into these categories will contract AIDS. These groups are merely considered at high risk because they have the greatest chance of coming in contact with the blood, semen, or vaginal fluids of an infected person.

There have been no reported cases of AIDS transmission through such casual contact as coughing, sneezing, hand-shaking, hugging, or kissing.

Testing for AIDS

HIV can be detected in the body before any symptoms of AIDS appear. Because the virus can lie dormant in the body for many years, apparently healthy individuals may be unwitting carriers and risk transmitting the disease to others. Early diagnosis may enable infected individuals to delay the onset of symptoms and the spread of the virus. The following tests are currently given to identify the presence of HIV:

ELISA

(Enzyme-linked immuno sorbent assay) This is a test used to indicate the presence of antibodies in the blood which are associated with the virus that causes AIDS.

WESTERN BLOT

This test is often used to confirm that the results of the ELISA test are accurate.

SKIN TESTS

Antigens (substances which stimulate the production of antibodies), such as those used to test for mumps, tetanus, diphtheria, and tuberculosis, cause swelling in people with healthy immune systems.

However, those infected with HIV will have little or no reaction to such injections.

RECOMBIGEN HIV-1

This test seeks HIV antibodies. A drop of blood is placed on a card and combined with a solution containing latex rubber particles. The results are apparent in minutes. If antibodies are present, they clump together with the antigens on the latex particles and produce a visible spot on the card. The percentage of error associated with the test is 0.4% and the test does not require expensive equipment or highly skilled technicians.

T4 HELPER CELL COUNT TEST

T4 cells are specific white blood cells which help to eradicate infections and viruses in the body. This test is used to determine if there has been a breakdown of the body's immune system. In AIDS patients, the level of T4 cells drops from the normal amount of about 1000 cells per cubic millimeter of blood to about 500 per cubic millimeter during the period when no symptoms are apparent. Cell counts below 200 per cubic millimeter are indicative of a severe collapse of the immune system.

MUREX TEST

This test detects HIV infection within ten minutes. Unlike other

torn by the issues

tests which require large samples of blood, the Murex test requires only a small amount of blood and is said to be 99.9% accurate.

SYMPTOM TESTS

These are obviously only effective when the infection has begun to outwardly manifest itself. Unusual disorders may appear, such as Kaposi's sarcoma, pneumocystis carinii pneumonia, cytomegalovirus, and thrush.

Treatment

At the present time there is no effective cure or vaccine for AIDS. Treatment involves attempting to alleviate or slow down replication of HIV and relieving the symptoms which occur as a result of the body's susceptibility to opportunistic infections. However, treatment of AIDS-related infections and illnesses is difficult and often discouraging because although treatments may prove helpful for a period of time, recurrences of infections and the existence of two or more illnesses at one time are common in AIDS patients. Some drugs used to treat AIDS include:

- **Azidothymidine (AZT)**—Taken orally, AZT stops HIV from replicating in the body. AZT does not kill the virus, however. If AZT treatment is stopped, the virus will begin replicating again, so the treatment must be continued for the remainder of life. AZT also seems to alleviate many of the opportunistic infections resulting from the virus. Once treatment is begun, results are usually noticeable within two weeks. Many patients treated with AZT have more energy, regain their appetites, gain weight, and have fewer infections.

  Side effects of the drug include: headaches, nausea, and reduction of red and white blood cells due to the toxicity of the drug to bone marrow which manufactures blood cells. Some individuals being treated with AZT may require blood transfusions to replenish lost blood cells.

At the present time there is no effective cure or vaccine for AIDS. Treatment involves attempting to alleviate or slow down replication of HIV and relieving the symptoms.

Non-medical

approaches such as

macrobiotic diets,

holistic treatments

…and vitamin

therapy…have been

attempted.

- **AL 721**—developed in Israel, AL 721 has not been approved for legal use in the U.S. It is made from egg yolks, and affects the protein coats of certain viruses including HIV, herpes virus, cytomegalovirus, and Epstein-Barr virus.
- **Bactrim**—still in the testing stage, it is thought to be effective against pneumocystis carinii pneumonia (PCP).
- **Dapsone, trimethoprim, sulfamethoxazole**—these drugs help to stop the pneumonia microbe from reproducing.
- **Erythropoietin**—effective against AIDS-related anemia.
- **Fluconazole**—helps to prevent fungal infections such as candidiasis.
- **Gancyclovir**—an antiviral drug developed to be used against Cytomegalovirus (CMV).
- **Hydroxynaphthoquinone**—a drug which has been shown to kill the pneumonia microbe and may prevent relapses of PCP.
- **Interferons**—proteins produced by cells infected with viruses which prevent viral replication. Interferons used in HIV treatment are made by genetically engineered bacteria. Treatments have been found to be effective against Kaposi's sarcoma and hairy-cell leukoplakia, two common AIDS-related diseases. Side effects of interferons include: flu-like symptoms including fever, headache, and nausea, and mild bone marrow toxicity.
- **Interleukin-2 (IL-2)**—a chemical produced by T-cells; it triggers the immune system response. When given to AIDS patients, it stimulates T-cell growth and regulates the function of T4 helper and T8 suppressor cells.
- **Megace**—a drug normally used to treat breast cancer patients, Megace helps to stimulate appetite and restore strength.
- **Pentamidine**—inhaled in the form of an aerosol, this drug helps PCP.

Non-medical approaches such as macrobiotic diets, holistic treatments, subliminal encouragement tapes, and vitamin therapy, have been attempted by many individuals with AIDS. Some of these

The only method

which is 100%

effective in protecting

against sexual

transmission of AIDS

is abstinence from

sex.

approaches have been shown to be somewhat effective for some individuals. Counseling individuals with AIDS is also an important aspect of treatment.

Prevention

Condom use is the best means of avoiding the transmission of AIDS and other sexually transmitted diseases when engaging in sexual intercourse. The condom protects against the transfer of bodily fluids, thus lessening the chance of contracting the disease. However, it is not uncommon for condoms to tear during intercourse or to be used incorrectly, which renders them virtually useless against AIDS. Therefore, condoms should be used carefully and according to package directions.

The only method which is 100% effective in protecting against sexual transmission of AIDS is abstinence from sex.

Individuals using intravenous drugs should never share hypodermic needles with others.

Individuals concerned about receiving contaminated blood or blood products through transfusion could arrange to store their own blood or that of a friend or family member if blood will be needed at some time in the future. However, all donated blood is now carefully screened for HIV infection.

AIDS Facts

- Scientists believe that 1977 was the first year the AIDS virus appeared in the United States.

- The first verifiable cases of AIDS in the U.S. were discovered in 1981. By 1982, 691 cases had been identified. By 1985, more than 15,000 cases of AIDS had been documented in the U.S.

None of the American individuals diagnosed with AIDS before 1983 is alive today.

Number of AIDS Cases
(1982 – 1993)

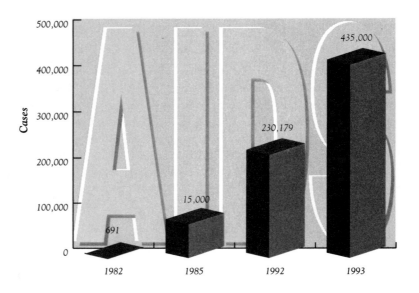

- None of the American individuals diagnosed with AIDS before 1983 is alive today.

- As of June 1992, a cumulative number of 230,179 U.S. AIDS cases had been reported to the Centers for Disease Control (CDC).

- The CDC estimates that between 1.0 and 1.5 million Americans are infected with HIV.

- Approximately one out of eight of all HIV-infected Americans is a woman.

- Studies show that women who are infected with HIV die more quickly than HIV-infected men.

- The Centers for Disease Control estimate that by 1993, between 390,000 and 480,000 cases of AIDS will be diagnosed in the U.S.,

torn by the issues

resulting in 285,000 to 340,000 deaths.

Although in the U.S.
AIDS is most
common among
homosexual men,
globally it is found
primarily in
heterosexuals.

- According to the Centers for Disease Control, the cumulative number of AIDS-related deaths as of June 30, 1992 was 152,153. Of these, 150,114 were adults, 2,039 were children.

- The World Health Organization estimates that 8 to 10 million adults may have been infected with the HIV virus worldwide over the past decade.

- AIDS cases among teens in the U.S. increased from 127 in 1987 to 789 in 1991.

- The average length of time the HIV virus remains in the body is four to eight years. However, in some cases, the latency period lasts for ten or more years. Because no symptoms are apparent during this time, it is unlikely an infected person will be aware that he or she has contracted the virus and thus may unknowingly infect others.

- Although in the U.S. AIDS is most common among homosexual men, globally it is found primarily in heterosexuals.

- A 1988 study of Massachusetts women giving birth showed that 1 in 476 was HIV-infected.

- In New York State, studies conducted since 1987 indicate that 1 of every 1000 babies born to fifteen-year-olds and 1 of every 100 babies born to nineteen-year-olds carries AIDS antibodies.

- Children who are infected with HIV by their mothers during fetal development or at birth usually develop symptoms of the virus within two years.

- In some African cities, 20% to 30% of pregnant women are infected with HIV.

Sources

Anderson, Roy M., and Robert M. May. "Understanding the AIDS Pandemic." *Scientific American*, May 1992.

Centers for Disease Control. *HIV/AIDS Surveillance Report*. January 1990.

——. *HIV/AIDS Surveillance Report*. January 1991.

——. *HIV/AIDS Surveillance Report*. January 1992.

——. *HIV/AIDS Surveillance Report*. July 1992.

Farizo, Karen M., M.D., et al. "Spectrum of Disease in Persons With Human Immunodeficiency Virus Infection in the United States." *The Journal of the American Medical Association*, 1 April 1992.

Flanders, Stephen A., and Carl N. Flanders. *AIDS*. New York: Facts on File, 1991.

Grmek, Mirko D. *History of AIDS*. Princeton: Princeton University Press, 1990.

Jennings, Chris. *Understanding and Preventing AIDS*. 2nd ed. Cambridge: Health Alert Press, 1988.

Kurland, Morton L., M.D. *Coping with AIDS: Facts and Fears*. New York: The Rosen Publishing Group, Inc., 1988.

Madaras, Lynda. *Lynda Madaras Talks to Teens About AIDS*. New York: Newmarket Press, 1988.

Mannix, Margaret, et al. "10-Minute Tests for the AIDS Virus." *U.S. News*, 8 June 1992.

Mayer, Kenneth H., and Charles C. J. Carpenter. "Women and AIDS." *Scientific American*, March 1992.

McGregor, Alan. "WHO: World Health Assembly." *The Lancet*, 23 May 1992.

Nourse, Alan E., M.D. *AIDS*. New York: Franklin Watts, 1989.

Silverstein, Alvin, and Virginia Silverstein. *AIDS: The Deadly Threat*. Hillside: Enslow Publishers, Inc., 1991.

homelessness

home-
less-
ness

t he number of homeless people in the U.S. is estimated at

between 50,000, according to U.S. Department of Housing and

Urban Development statistics, and 4 million, according to home-

less advocacy groups. The disparity in the numbers reveals the diffi-

culty in defining and categorizing the homeless population. Some

studies, like the 1990 U.S. census, have attempted to count the

The disparity in the numbers reveals the difficulty in defining and categorizing the homeless population.

number of people staying in shelters or on the street on a given night. This method resulted in a count of 250,000 to 350,000. Another study, undertaken by the Coalition for the Homeless, included those who are without permanent housing or who are "precariously housed"—that is, in serious danger of becoming homeless. This would include those in temporary shelters or welfare hotels or staying with friends. The count reaches 3 to 4 million using these methods. Other studies give a range of 600,000 to 750,000 people homeless on any given night. The U.S. General Accounting Office suggests the homeless population is growing by 10% annually. The working poor, a significant segment of working America, are increasingly finding themselves in shelters or in food lines, and they are about to be joined by thousands more, projecting present trends.

Studies reveal three patterns of homelessness: temporary, episodic, and chronic. In the first category fall people displaced from their homes by natural and man-made disasters, like hurricanes or fires. Once a low-income person or family is temporarily homeless, it often becomes difficult to resettle into permanent living quarters because of loss of possessions, loss of employment, inability to pay move-in costs, family breakup, and substance abuse. Episodically homeless people are frequently welfare recipients who run out of funds halfway through the month, as well as abused wives, who move in and out of family situations, and runaway or throwaway youths. Throwaway children are those rejected or abandoned by parents. The chronically homeless are more likely to suffer from substance abuse and mental illness than members of the other groups.

Various theories are proposed as to why we are experiencing an increase in homelessness. Studies reveal a direct correlation between the decrease in low-cost housing and the increase in the homeless population. About a half million of these low-cost units are lost annually to conversion, abandonment, fire, or demolition.

Another cause may be the shift taking place in the U.S. from an industrial-based economy to a post-industrial service economy. This shift is gradual and not total, but the change may be enough to trigger the increase we are seeing in the homeless population. This shift may be responsible for the disparity between average wages, which are stagnant or decreasing, and housing costs, which continue to rise. In 1990, HUD identified 5 million households that pay more than 25% of their income for rent. A 1987 study reported that 4 million households were paying over 70% of their income for rent.

Median Rent: 1970 – 1990
(In constant 1990 dollars)

Increase: 30%

Median Household Income: 1970 – 1990
(In constant 1990 dollars)

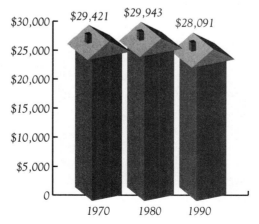

Decrease: 2%

Other contributing factors:

- Families are increasingly broken and dysfunctional. Traditional family support systems are disappearing. This may be a byproduct of industrialization, urbanization, and overpopulation. Housing codes, developed to prevent the negative aspects of overcrowding in urban areas, sometimes hinder or prevent the shared dwelling of extended families that was once the rule in America.

- Traditional education is not preparing people adequately for an increasingly high-tech workplace.

- Over the last twenty years in the U.S., there has been a dramatic increase in service-sector jobs and a loss of jobs in the manufacturing, mining, logging, fishing, agriculture, and defense industries. Many of the jobs in these industries required low skills or minimal training, yet paid well enough to allow rental of minimally adequate housing. Between 1979 and 1984, over 11.5 million workers lost jobs due to plant shutdowns, company relocations, or increased automation. This trend continues.

- The manufacturing sector employed 28.2% of all workers in 1960. By 1987, this industry employed only 19% of all workers.

- More low-wage jobs than high-wage jobs are being created. Between 1963 and 1973, 20% of newly created jobs were at poverty-level wages. Between 1979 and 1985, 44% of newly created jobs paid poverty-level wages. Projections from the U.S. Bureau of Labor show that nearly 70% of new jobs becoming available by the year 2000 will be low-wage jobs in the retail trades and services. Using 1989 statistics, the average gross weekly earnings in the retail trades were not enough to rent an average two-bedroom unit in all fifty states.

- There is growing competition for low-end jobs because of increasing immigration levels. Undocumented immigrants are often willing to work for less than minimum wage, creating even greater competition.

- Since 1973, there has been an increase of 224% of people living in extreme poverty, defined as an annual income of one-half or less of the poverty line. An estimated 3 million people live in extreme poverty and are considered precariously housed.

- A person working full-time, year-round, at the current minimum wage ($4.25/hour) and paying the national median rent of $447.00

per month, would have $8.71 left per day to pay for food, health care, clothing and other necessities of life.

- The average weekly wage from a manufacturing job is roughly $450 a week. From a mid-level service job, the same worker will make about $325 a week. Low-end service jobs pay minimum wage, $170 a week or less. If a small apartment can be afforded, often the "key money" (security deposits and the like) is not available. At the current minimum wage, a couple working full-time could not afford a two-bedroom apartment (at fair-market rents and paying 30% of their income for rent) in any of the country's largest metropolitan areas.

- A study by the Institute of Medicine in 1988 reported that there is a direct correlation between the reduced availability of low-cost housing and the increased number of homeless. The number of low-cost housing units has been decreasing by as many as half-a-million units annually. A 60% reduction of federal subsidy since 1980 contributes to the decrease. Every city surveyed by the 1991 Conference of Mayors cited the lack of affordable housing for low income people as the main cause of homelessness.

- Elderly homeless are reported to be between 12% and 19% of the homeless population. Three-quarters of the nation's elderly live in urban areas. They are often alone. Without family assistance, they live on minimal social security benefits. Many elderly homeless who have been found on the streets are people who traditionally rented rooms in single-room-occupancy hotels (SROs). These hotels are being torn down at a rapid rate due to urban redevelopment. The number of rooms lost, city by city, nationwide, bears a striking resemblance to the number of homeless in those respective cities.

- Where these SROs have been upgraded, room rents have doubled or tripled in ten years. Seniors who are lucky enough to be able to keep one are often paying 60% to 70% of their income for rent. Many will rent a room for part of the month and then live on the street for the remainder of the month.

- During recent decades, there has been a trend toward removing some of the less severely mentally ill from institutions because of the recognition that these institutions were often cruel and inhumane places in which people did not fare well. It was believed that many of the mentally ill could be better treated by community facilities on an outpatient basis, while they remained living in their own homes.

However, community treatment facilities and supportive home environments have not materialized in many cases; mentally afflicted people have been left to wander the streets, unable to help themselves. Averages taken from a wide range of studies indicate that between 25% and 35% of the homeless population could be classified as having chronic mental illness.

- Alcoholism and drug abuse, perennial problems in human society, have reached epidemic proportions in recent years. This has contributed to the upsurge in homelessness, particularly when coupled with the loss of low-end jobs and housing. It is estimated that 30% to 40% of the homeless population are drug and/or alcohol abusers.

- Veterans make up about 25% of the homeless. One out of three of the males on the street is a veteran. Many of them are substance abusers, suffering from post-traumatic stress syndrome, and from a profound distrust of other people, even those offering assistance.

- The fastest growing segment of the homeless population is made up of families, typically women with children. Many of the women are escaping from domestic violence. Children make up about one fourth of the homeless population. About 3% of the homeless population are runaway or throwaway youths.

- The precariously housed—those living with friends or relatives, in cars, in abandoned buildings, facing eviction or foreclosure, or in transitional housing—are now estimated at 7 million people.

- Rural homelessness is on the rise, now estimated at 10% to 20% of the nation's homeless population.

- For many Americans, the task of finding an affordable home in a reasonably safe neighborhood is formidable. The cost of housing has risen nearly three times faster than incomes over the last fifteen years. The traditional rule of thumb of spending 25% of one's income for housing is often no longer possible. One half of the household residents who rent pay more than 25% of their income.

torn by the issues

For many

Americans, the task

of finding an

affordable home in a

reasonably safe

neighborhood is

formidable.

Home Ownership

The average mortgage payment is over $1,000 per month, including taxes, or $12,000 per year. A minimum wage job pays $8,840 per year, before taxes. Even if monthly payments could be met, the move-in costs are prohibitive.

Median monthly mortgage payments for first-time buyers grew from $122 in 1970 to $451 in 1987. The average sale price of an existing single-family home was $23,000 in 1970, and $65,000 in 1980, and $85,000 in 1987. By 1991, the average price had risen to $100,000. The average sale price of a new single-family home rose from $23,000 in 1970 to $147,200 in 1991. In New England, the average price of a new single-family home was $188,800 in 1991.

Average Sale Price of an Existing Family Home

1970–1991

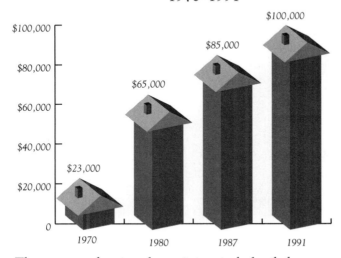

The average sale price of an existing single family home rose from $23,000 in 1970 to $100,000 in 1991. The average sale price of a new home rose to 147,200.

Over the last 20 years, the average price of a residential lot has risen over 800%, from $5,200 in 1969, to $42,300 in 1989.

Nearly half of all families in America cannot afford to buy a median-priced home. Over 70% of the country's 25- to 34-year-old householders cannot afford to buy a home.

Timeline

1346

England enacts the first vagrancy laws.

1865

Widespread homelessness in the U.S. begins with the conclusion of the Civil War.

1896

New York City closes its police stations to the homeless. It had been common practice for police stations to act as shelters, allowing the homeless a place to sleep. By the late 1800s, the numbers of homeless grew to such an extent that this practice was no longer viable.

1901

The Municipal Lodging House opens in Chicago. Lodgers have to do a day's work for a night of lodging. Other similar community shelters open up around the country to assist the destitute.

1933

Demand for emergency shelters surges as the unemployment rate soars during the Great Depression.

1934

A survey conducted by the Committee on the Care of Transients and Homeless reports between 200,000 and 1.5 million homeless people in America. The country's population was half its current size.

The Federal Housing Administration (FHA) is created to support financial institutions involved in the construction of housing and offering mortgages for home purchases. The FHA guarantees these loans, as well as loans for rehabilitating existing housing.

1937

The U.S. Housing Act creates the Public Housing Program. Over one million units of public housing have been built since this program was created.

1947

Congress announces a new national goal for housing: "A decent home and suitable living environment for every American family."

1949

Another Housing Act is passed, appropriating funds to augment and upgrade the general housing stock in the U.S.

1968

The National Housing Act is passed. This program is designed to assist developers of housing for low- and moderate-income tenants. The developers will receive below-market interest rates in exchange for charging the tenants lower than Fair Market Rent. The contract requires the apartments be rented to low- and moderate-income families for 20 years. After this period, the owners have the option of prepaying the balance of the mortgage and gaining release from any federal restrictions on the use of the property. The goal was to provide 26 million new housing units. The goal was achieved; however, many are predicting that 800,000 or more of these low-income units may be lost as the original contracts expire and conversion to more lucrative uses is allowed.

In 1947, Congress announces a new national goal for housing: "A decent home and suitable living environment for every American family."

1972

The Supreme Court rules that there is no constitutional right to adequate housing. "The Constitution does not provide judicial remedies for every social and economic ill."

1974

The Housing and Community Development Act is passed. Section 8 of this program provides vouchers, in lieu of cash, to low-income families for rent. To qualify, a family must find an apartment in a designated time period that is renting for less than the designated fair market value. The apartment must also meet minimum standards of housing quality. The household is responsible for paying 30% of their income for rent, and the remainder is paid by the government. Section 8 vouchers are limited and are given mainly to families with children. Critics of the program assert that there is a critical shortage of apartments that meet the mandated quality and cost standards. Nearly half of those receiving Section 8 vouchers return them unused because they cannot find housing that qualifies for the program. Currently, one million households receive rent vouchers. The number of new certificates was reduced from 110,000 in 1981 to 10,000 in 1988.

The average monthly cost of a housing voucher is estimated to be $360 a month.

In many cities, there is a waiting list for Section 8 vouchers. In Washington, D.C. the wait is 8 years. In Chicago, it is 10 years.

1981

Seven dollars of federal money is spent on defense for every dollar spent on housing programs.

1987

The International Year of the Homeless is declared by UNESCO.

Congress passes the Stewart B. McKinney Act, responding to the social service and health needs of the nation's homeless. The act includes nearly 20 different provisions for emergency shelter, food, health care, housing, educational programs, job training, and other community services.

torn by the issues

1989

Forty dollars is spent on defense for every dollar spent on housing programs.

The U.S. Conference of Mayors reports a 24% rise in requests for emergency shelter.

1990

The Cranston-Gonzalez National Affordable Housing Act is passed. Its purposes are:

- To facilitate saving payments for home purchase.

- To extend public and private partnerships to produce and operate housing affordable for low- and moderate-income families.

- To expand and improve federal rental assistance for very-low-income families.

- To increase the supply of supportive housing and services to allow persons with special needs to live in dignity and independence.

- To create model housing programs appropriate to local circumstances and to increase private investment.

1991

$650 million is spent on homeless programs.

1992

Washington D.C. reports a 49% increase in requests for emergency shelter by families between December of 1990 and December of 1992.

1993

Government attempts to deal with the homeless problem have led to the development of many programs on the local, state, and federal levels. Aid has been provided for people in need, with an expansion in the number of temporary shelters and transitional housing units, as well as health services, crisis counseling, and food distribution. The federal government alone will spend over $1 billion in 1993 to help the homeless. Nevertheless, in New York City, there are 200,000 people on an 18-year waiting list for a public housing unit.

Sources

Adler, Wendy Chris. *Addressing Homelessness: Status of Programs Under the Stewart B. McKinney Homeless Assistance Act and Related Legislation.* Washington, D.C.: National Governors Association, 1991.

Barak, Greg. *Gimme Shelter: A Social History of Homelessness in Contemporary America.* New York: Praeger Publishers, 1991.

Blau, Joel. *The Visible Poor: Homelessness in the United States.* New York: Oxford University Press, 1992.

Coates, Judge Robert C. *A Street is Not a Home.* Buffalo, NY: Prometheus Books, 1990.

DiLulio, John J. Jr. "There But for Fortune—The Homeless: Who They Are and How to Help Them." *The New Republic*, 24 June 1991.

Doblin, Bruce H., et al. "Patient Care and Staffing Patterns in McKinney Act Clinics Providing Primary Care to the Homeless." *The Journal of the American Medical Association*, 5 February 1992.

Dolbeare, Cushing N., and Joan Alker. *The Closing Door: Economic Causes of Homelessness.* Washington, D.C.: National Coalition for the Homeless, 1990.

Drier, Peter, and Richard Applebaum. "American Nightmare: Homelessness." *Challenge*, March/April 1991.

Giamo, Benedict, and Jeffery Grunberg. *Beyond Homelessness: Frames of Reference.* Iowa City: University of Iowa Press, 1992.

Hoffman, Mark S. *The World Almanac, 1993.* New York: Pharos Books, 1993.

Horowitz, Carl F. , et. al. "Inventing Homelessness." *National Review*, 31 August 1991.

Orr, Lisa, ed. *The Homeless: Opposing Viewpoints*. San Diego, CA: Greenhaven Press, Inc., 1990.

Torrey, E. Fuller. "Who Goes Homeless?" *National Review*, 26 August 1991.

Wright, John W., ed. *The Universal Almanac, 1993*. Kansas City: Andrews and McMeel, 1993.

congressional pay

although the salaries, fringe benefits, and other privileges of the members of the United States Congress are, by law, a matter of public record, very few citizens actually know what they are. The salaries and perquisites in both the House of Representatives and the Senate are outlined and enumerated in their respective handbooks. These handbooks are generally unavailable to the public.

The Commission on Executive, Legislative, and Judicial Salaries meets every four years to review and make recommendations on pay raises. If these recommendations are not voted on within thirty days, they automatically go into effect.

Many of the services available to members of Congress are necessary to carry out their official duties while many others are not. All perquisites are either partially, or entirely, subsidized by taxpayer money. These salaries and privileges have been legislated into existence by those who profit from them. The U.S. House of Representatives allows perks and privileges that amount to $2,044,288 per member per year, making it the world's most highly paid legislative body.

Perquisites are intended to reduce congresspersons' personal expenses that would ordinarily have to be paid out of their salaries. However, perks tend to rise concurrently with salaries.

In addition to salaries and perquisites, members of Congress are entitled to pensions and health care services which compare favorably with the same benefits in the private sector. Members of Congress are also entitled to employ assistants to help operate their offices and provide intelligence for legislative decision-making. There are now nearly 10,000 congressional staffers, and 15,000 congressional employees altogether.

F*acts*

- Congressional salaries were 48% higher in 1989 than they were in 1980.

- One out of every three U.S. senators is a millionaire.

- Ninety-nine percent of the population of the U.S. earn less than members of Congress.

- Salaries in both the House of Representatives and the Senate are $129,500, effective January 1, 1992.

- The annual salary for the Speaker of the House is $166,200 as of 1992.

- The annual salary for the House minority leader is $143,800 annually as of 1992.

- The Senate majority and minority leaders and the president pro tempore currently earn $143,800 per year.

- Members of the British Parliament earn approximately one third that of their American counterparts.

- Members of the Canadian Parliament are paid approximately half that of U.S. Congress members.

- Congressional pay raises that issue from the Commission on Executive, Legislative, and Judicial Salaries recommendations become law if not voted on within the thirty-day time allotment.

- Seventy-two percent of voters polled in 1989 opposed any congressional pay hike.

Honoraria

- Honoraria are fees paid for appearances by congressional members, usually for speaking engagements. Although both House and Senate banned acceptance of honoraria in 1991, members may still receive gifts of travel and lodging expenses from special interest groups.

- Prior to the banning of honoraria, members could keep up to $30,000 of such earnings annually. Any amount over that could be donated to charity. In lieu of honoraria, special interest groups may make charitable contributions on behalf of members. These gifts are often much larger than the amounts previously paid for honoraria.

Pensions

- Members of Congress are covered under Social Security and are required to pay the Social Security tax.

- As of 1987, members of both House and Senate can invest up to 10% of their base pay (untaxed until withdrawn) in a 401(k) pension plan.

- Taxpayers match up to the first 5% of the member's salary. Under current pay schedules, that amount can be up to $6,200 annually.

- Members also have the option of participating in civil service retirement programs, in which 8% of their base pay is deducted each year.

- Members of Congress are eligible for pension benefits at age 50 after 20 years, or age 60 after 10 years. Annual payments average $50,000.

- To date, some former members have received over $1,000,000 in pension benefits, and many others are approaching the $1,000,000 mark.

Air Travel

- Members of Congress may travel to foreign countries either on congressional business or by executive request or appointment and are required to submit itemized reports on foreign travel that are open to public inspection.

- Congressional committee reports show that $13.5 million was spent on congressional foreign travel during the 100th Congress. These funds are appropriated by Congress as a part of the Department of State budget and are financed by taxpayers.

- The Government of the United States maintains the 89th Airlift Wing for domestic transportation of members of Congress, among others. At an estimated 10,000 passengers per year, the operating costs run $500 million per year, more than twenty times that of using commercial airlines. Even if estimates of the number of passengers were doubled, the typical traveller flying with the 89th would cost the taxpayer about $25,000 per flight.

Medical Benefits

- Members of Congress are eligible to participate in the Federal Employees Health Program on a voluntary, contributory basis.

- The Attending Physicians Service staff, whose offices are located on Capitol Hill, are available to meet the members' medical needs. This program is totally subsidized at the taxpayers' expense and includes a medical response team, ambulance service, complete laboratory services, X-ray, pharmacy services, and immunization and allergy injections. Senators and their staff members may use, at no cost, the Senate Health Club, where they may receive free medical testing services and free blood. They may also use several Washington-area hospitals free of charge.

- A basic life insurance policy of $99,000 is provided to all members of Congress. Members are required to pay two thirds of the costs of the insurance, and taxpayers pick up the remaining third.

- Congress began a tradition in 1817 of awarding a year's salary to a surviving spouse of any member who dies in office.

The Attending Physicians Service staff, whose offices are located on Capitol Hill, are available to meet Congressmen's medical needs. This program is totally subsidized at the taxpayers' expense.

Franking privilege

- This privilege, known as the "frank," permits members to use their signature as postage. This allows them to mail legislative and campaigning information to their constituents at taxpayers' expense. Franking privileges cost the American taxpayer $89.5 million in 1989.

- Through 1990, House members could send unlimited amounts of mail addressed to particular constituents, plus three additional district-wide mailings to each address in their district when marked "resident."

During every tax

season, the Internal

Revenue Service

opens an office in the

Cannon House office

building to personally

assist members and

staff to prepare their

income taxes.

- After January 1, 1991, each representative received a mailing account entitling him or her to an amount equal to three times the number of non-commercial addresses in their district multiplied by the first-class stamp rate. The average account is $178,000 per year.

- Senate members receive an allocation of between $100,000 and $1,217,147 by a formula based on the number of non-business addresses in their state.

- House members also receive $178,775 annually for "office rent," monies which were allowed, before recent legislation, to be diverted (by House "rules") into mailing funds, staff salaries, or other perks.

- During FY 1987, members of Congress sent out 595 million unsolicited letters, newsletters, or postcards to constituents.

- House members must now file quarterly reports that detail mailing activities and notify the Commission on Congressional Mailing Standards before sending more than 500 pieces of any one correspondence.

Taxes

- During every tax season, the Internal Revenue Service opens an office in the Cannon House office building to personally assist members and staff to prepare their income taxes.

- Members of Congress are allowed a tax deduction of up to $3,000 annually for living expenses while away from their congressional districts or home states.

Gifts

- House members may accept personal gifts of unlimited value from parties who have no direct interest in legislation before Congress.

- Gifts from parties who have a direct interest in legislation before Congress are limited to $200 per year. Gifts valued at under $75 do not have to be included when calculating the aggregate total of $200.

- Senators may accept gifts valued at up to $300 per year from any one source other than relatives.

- Senators are prohibited from accepting gifts valued at over $100 from individuals with a direct interest in legislation. House members may accept and keep gifts from foreign governments of up to $200. Gifts of over $200 may be accepted but must be turned over to the U.S. Government. Senators may not accept gifts from foreign governments valued at over $100.

- Both House and Senate members, their spouses, and dependents may accept gifts of travel (which include food, lodging, transportation, and entertainment) within foreign countries, offered by foreign governments or other foreign entities, when the travel relates to official duties of the member.

Both House and Senate members, their spouses, and dependents may accept gifts of travel within foreign countries, offered by foreign governments or other foreign entities, when the travel relates to official duties of the member.

Expense Allowances

- The Official Expense Allowance for House members is:

  - A base amount of $67,000.

  - A minimum of $6,200 for travel, or an amount equivalent to the cost of 32 round trips from Washington to the member's home district (based on a formula that ranges from $0.23 to $0.39 per mile).

  - The dollar equivalent of renting 2500 square feet of office space in the member's district at the highest rate charged by the Government Accounting Office for federal space.

Based on these three factors, the Official Expense Allowance varies from a low of $106,000 per year to a high of $302,000 per year, averaging $146,388 per year.

- The following items may be charged to the House member's Official Expense Allowance: office equipment, stationery supplies, office space, mobile offices, furniture for district offices, travel expenses, automobiles, television production costs, education expenses, food and beverage expenses, plants and picture frames, photographs, books and newspapers, town meetings.

- Senators receive office space allowance based on the population of each senator's state, with the minimum being 4800 square feet for states with a population of less than 2 million, and a maximum of 8000 square feet for states with population of over 17 million. Funds for these offices are disbursed from legislative appropriations administered by the Senate Sergeant-at-Arms.

- Senators receive an allowance for furniture and furnishings (carpets, draperies, and other office equipment) through the General Services Administration. This allowance is based on a $30,000 minimum allowance for an office not in excess of 4800 square feet, and is increased by $734 for each authorized increase of 200 square feet.

- The Administrative and Clerical Assistance Allowance is used by Senate members to hire staff employees. The amounts of this allowance vary according to state population and range between $814,000 and $1.7 million.

- The Legislative Assistance Allowance in the amount of $269,000 is given to each senator to hire committee staff employees.

- The Senatorial Official Office Expense Allowance is based on the distance of the senator's home state from Washington, D.C. The amounts of this allowance range from $33,000 (Delaware) to $156,000 (Hawaii). The items covered by this account are round-trip transportation and per diem expenses, stationery, telephone and telegrams, mailing privileges other than franking, newspaper and periodical subscriptions, reimbursements to individuals appointed by senators to serve on panels or other bodies that officiate nominating procedures (judgeships, service academies, etc.).

- For correspondence, each senator receives one and one-third blank sheets of paper per constituent per year, or 1.8 million sheets per year, whichever is larger. This does not include an undisclosed amount of free letterhead sheets, envelopes, or paper used for town meeting notices.

The Legislative

Assistance

Allowance in the

amount of $269,000

is given to each

senator to hire

committee staff

employees.

- Any senator who does not have the resources to respond to an organized mail campaign may request assistance from the Senate Sergeant-at-Arms. Any assistance rendered includes free paper used for responses.

- All general office equipment used in Senate offices (including home offices) is issued and maintained by the Senate Sergeant-at-Arms. Equipment included in this category are signature-signing machine, letter folder, letter inserter and sealer, paper cutter with stand, electric or manual typewriters, calculators, copy holders, mimeograph machines, noise suppressor, electric pencil sharpeners, recorders and transcribers, electric staplers, telephone answering machines, time recorders.

- Each senator is allowed one mobile office, leased and paid for by the Sergeant-at-Arms.

Off-budget Perks & Benefits

- Each House member is provided with one free garage space for personal use, plus four garage spaces and two outside spaces for staff members. Each senator is provided with four garage spaces for personal use and the use of senior staff, and additional outside spaces depending on the number of staff. The GSA also provides one space for each senator's home state office in a federally owned or leased office. Reserved spaces on Capitol Hill are worth approximately $1,500 per year. Congressmen receive the use of government-supplied office furniture for their Washington offices. Members of the House receive furniture from the Clerk of the House, and senators are supplied by the Superintendent of Buildings, who represents the Architect of the Capitol. Basic furnishings include executive desks, draperies, typing chairs, bookcases, leather couches, table lamps, desks, coat trees, leather lounge chairs, rugs, occasional chairs, made-to-order bookcases, refrigerators, smoking stands, carpets, metal file cabinets, tables, executive swivel chairs, venetian blinds, conference tables, coffee tables.

Each senator is

provided with four

garage spaces for

personal use and the

use of senior staff,

and additional outside

spaces depending on

the number of staff.

Reserved spaces on

Capitol Hill are

worth approximately

$1,500 per year.

- Indoor plants are supplied by the U.S. Botanical Gardens on loan.

- Two framed reproductions from the National Gallery of Art are available on request.

- Maps are furnished at no cost.

- The Superintendent of Buildings provides members with picture framing services for photos, maps, posters, etc. for use in Washington offices.

- Members leaving Congress may purchase their office furniture at a depreciated, or fair-market, value.

- Members are entitled to an undisclosed amount of envelopes for "franked" mail.

- For $50 per year House members may use health club facilities located in various government buildings on Capitol Hill. Senators' gym facilities include swimming pool, steam room, and courts for handball, volleyball, and basketball.

- Congressional members and their families may borrow materials for personal use from the Library of Congress. The public is not allowed to borrow materials from this library.

- Members may purchase airline tickets at a special ticketing office located in the Longworth House office building. Members of Congress get free upgrades on airline travel to first class.

- Members and their families may use facilities on U.S. military installations around the world.

- Members and their staffs may shop at their own discount store to purchase nominally priced (taxpayer subsidized) merchandise such as is generally found in department stores.

- Members may obtain discounted haircuts and shoe repairs at shops located in the House and Senate office buildings. Limousines and drivers are provided to the Speaker of the House, the House majority and minority leaders, the president pro tempore of the Senate, the majority and minority leaders of the Senate, and the Senate majority and minority whips.

- Flags that have been flown over the Capitol are available to members to be used as gifts.

Members receive special

license tags that allow

them to park almost

anywhere in the District

of Columbia without

being ticketed.

- Special parking lots located next to the terminals at Washington National and Dulles airports are provided to members of Congress, a savings of $20 to $26 per day.

- Members receive special license tags that allow them to park almost anywhere in the District of Columbia without being ticketed.

- Members who travel more than twice a year are entitled to receive a government-owned Diners Club charge card to pay for authorized business travel.

- Free passports are provided to members in the House post office. State Department staff are available to members to expedite processing of passports.

- "Orange-bagged" franked mail is assured one-day service by the U.S. Post Office.

- Members and their staff and guests eat taxpayer-subsidized meals at congressional restaurants.

- General banking services are available to members through the Wright Patman Congressional Credit Union. House members used the Sergeant-at-Arms Bank until abuses caused its closing in October, 1991. In March, 1992, the House Ethics Committee disclosed the names of 355 members who had written checks on overdrawn accounts. The checks were paid without penalty.

- In 1993, the government will give George Bush $463,000 and Ronald Reagan $633,000 for office rent, staff, and travel. In addition the Republican National Committee gives them each $150,000 a year. They each draw a pension of $148,000.

Sources

"Are They Worth It?" *Time*, 23 January 1989.

Congressional Accountability Project. *Feathering Their Own Nests; The Facts on Congressional Pay and Perks*. Washington, D.C.: Congressional Accountability Project, March 1992.

Gross, Martin L. *The Government Racket: Washington Waste from A to Z.* New York: Bantam, 1992.

Jackley, John L. *Hill Rat: Blowing the Lid Off Congress.* Washington, D.C.: Regnery Gateway, 1992.

"Just Say No." *The New Republic,* 6 February 1989.

"Should Congress Get a 51% Raise?" *U.S. News & World Report,* 13 February 1989.

"The Packaging of a Pay Raise." *U.S. News & World Report,* 27 November 1989.

during the first 2 to 5 million years of human history,

the total population of the world never exceeded about 10 million

people. About 8000 B.C., when humans began to farm and raise

animals, significant population increases began. Because of

improved nutrition and a more settled lifestyle, death rates began to

fall. World population reached its first billion about 1800. It took all of human history to reach that first billion. Now, each billion is added in just over a decade.

That the population is growing dramatically is not in dispute; what is disputed is whether this spells disaster for the human species and the planet. Some feel that more people will simply mean more productivity and more technology. A study of population fluctuations seems to indicate that there will eventually be a stabilization and subsequent decline of population rates. World population in 1990 was 5.4 billion. It is expected that the population will grow to approximately 11 to 13 billion by 2100, approximately doubling today's numbers, before the decline in growth rates begins.

World Population Growth Through History

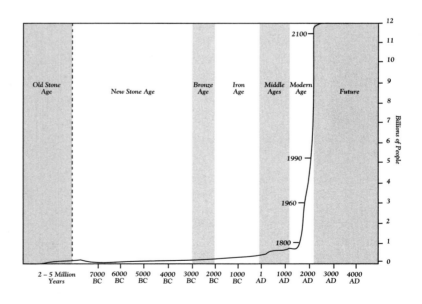

Plague, famine, war,

and other natural

disasters are not

counted as factors in

projections, as they

are unforeseeable.

Timeline

AD 1

Estimated population: 200-300 million.

1650

Estimated population: 500 million. It has doubled in 1650 years.

1850

Estimated population: 1 billion. It has doubled in 200 years.

1965

Estimated population: 3 billion. It has tripled in 115 years.

2000

Population projection: 6 billion. It will double in thirty-five years.

Projections

During all of human history before 1965, a span of perhaps two million years, the total population grew to three billion. It will take thirty-five years to add the next three billion.

There is a tendency for the media to take population projections as exact predictions. There are so many variables in population projections that a single figure cannot be accurately derived. All projections in scientific reports and studies are presented as a range of possibilities with several factors seen as unpredictable variables. Usually the media when delivering information to the public will present the middle projection as fact, although it is just one of several equally likely possibilities. Plague, famine, war, and other natural disasters are not counted as factors in projections, as they are unforeseeable. These factors do, however, enter into human history with great regularity, and they are often significant regulators of population size. Human populations also regulate themselves naturally over time, growing or diminishing with the advent of social, technological, or environmental changes.

Developing countries will account for 90% to 95% of the total population increase between now and the twenty-first century. Traditional agricultural societies often favor large families because more workers within the family unit means more wealth. Often family planning programs meet resistance because the planner perceives a problem and the indigenous people don't.

Europe is now experiencing a decline in population growth rates, and in some areas is instituting policies that encourage increased birth rates. These policies do not seem to be taking hold, and Europe's population continues to decline. Between 1975 and 2000, annual growth rates are projected as follows:

Projected Annual Growth Rates

AREA	GROWTH RATE
North America	1.2%
Europe	1.0%
Asia	3.0%
Africa	2.8%
Latin America*	3.8%

(population will double every 18 years)

Due to advances in medical science, death rates have fallen in both the developed and undeveloped world. However, an equivalent decline in birth rates did not begin until recent years. This accounts at least partially for the dramatic growth rates in the last 200 years. Annual population increases (worldwide) are expected to grow to a high of 90–100 million per year in the late 1990s, then begin a gradual decline (that is, the rate of increase will gradually decline).

American women

averaged more than

seven children each

until the early decades

of the nineteenth

century.

The Most Populous Countries in 2034 (Projected)

1. India ....1.3 billion
2. China...1.3 billion
3. United States ....270 million
4. Nigeria...265 million
5. Brazil... 260 million
6. Indonesia ....230 million
7. Bangladesh ....220 million
8. Pakistan...200 million
9. Mexico...165 million

Fertility Rate refers to the average number of children a group of women will have during their child-bearing years (15–49).

Death Rate refers to the number of deaths that occur in any given age group from infancy through old age, in a given year. Death rates are higher when larger numbers die at younger ages, and they decline when greater numbers have longer life spans.

If two parents have two offspring, thereby replacing themselves, this is considered a replacement-level fertility rate. The rate actually cited as replacement level is 2.1; it allows for some instance of infant mortality. This replacement-level rate is also referred to as zero population growth or no-growth equilibrium. The momentum of population growth continues for some time even after fertility rates go below replacement level.

In 1990, the worldwide fertility rate average was 3.6, ranging from 1.3 in Italy to a little over 8.0 in Rwanda. The fertility rate in the U.S. was 2.1. About 90 to 95 million people are being added to the world's population each year.

The United Nations (U.N.) Population Division offers four population projections or scenarios for the year 2100, ranging from 7.2 billion to 14.9 billion. This largest figure would triple 1990 levels in 110 years. The U.N. midrange scenario or medium variant offers a world population stabilizing (birth rates equal death rates) at 10.2 billion in 2100, which would double today's population. This stabilization scenario requires a no-growth fertility rate of 2.1 by 2035.

If the date for achieving a replacement-level fertility rate is delayed by twenty years (2055), the global population by 2100 will be 13 billion. If it is achieved twenty years earlier (2015), the 2100 population would be 8 billion. The difference between these scenarios is approximately equal to today's world population.

American women averaged more than seven children each until the early decades of the nineteenth century. Fertility rates declined thereafter, interrupted only by the baby boom after World War II. The U.S. fertility rate reached an all-time low in 1976, and rose to 2.1 in 1990.

A young woman of today who bears two children instead of the six her mother might have borne will, if this rate stays constant, have eight great-grandchildren rather than the 216 her mother could have produced.

Population Growth & Water

To support the expanding human enterprise, water is being withdrawn from underground stores called aquifers many times faster than it is being replaced by nature.

More than 1000 cities in the U.S. have had to curtail water service. In Chicago, in areas where artesian wells flowed under their own pressure a hundred years ago, new wells must go down 2000 feet to reach the water table.

Much of the newly cultivated arable land in the world has to be irrigated, as rainwater is often insufficient. The water in the Ogallala aquifer underlying the Great Plains in the U.S. accumulated in the last Ice Age. In some places, particularly the southern high plains, the Ogallala takes in about a half-inch a year due to natural processes. The water level drops four to six feet annually as pumps take out the water to irrigate crop land.

In California's San Joaquin Valley, aquifers are being pumped out at a rate that exceeds natural replacement by more than 500 billion gallons annually, and the rate is rising. The amount of water removed, less the amount that is naturally replaced, is roughly double the amount of oil that flows into the American economy each year.

Rainwater is essentially distilled. It has been accumulated through evaporation and contains no appreciable level of salts. Irrigation water, drawn from underground sources, has leached through the earth and has accumulated salts. When it evaporates, it leaves the salts behind, on the ground. This process is called salination. Salvaging saline fields by a flushing process costs more than most farmers can pay. California's fertile Imperial Valley, where the most modern irrigation methods are practiced, is currently threatened by salination. Many aquifers underlying irrigated areas have become so brackish that their usefulness has been impaired or destroyed.

The problem with salinity is not a new phenomenon. The ancient Sumerian culture that thrived 6000 years ago in the Tigris-Euphrates flood plain (present day Iraq) used irrigation practices that led to salt build-up in water and soil and subsequent desertification. This undoubtedly contributed to their eventual cultural decline.

Salinization is causing declining yields in India, China, Central Asia, Asia Minor, the Middle East, North Africa and North America.

The oceans are a source of water that has barely been tapped. No one really knows what the desalination of sea water may mean to the reclamation of deserts, but it is considered one of the major hopes of the future. The high levels of salt will be costly to remove from this water, and rich countries will be able to absorb this cost better than poor countries.

Over the centuries, human activities such as deforestation, overgrazing, and overcultivation have created the desert-like conditions that exist today in the Near and Middle East, some parts of the American southwest, and elsewhere.

Population Growth & Land

As rural areas are losing people, they are also losing land. The U.N. Food and Agricultural Organization estimates that about 1.4 billion hectares of arable land will be claimed by urban development worldwide between 1980 and 2000.

According to the U.S. Census Bureau, 29% of the world's population lived in urban areas in 1950. Demographers estimate that by 2000, half the world's people will be living in urban areas.

About 35% to 40% of the land surface on the planet is said to be virtually unavailable for agricultural use, given current technology. Such land is too arid, too cold, too mountainous, or already occupied by cities or inland waters. Of the 60% remaining, one sixth is cultivated for crop production, one third is described as meadows or pasture land for the grazing of domesticated animals, and one half is covered by forests.

The size of arable land and the size and quality of other natural resources dictate where human populations concentrate. These viable areas tend to be below 1500 feet in altitude, and in the middle latitudes, the subtropics, and a few areas of the tropics. Productivity in more difficult areas requires more cost in money and human energy.

Per-capita grain production increased three to four times from 1950 to 1975. This is often referred to as the "green revolution." The dramatic increase was due to technological advances in agricultural methods, and it gave great hope to the world that the burgeoning population could easily be fed. However, in the 1980s, many areas experienced declines in crop yields despite high-yield technologies. Salination, loss of top soil, and widespread drought were seen as the causes.

Since 1984, according to the environmental research organization called Worldwatch, world grain production per capita has fallen one percent a year. In 1990, eighty-six nations grew less food per person than they did a decade before.

Desertification is the creep of desert-like conditions into areas where they should not climatologically exist. Plants, by shading the ground, keep evaporation of excess water to a minimum. By removing the plants through deforestation or overgrazing, the sun hits the soil directly and dries it out, producing desert-like conditions. Over the centuries, human activities such as deforestation, overgrazing, and overcultivation have created the desert-like conditions that exist today in the Near and Middle East, some parts of the American southwest, and elsewhere.

The extensive deforestation that has taken place on the planet to serve the growing human population has been necessary to create more and more arable land, to create grazing land for animals, and to provide fuel. In recent years, there has been extensive re-planting of forests in the U.S., partially due to the efforts of environmentalists to counter the negative effects of deforestation, and also because it is becoming a profitable business investment as the price of wood rises.

There has been extensive natural regrowth of forests in the eastern U.S. as the major agricultural activity moved westward as the country expanded.

In Malthus' view,

population growth

would be corrected by

famine, disease, war,

or other similar forms

of "misery and vice."

The rapid deforestation in tropical areas causes scientists particular concern. The soils beneath tropical rain forests are generally poor and thin. The rain forest nutrients are stored largely in the vegetation, not in the soil. When the forests are cleared, the remaining nutrients in the soils are quickly leached away by heavy tropical rainfall. Thus far, permanent agriculture in these regions has been unsuccessful, although policy makers still remain hopeful. Some scientists are trying to restore traditional farming practices in some areas that apparently supported a large indigenous population before the Spanish conquest. Many of these practices, however, require the existence of the forest canopy to protect topsoil. This canopy is rapidly diminishing.

Some projections of post WWII rates of increase give a population of one person per square foot of land surface of the earth in less than 800 years. (Of course, the planet could not sustain this number, given current and foreseeable technology.)

In the Netherlands, there are 14 million people living on land the size of Maryland (pop. 4 million). In the former West Germany, there are 60 million living on land the size of Oregon (pop. 3 million). These large numbers have not prevented these countries from functioning well and maintaining a fairly high standard of living. However, these land areas do not entirely support these numbers. Much of their food, mineral and energy supply is imported from other countries with less dense populations and surpluses available for export.

Theories About Population Growth

The Malthusian Catastrophe

The Malthusian doctrine was expounded in 1798 by Thomas Malthus, a Christian minister in England. At this time England was suffering from a series of climate-related food shortages and economic crises. By 1803, one out of every seven people receiving poverty relief was from a local parish.

Malthus theorized that human populations, like populations of all living species, would expand up to and slightly beyond the available food supply. He proclaimed that "the power of population is indefinitely greater than the power of earth to produce subsistence for man."

This theory is often reproduced in economic textbooks as a graph. One line shows the planet food-production capacity rising slowly as humans clear more land and learn more productive farming techniques. The second line, representing human population, starts out low, climbs to meet the first quickly, and then rapidly rises above it. At some point there is no hope of closing the gap between the two lines, and humanity is doomed to live on the brink of starvation or beyond. He felt that public charity was not the answer, as this only produced higher birth rates and encouraged pauperization, which worsened the problem.

In Malthus' view, population growth would be corrected by famine, disease, war, or other similar forms of "misery and vice." He felt this was inevitable despite intervention by government or technology. The "Malthusian catastrophe" is widely cited in population growth studies.

High-Tech Solutions

Opposing theories claim that technology and human creativity can handle almost unlimited growth, because technology, like population, can also grow exponentially and can sustain population growth. For example, one silicon chip now holds close to half a million data bits through which information is sorted. By the turn of the century, it is expected that some two billion data bits will fit on one chip.

Some theorists predict extremely large but viable populations in 200–300 years, based on assumptions that capturing solar or nuclear energy will produce extremely cheap power. It would then be feasible to obtain all things we need from rock, sea, and air. According to this theory, humanity will subsist largely on food products from algae farms, yeast factories, and the like, and future developments will enable colonization of other planets.

One American researcher in the mid-1970s argued that by using present high-yield technology and irrigation, the world could produce 2500 calories per person per day for 40 billion people. Other researchers, who see that as a nightmarish prospect, dispute the estimates of yield as well. An estimate of 9000 calories per person per day is suggested as more realistic when animal feed and seed are included. The predicted yield could then support only about 7 billion people. As of 1990, scientists are observing reduced yields as soil nutrients decline and salination from irrigation water renders more and more acreage unusable.

In nature, populations of any living species are limited by the available food supply, and humans are no exception. However, the human species has demonstrated enormous powers of intellect and creativity to overcome food supply problems and other threats to its survival as they arise. Future technological possibilities include:

- Aquaculture or "hydroponics," eliminating the need for topsoil.
- New techniques for tropical agriculture.
- More conservation and recycling of water, cutting down on salination.
- Bioengineering through the ability to control DNA, which will perhaps be more significant than the discovery of fire or the invention of the printing press.

Such technological advances require that a sizable portion of the population is well-nourished, energetic, and free to work on projects other than the actual production of food. In wealthy developed countries like the U.S., an estimated 2875 people per million are engaged in research and development. In developing countries, 121 people per million are engaged in research and development.

Demographic Transition

The phenomenon of demographic transition can be observed currently in the developed world. It appears to refute the Malthusian doctrine. This four-staged model describes and explains how populations naturally grow and decline.

In wealthy developed countries like the U.S., an estimated 2875 people per million are engaged in research and development. In developing countries, the average is 121 people per million.

Since many worry

that the aging of the

population will place

an intolerable burden

on the Social Security

system, encouraging

the immigration of

younger workers is

seen as a possible

correction of this

imbalance.

In the first stage, birth and death rates remain at relatively constant high levels, and populations remain stable. Death rates are high because of harsh living conditions. High birth rates are encouraged by societies through religious teachings and social pressure. Large families serve a practical function, furnishing free labor to families and support of aged parents. Collectively, large families increase the military, economic, and political power of tribal groups.

During the second stage, death rates drop in response to improved living conditions, but birth rates do not. Population increases.

In the third stage, birth rates begin to decline due to the perceptions that more children will survive and that fewer children are required for labor as rural populations move to urban areas. Growth rates begin to decline.

By the fourth stage, birth and death rates are about equal again; they vary at a relatively constant low level. Population stabilizes. The former West Germany and Hungary have passed through this fourth stage into a decline in population. Were it not for high immigration levels, the U.S. also would face negative population growth in the 21st century. Some would welcome this decline in numbers, believing it would ease the pressure on already overloaded ecosystems. Others see population decline as a threat to economic systems, defense systems, and even to national identities.

The U.S. population is currently about 250 million. The U.S. census bureau predicted in 1982 that the U.S. population would stop growing at about 309 million by 2050 and then begin to decline, even with a net immigration of 450,000 per year.

Currently the U.S. continues to accept 500,000 to 750,000 immigrants per year. The immigration factor keeps the U.S. population younger than its European counterparts. Since many worry that the aging of the population will place an intolerable burden on the Social Security system, encouraging the immigration of younger workers is seen as a possible correction of this imbalance.

The Organic Model

This model likens population growth to the growth of individual organisms. Human societies are born after a very long pregnancy, and rapid population growth immediately occurs. This is followed by an adolescent period when growth takes place at a slower rate. According to this model, the U.S. is now emerging from adolescence. Adulthood arrived in Europe in the late 1960s. No further growth is observed. According to this theory, all nations in the developed world are "adults" and now face "old age" and population decline. Some societies disappear or are absorbed in newer ones, and the growth cycle may begin again.

More Facts

- Population in the U.S. in 1970 was 203,302,000. In 1980, it was 226,546,000. In 1991 it was 252,177,000. This is an increase of approximately 25% in 20 years.

- There were 32,000 centenarians in the U.S. in 1980; 1.9 million are projected by 2080.

- Half of the world's people are concentrated on 5% of the earth's surface. About 25% is suitable for human habitation, given current technology. Most of that is needed for agricultural land.

- In 1965, two thirds of the world's population are considered hungry by U.N. standards.

- In 1950, annual per capita income worldwide was estimated at $223. The North American per capita income was $1100. Had each person on the globe enjoyed the North American level of income, the aggregate world product would have supported only 500 million persons, as contrasted with 1950's world population level of 2.5 billion. The current world population is 5.4 billion.

- Nature has three ways of controlling populations: war (or predation), disease, and famine.

- The world's population growth rate has begun to decline. It was 2% worldwide in the 1960s. In the early 1980s it was 1.7%.

Looking Ahead

The population growth in developing countries may be appropriate according to these models of population growth and decline, but many are beginning to feel that the burden of the rapidly increasing numbers on the planet is becoming unsustainable. If population growth outstrips food production, particularly in poorer nations, this may mean the total disappearance of those most severely affected societies in the near future.

Most scientists agree that the rapid increase in population over the 200 years since Thomas Malthus wrote his famous essay has placed extreme strain on ecological systems that somehow have to provide sustenance to those numbers. The most optimistic scenarios describe the pressing need for conservation far beyond today's efforts, and most depend upon some decline in fertility rates. They also rely on the development of very young technologies. For these technologies to mature, a well-nourished population with excess wealth is required.

Natural checks on human population size are expressed in terms of numbers and percentages, but they often manifest as extreme human suffering. Since 1968, at least 200 million people have died of hunger or hunger-related diseases; of these, most victims were children.

Life Expectancy in Selected Countries

Country	Life Expectancy
Chad	39.8
Cambodia	49.3
Ethiopia	51.3
Bangladesh	53.0
India	57.2
Brazil	65.2
China (mainland)	70.0
Ireland	75.5
U.S.	75.7
Germany	75.8
United Kingdom	76.5
France	77.8
Italy	78.1
Japan	79.2

torn by the issues

Population per Square Mile in Selected Countries

Western Sahara 2

Australia 6

Iceland 7

Canada..8

Sweden 54

U.S..71

United Arab Emirates 74

Colombia 84

Kenya...115

Mexico...121

Greece..199

France 269

Denmark 314

China (mainland) 320

Germany 588

India...757

Japan 814

Hong Kong 15,335

Monaco..38,477

Macao 72,239

The most optimistic scenarios describe the pressing need for conservation far beyond today's efforts.

Sources

Erlich, Paul, and Anne Erlich. *The Population Explosion.* New York: Simon and Schuster, 1990.

Glantz, Michael H., ed. *Desertification: Environmental Degradation in and Around Arid Lands.* Boulder: Westview Press, 1977.

Malthus, Thomas Robert. *Population: The First Essay.* London, 1798.

Mamdani, Mahmood. *The Myth of Population Control: Family, Caste and Class in an Indian Village.* New York: Monthly Review Press, 1973.

Mann, Charles C. "How Many Is Too Many?" *Atlantic Monthly*, February 1993.

Ng, Larry K.Y., and Stuart Mudd, eds. *The Population Crisis: Implications and Plans for Action*. Indianapolis: Indiana University Press, 1965.

Kent, Mary M., ed. "Population, Resources, Environment." *Population Bulletin* 1987:2. Washington, D.C.: Population Reference Bureau, 1987.

——. "Understanding Population Projections." *Population Bulletin* 1987:4. Washington, D.C.: Population Reference Bureau, 1987.

——. "Food and Population—Beyond Five Million." *Population Bulletin* 1988:2. Washington, D.C.: Population Reference Bureau, 1988.

——. "Population, a Lively Introduction." *Population Bulletin* 1991:1. Washington, D.C.: Population Reference Bureau, 1991.

Wright, John W., ed. *The Universal Almanac, 1990*. Kansas City, Kansas: Andrews & McMeel, 1990.

global warming

the climate is governed by many factors, one of which is

the relative quantity of different gases in the atmosphere. All of

these gases have more or less ability to "trap" heat, hence the name

"greenhouse gases." If it weren't for this natural greenhouse effect,

the earth's temperature would be approximately 0° F on average,

instead of its current average temperature of 59° F. Since the

It was in this

greenhouse-like

environment, where

the sun's radiation is

limited, and much of

the earth's outward

radiation is trapped,

that biological life, as

we know it, appeared

on the planet.

Industrial Revolution, there has been an unprecedented increase in four major greenhouse gases. These are carbon dioxide, chlorofluorocarbons (CFCs), methane, and nitrous oxide.

Solar radiation is the main source of energy for the planet. This radiation is partially absorbed and partially reflected by the earth. Interactions of incoming solar energy, and outwardly radiated heat from the earth, with air, sea, ice, land, and life, create climate. All these interactions create feedback loops of enormous complexity. Positive feedback loops amplify effects and changes, and negative feedback loops dampen or eliminate effects and changes.

A dramatic change in climate can be caused by even slight changes in these processes. To attempt to predict climate changes, extremely sophisticated computer models are created with as many of the known feedback loops as possible taken into account. Models are presently limited by computing power, computer time and research money available to scientists, so scientists idealize by picking and choosing the parameters they feel are most important. The computer is then asked what might happen ten, twenty, fifty, or one hundred years from now.

Mistakes, oversights, and limitations are unavoidable in the creation of these models. Scientists, through the process of worldwide communication and peer review within the scientific community, are constantly comparing data, receiving and reviewing criticisms, correcting errors, and improving and refining computer models.

The average surface temperature of the sun is 6000° C. The sun emits massive amounts of electromagnetic energy across a broad range of wavelengths. A limited band of the sun's emissions penetrates our protective atmosphere and touches the earth. Our flesh has evolved in this atmosphere, so these rays are usually not harmful to us. (The exception is the sunburn that fair-skinned people experience when exposed to more or stronger sunlight than usual.)

The earth is heated through the molecular activity stimulated by this radiation. It then emits its own radiation and heats its surrounding air from the ground up. If the earth were covered with plowed fields, it would be darker and absorb more light, and the atmosphere would be much hotter. If the earth were covered with more ice, it would be lighter, reflect more light without causing increased molecular activity within the earth, and the atmosphere would be cooler.

At the height of the

last Ice Age, 18,000

years ago, the

average surface

temperature of the

earth was only 5°C

colder than it is now.

The heat from the earth is radiated out in the form of lower frequency wavelengths that do not readily penetrate the atmosphere as they move outward. They are effectively "trapped." It was in this greenhouse-like environment, where the sun's radiation is limited, and much of the earth's outward radiation is trapped, that biological life, as we know it, appeared on the planet.

Increased production of carbon dioxide (CO_2) by burning wood and fossil fuels, and the increased production of other greenhouse gases, are effects of the expanding human population. The rapid increase in these substances may alter the greenhouse effect provided by our atmosphere, and cause the much-feared global warming trend predicted by many, but not all, scientists. Weaknesses of computer models include:

- Ocean dynamics have not been sufficiently studied. These are critical to the understanding of what happens to the excess temperature caused by greenhouse gases, and the excess CO_2.

- There is poor understanding of clouds. More heat leads to more evaporation, more clouds, whiter earth, more reflection of sunlight, and possibly, a cooler climate. These are also insufficiently studied phenomena.

- Expanding small, localized grids to regional and then to global grids creates inaccuracies.

One of the methods used to determine past climate conditions involves the use of ice core samples taken from the ice layer at polar regions. Air bubbles trapped in these cores can provide information about the chemical properties and temperatures of the atmosphere at the time the air bubble was formed. Scientists can gather data about the earth's atmosphere thousands of years ago using this method.

At the height of the last Ice Age, 18,000 years ago, the average surface temperature of the earth was only 5° C colder than it is now.

Interglacial periods, such as the one we are living in now, have typically lasted approximately 10,000 years in "recent" geological history. We are now 10,000 years into our interglacial period, and we may be at the beginning of another cooling period. The addition of the human factor during this interglacial period, and the ensuing industrialization, will probably affect the heating and cooling process in some way.

Though not as

sudden as a collision

with a meteor, a

rapid change in

atmospheric

chemistry would alter

interactive processes

with consequences

that are impossible to

predict with certainty.

About 6000 years ago, there seems to have been a global warming of about 1°C to 2°C. The cause is uncertain, but it did produce aridity on the U.S. plains and a wetter Africa, among other climatological effects. A +2°C warming has never happened in recorded history and this is the level of warming predicted by some scientists as a result of the greenhouse effect.

Between 65 and 220 million years ago, long before the appearance of humans, dinosaurs thrived, along with many other now-extinct species. There apparently was a catastrophic event that caused the rather sudden disappearance of dinosaurs and 75% of the other existing species on the planet. A meteorite striking somewhere on the planet might have caused widespread extinction of species through such short-term effects as destruction of land area, formation of tidal waves, a rain of debris, and a thick planetary cloud. Such a cloud could have quickly disrupted the food chain by blocking sunlight to plants. There have been many equally catastrophic events in geological history caused by a sudden or rapid change in one or another of these complex systems.

The rapidity of the human population growth in the last few hundred years, with its attendant production of large amounts of greenhouse gases over and above "natural" processes, could be a catalyst for one of these catastrophic events. This is what is worrisome to many in the scientific community. Though not as sudden as a collision with a meteor, a rapid change in atmospheric chemistry would alter interactive processes, with consequences that are impossible to predict with certainty.

Other greenhouse gases that are increasing due to human activity are chlorofluorocarbons and methane. Methane exists at about 1% of CO_2, but it has twenty to thirty times more heat-trapping effect. Methane concentration in the atmosphere doubled from the mid-glacial period (18,000 years ago) to the pre-industrial period. It has since nearly doubled again. At today's concentration, it accounts for about one third of the greenhouse effect. Its increase in the atmosphere can be directly related to population growth.

Methane is produced by bacteria that like to live in relatively oxygen-free places like the intestines of humans, cows, and termites, in rice paddies under irrigation, under perma-frost in the Arctic regions, and in landfills and garbage dumps. It is also known as natural gas, and

Some laboratory

testing shows that

CO_2 actually acts

like a fertilizer and

may benefit plants,

causing them to grow

bigger and bigger.

is drawn from underground stores and used as an energy fuel. It can be released into the atmosphere in the process of mining or transport.

Chlorofluorocarbons are destructive to the ozone layer which shields the earth from most of the sun's ultraviolet rays. Large levels of ultraviolet radiation are lethal to biological life as we know it. Our life form has evolved in an atmosphere largely protected from these rays. It could not sustain itself if this radiation was released through a destruction of the layer of ozone that blankets the earth.

The greenhouse gases interact with one another and with the earth in complex chemical, biological, and energetic ways. (Heating and cooling processes are caused by faster or slower motion of molecules and atoms. These could be called energy processes). A natural slow removal of CO_2 from the atmosphere is accomplished through biological and chemical processes. Plants absorb it and make use of it in their growth process. Oceans absorb it and deposit it as sediment in the form of calcium carbonate (shells, etc.). Half of the newly injected CO_2 may be absorbed by the oceans. This takes decades to centuries. The effect of this increased absorption is unknown.

Plants absorb CO_2 by the process of photosynthesis. The absorption of CO_2 by plants would increase with increased amounts of CO_2 in the air. Some laboratory testing shows that CO_2 actually acts like a fertilizer and may benefit plants, causing them to grow bigger and bigger. (Plants make plant tissue by this process of photosynthesis. They use the carbon and release the oxygen). Some say this would mitigate the greenhouse effect and even be a benefit to society. This is an example of a negative feedback loop. (More CO_2 = bigger plants = more photosynthesis = less CO_2).

But considerably more carbon is stored in dead organic matter (soil, sediment, fossil fuels) than in living organic matter, the atmosphere, or the oceans. This is eventually transformed back into CO_2 and methane by heat and microorganism activity. Rates of bacterial activity increase when soil is heated, and this activity further heats soil so this would produce more CO_2 and methane. This is an example of a positive feedback loop. (More CO_2 in the atmosphere = increased greenhouse effect = more heat in soil = increased microorganism activity = more CO_2, more methane = increased greenhouse effect = more heat = more microorganism activity = more CO_2, more methane = more heat, etc.)

Trees are a major

natural absorbent for

the excess CO_2. The

burning of forests

releases massive

amount of CO_2 into

the atmosphere.

Extensive deforestation is eliminating a natural "sink" for CO_2. Trees are a major natural absorbent for the excess CO_2. The burning of forests releases massive amounts of CO_2 into the atmosphere. The termite population is expanding in geometric proportions, (feeding on the dead wood left behind after burning) and termites, believe it or not, are a major source of methane. Also much of the wood is left to rot after clearing. All of these processes, burning, termite activity, and rotting, release stored carbon and methane back into the atmosphere. Thus widespread, rapid deforestation plays a role in many complex, interrelated feedback loops that affect climate changes.

Over the past hundred years, most scientific studies show an average global warming of 0.5° C (1° F). This amount of change is still obscured by natural year-to-year fluctuations, so there is continuing study and dispute about the accuracy and significance of this data.

Most climatologists do not claim with absolute certainty that there is an average rise in temperature, or that any perceived rise is caused by increased greenhouse gases. This warming could still be a chance occurrence. Most feel that another decade or two of careful measuring will tell more clearly what is signal (real trends) and what is noise (random occurrences). But all agree that greenhouse gases are likely to double in the next century, and when this likelihood is included in computer models, they invariably predict warming. When this is considered together with an apparent hundred-year warming trend of 0.5° C, then it becomes a better-than-even bet that the global warming theory is a valid one.

The following are some predicted effects of warming:

- Water supplies will change globally. (Some areas will dry up, others will have increased rainfall). This will affect crop production.
- Forests will die or spring up in different locations.
- Floods and storms may increase in severity and frequency.
- Precipitation may increase or decrease. This might mean less rain in the midwestern U.S. breadbasket. Global economies could be affected as agricultural areas move to higher latitudes.

- Tropical pests may multiply and thrive in new regions.

- Sea levels will rise. Water expands with even slight warming so this rise may measure a few inches. This rise of a few inches could have a major impact, given huge concentrations of populations worldwide at sea-level ports. New York City is an example. A three-foot rise would inundate an area the size of Massachusetts. With excessive melting of the polar ice caps, the rise may measure several hundred feet.

It is important to note that change is inherent in dynamic natural systems. It is "in the nature of things" to change. The human race has developed its present civilization over the last 10,000 years in this most recent interglacial period, and this climatological circumstance will change, and civilization will change along with it. In the field of climate prediction, there are several points on which all scientists can agree:

- Levels of trace gases (carbon dioxide [CO_2], methane, chlorofluorocarbons, and others) have increased in the atmosphere as a result of human activity.

- Although they are only trace gases, substantial changes in their concentration are likely to affect climate. They have significant heat-trapping capabilities.

- In pre-industrial times, the incidence of CO_2 in the atmosphere was 280 parts per million (ppm). In the late 1980s the incidence is 350 ppm. This is a 25% increase.

- Current projections of fossil fuel consumption suggest that a doubling of CO_2 from pre-industrial levels (1800–1850) may occur between 2020 and 2080.

- When the researchers test an equivalent increase of CO_2 and other gases in their computer modeling, they have found that the effect of such an increase is a warming of several degrees over the next fifty years. (The range frequently mentioned is 5°C to 9°C). The cooling during the Ice Age was a 5°C difference from today's climate. This was not an evenly distributed cooling. The changes were greater at the poles and smaller at the equator.

In pre-industrial times, the incidence of CO_2 in the atmosphere was 280 parts per million (ppm). In the late 1980s the incidence is 350 ppm. This is a 25% increase.

global warming

The climate of the

planet has changed

radically many times

over the past millions

of years of its

existence.

- The climate of the planet has changed radically many times over the past millions of years of its existence. It will continue to go through recurring changes.
- The very rapid growth of the human population may affect climate in some way, and the effects might be faster and more traumatic than when changes occur over eons.

Sources

Fisher, David E. *Fire and Ice*. New York: Harper and Row, 1990.

Glantz, Michael H., ed. *Desertification: Environmental Degradation in and Around Arid Lands*. Boulder, CO: Westview Press, 1977.

Roan, Sharon. *Ozone Crisis*. New York: John Wiley and Sons, 1989.

Mann, Charles C. "How Many is Too Many?" *Atlantic Monthly*, February 1993.

Schneider, Stephen H. *Global Warming*. San Francisco: Sierra Club Books, 1989.

Wright, John W., ed. *The Universal Almanac, 1993*. Kansas City: Andrews and McMeel, 1993.

ozone depletion

Ozone is an oxygen compound (O_3). As a component of the lower atmosphere, ozone is critical to life on earth. If there is an overabundance of it, as in smoggy urban areas, it can cause harm to plants, damage to human lungs, and a burning sensation in the eyes. This overabundance that occurs occasionally in the lower atmosphere is caused by burning fossil fuel.

The filmy veil of ozone that blankets the outside of the lower atmosphere protects the biosphere (all living things). It very effectively filters out most of the ultraviolet light waves from the sun. It has done so for perhaps as long as a billion years. The ozone layer is life-sustaining in that our form of biological life cannot survive exposure to large quantities of ultraviolet light. A 2.5% depletion of the ozone layer is predicted to cause 15,000 new cases of melanomas (skin cancers) each year. Immune system damage, cataracts, and damage to other species is also predicted.

A hole in the ozone layer has recently been discovered over Antarctica. It appears for a few months starting in November and then it closes up again. The reason for its appearance is not known and is currently being studied by scientists worldwide. It may be a result of man-made chemicals or it may be a result of wind or ocean currents or other climatological processes. The hole is getting larger each year.

In Tasmania, close to the hole, the incidence of melanoma has doubled in the last ten years.

An overall depletion has recently been measured by scientists. The level of depletion is disputed. This phenomenon first attracted the attention of scientists in the early 1970s when scientists from the fields of chemistry and meteorology started talking to one another about the possible effects of man-made chemicals on the atmosphere. The nitrous oxides that would be injected into the stratosphere by the exhaust from the newly invented supersonic jets and orbiting satellites were seen as possibly damaging to the ozone layer.

At about this same time, several scientists began to study the possible effect of clorofluorocarbons (CFCs), the chemical used for spray products and refrigerants, suspecting that these were a greater danger than the nitrous oxides.

The CFCs and nitrous oxides, so plentifully produced in modern times, do not break up in the lower atmosphere. They float up slowly to the upper atmosphere (the stratosphere) and are then broken down by the sun's ultraviolet radiation. In this process, free chlorine atoms are released. The chlorine atoms attack ozone, and the product of this interaction is ordinary oxygen and chlorine. The chlorine is free to attack ozone molecules again and again. The ozone is thus depleted and its shielding power is gradually eliminated. The chain reaction created by chlorine acting on ozone poses a threat to human life that cannot, according to these scientists, be overstated.

354

Due to the increasing levels of skin cancers and cataract blindness being reported worldwide over the last fifteen years, the use of CFCs has largely been banned. The extent of ozone layer damage, present and future, is still being discussed and disputed, but the risk was seen as great enough to eliminate the production of this chemical throughout most of the world. It is still being used in some underdeveloped countries that are so economically dependent on it that they refuse to stop producing and using it.

The length of time it takes for the CFCs to travel up through the atmosphere to the outer layer is very long. The CFCs already released into the atmosphere will take another fifty to one hundred years to complete their journey to the ozone level, even if all production of these chemicals were to cease immediately. It is predicted by most scientists that this chemical process that destroys ozone will continue far into the future.

The CFCs already released into the atmosphere will take another fifty to one hundred years to complete their journey to the ozone level, even if all production of these chemicals were to cease immediately.

Timeline

1930s

CFCs are introduced as a substitute for ammonia in refrigeration use. This family of chemicals is found to have many applications beyond refrigeration. Chemically inert, nontoxic, and easily liquefied, CFCs are used widely in air conditioning, packaging, and insulation, as a solvent for cleaning electronic circuit boards, and as an aerosol propellant.

1974

F. Sherwood Rowland and Mario Molinas, in an article in *Nature Magazine*, announce a theory that CFC molecules could be destroying ozone molecules in the stratosphere. A government committee recommends that the theory be studied by the National Academy of Sciences (NAS). The theory is hotly debated in scientific and industry circles.

1975

Johnson Wax, the nation's fifth largest manufacturer of aerosol sprays, announces it will stop using CFCs in its products.

Oregon bans CFCs in aerosol sprays.

The Consumer Product Safety Commission announces there is insufficient evidence that CFCs harm the ozone layer.

1976

NAS verifies the Rowland-Molina hypothesis, but says government regulations should be postponed pending further study.

1978

After considerable debate, CFCs used in aerosols are banned in the U.S.

1979

A NAS report estimates eventual ozone depletion at 16.5%. This report advises that a further postponement of regulations is not practical.

1981

NASA scientist Donald Heath announces that satellite records show ozone has declined 1 percent.

1982

NAS releases a third report predicting eventual ozone depletion of 5% to 9%.

1984

A fourth NAS report downplays the potential harm of CFCs to the ozone layer by lowering depletion estimates to 2% to 4%.

In 1988, three weeks

after it denies the

previous request,

DuPont agrees to

cease production

of CFCs.

1985

British Scientist Joe Farman publishes study results showing 40% loss of ozone over Antarctica during the austral spring.

Satellite photos confirm the existence of this hole.

1986

A major CFC industry lobbying group announces it will support limits on CFC growth. The DuPont Corporation announces it will call for limits on worldwide CFC production.

Scientists dispute causes of the hole. Some say it is chemically caused, and some say normal weather processes are causing it.

1987

New evidence supports the chemical explanation.

NASA satellite photos show 4% ozone loss worldwide, detected over a seven-year period.

McDonald's Corporation announces it will stop using CFCs in its containers.

An expedition to Antarctica to study the ozone hole reports that man-made chemicals are the primary cause of ozone depletion.

1988

Three U.S. senators ask DuPont to stop making CFCs. DuPont refuses.

The NASA-sponsored Ozone Trends Panel announces it has found ozone losses of 1.7% to 3% over the northern hemisphere.

Three weeks after it denies the previous request, DuPont agrees to cease production of CFCs.

Scientists meeting in the Netherlands confirm the Ozone Trends Panel findings of ozone losses in the northern hemisphere.

1989

European countries and the U.S. agree to faster reductions in use of CFCs, but developing countries oppose reductions, citing cost of substitutes and scientific uncertainty.

1993

The hole in the ozone layer over Antarctica continues to grow every year. Scientists continue to debate the significance of this phenomenon.

Sources

Fisher, David E. *Fire and Ice*. New York: Harper and Row, 1990.

Mann, Charles C. "How Many Is Too Many?" *Atlantic Monthly*, February 1993.

Roan, Sharon. *Ozone Crisis*. New York: John Wiley and Sons, 1989.

Schneider, Stephen. *Global Warming*. San Francisco: Sierra Club Books, 1989.

anatomy of a
supreme court decision

in 1787, the new Constitution of the United States was created and sent to the states for ratification. By 1789, when it had been ratified by nine of the thirteen states, it officially became the supreme law of the land. It was paramount to the framers of the Constitution that the tyrannical forms of government so prevalent in human history would not develop in America.

To this end, the newly formed federal government was divided into three parts so that each part could provide checks and balances for the others. These parts are the executive, the legislative and the judicial branches. The president and the legislature are elected for limited terms by the people. The Supreme Court justices are appointed for life by the duly elected president.

Those people who were enthusiastically in favor of ratifying the Constitution and forming a strong union of states under a centralized government were called Federalists. Alexander Hamilton was one of their most eloquent spokesmen. He and James Madison wrote the classic American political treatise called *The Federalist Papers*. These essays extolling the virtues of the new Constitution were published in the contemporary press. A strong federal government was promoted as an enhancement to trade between the states, currency stability and national security, thus providing an environment in which the new American republic could grow and prosper. The political party that grew under the leadership of the Federalists came to be known as the Republican party.

There were many who were fearful that individual human rights were not sufficiently protected under the new constitution. This reservation delayed ratification in some states by many months while public discussions were held on this matter. Many colonists were suspicious that a strong centralized government would rob them of their hard-won victory against oppression. These men, sometimes called anti-Federalists, fought for the addition of the first ten amendments to the Constitution, usually called the Bill of Rights. These amendments, adopted in 1791, specifically protected individual human rights against the tyrannical tendencies of centralized governments. Thomas Jefferson was a leading spokesman for the Bill of Rights. His political approach, which strongly supported individual and states' rights under a weaker Federal union, came to be known as Jeffersonian democracy, and formed the basis of what came to be known as the Democratic Party.

Both political parties have obviously evolved and changed their philosophical and political orientations, but the Constitution and the Bill of Rights have endured through this political evolution. Formed under the rules laid down in this carefully written document, the American government remains one of the most stable and just in human history.

torn by the issues

*J*udicial review, the

right and duty of the

Supreme Court to

rule on the

constitutionality of

laws or policies, was

not explicit in that

language.

Under the Constitution, the powers of the three branches of government were established, but the language was intentionally flexible and broad to allow for the expected growth and change within the national culture. The legislative branch was empowered to make laws. The executive branch, including the president, vice president and cabinet, was mandated to execute the laws, recommend legislation, make treaties with foreign nations, and appoint Supreme Court judges. The president is also the commander in chief of the armed forces. Advice and consent, veto, and impeachment powers were put in place so that actions of either branch can be checked by the other. The Supreme Court was designated the ultimate arbiter in ensuring the Constitution is upheld as the supreme law of the land.

In Article III of the Constitution, the Supreme Court was charged as follows:

> "The judicial power of the United States shall be vested in one supreme court, and in such inferior courts as the Congress may, from time to time, establish.... The judicial power shall extend to all cases, in law and equity, arising under this constitution, the laws of the United States, and treaties made, or which shall be made under their authority...."

Judicial review, the right and duty of the Supreme Court to rule on the constitutionality of laws or policies, was not explicit in that language. In 1803, in *Marbury v. Madison*, the Supreme Court declared that the Constitution had indeed implicitly authorized it to determine when a challenged law or policy was "repugnant to the Constitution" and therefore void. Chief Justice John Marshall offered several justifications for the Court's exercise of this power of judicial review:

- The Constitution is the supreme law of the land.
- As the supreme law it also binds the Supreme Court.
- When a federal statute conflicts with the Constitution it is void.
- When confronted with a case that involves a federal statute which, by the Court's interpretation, is in conflict with the Constitution, the Court is dutybound to give force to the Constitution.

Some scholars have criticized this justification on the grounds that it has not been determined that the Court's interpretation of the Constitution is necessarily superior to the legislature's interpretation.

anatomy of a supreme court decision

Almost 200 years later, there is still dispute over the concept of judicial review.

The conflicts on which the Supreme Court rules begin with a dispute over something a government (federal, state, or local) has done. The dispute may be brought to court by another branch of government, a private person, or a private business, but the genesis of the dispute must be in the official act of a government or government representative. The Constitution is a charter for governmental behavior, not a charter for regulating purely private relationships.

Because the American people demand accountability, the Court writes opinions explaining and justifying the decisions that it reaches. The decision of the majority of the nine justices is the official decision of the court. These majority opinions set precedent for lower courts, and lawyers advise their clients what is constitutionally permitted or prohibited according to these precedents. Dissenting opinions are also written when the decision is not unanimous, and dissenting opinions have also played a part in the evolution of constitutional law.

Due Process & the Right to Privacy

The following amendments to the Constitution contain the constitutional issues considered applicable to the laws concerning abortion. The constitutionality of lower court decisions is the only matter properly taken under consideration by the Supreme Court.

THE FIRST AMENDMENT

Congress shall make no law respecting an establishment of religion, or prohibiting the free exercise thereof; or abridging the freedom of speech, or of the press; or the right of people to peaceably assemble, and to petition the government for a redress of grievances.

The due process

clause, included in

the Fifth and

Fourteenth

Amendments, has

been a bone of

contention since the

beginning of our

nation's history.

THE FOURTH AMENDMENT

The right of the people to be secure in their persons, houses, papers and effects, against unreasonable searches and seizures, shall not be violated, and no warrants shall issue but upon probable cause, supported by oath or affirmation, and particularly describing the place to be searched, and the persons or things to be searched.

THE FIFTH AMENDMENT

No person shall be deprived of life, liberty or property without due process of law.

THE NINTH AMENDMENT

The enumeration in the Constitution of certain rights shall not be construed to deny or disparage others retained by the people.

THE FOURTEENTH AMENDMENT (SEC. 1)

All persons born or naturalized in the United States, and subject to the jurisdiction thereof, are citizens of the United States and of the state wherein they reside. No state shall make or enforce any law which shall abridge the privileges or immunities of citizens of the United States; nor shall any state deprive any person of life, liberty or property without the due process of law; nor deny to any person within its jurisdiction the equal protection of the laws.

The first ten amendments (called the Bill of Rights) were added in 1791, shortly after the original Constitution was ratified. The Thirteenth and Fourteenth Amendments were added to the Constitution after the Civil War, in 1865 and 1868, respectively. They were added to nullify the many existing state laws that denied the recently freed slaves their basic rights as American citizens.

The due process clause, included in the Fifth and Fourteenth Amendments, has been a bone of contention since the beginning of our nation's history. If a citizen feels that a state law impinges his constitutional rights, then the law can be challenged on the basis that it takes away his rights without due process of law. The constitutionality of many state laws are challenged in the courts on this basis.

Many eloquent opinions, pro and con, have been written about the appropriate use of this clause as a justification for overturning state laws. Some of these opinions limit the applicability of the due process clause, while others expand it.

The following excerpt is taken from an opinion written in 1963 by Justice Hugo Black, in the case of *Ferguson v. Skrupa*. (Justice Black was appointed by President Franklin Roosevelt.)

> Under the system of government created by our Constitution, it is up to legislatures, not courts, to decide on the wisdom and utility of legislation. There was a time when the due process clause was used by this Court to strike down laws which were thought unreasonable, that is, unwise or incompatible with some particular economic or social philosophy. In this manner the due process clause was used, for example, to nullify laws prescribing maximum hours for work in bakeries (*Lochner v. New York*, 1905), setting minimum wages for women (*Adkins v. Children's Hospital*, 1923), and fixing the weight of loaves of bread (*Jay Burns Baking Co. v. Bryan*, 1924). This intrusion of the judiciary into the realm of legislative value judgments was strongly objected to at the time.

Another statement on the use of the due process clause to overturn state laws can be found in a dissenting opinion written by Justice Oliver Wendell Holmes in 1905, in the case of *Lochner v. New York*. (Justice Holmes was appointed by President Theodore Roosevelt.)

> ...It is settled by various decisions of this Court that state constitutions and state laws may regulate life in many ways which we as legislators may think of as injudicious, or, if you like, tyrannical.... Sunday and usury laws are ancient examples. A more modern one is the prohibition of lotteries.... The Constitution is made for people of fundamentally different views....

The opposing view can be found in the following excerpt from the dissenting opinion written by Justice Stephen Field in 1873, in *Slaughter Houses v. the City of New Orleans*. (Justice Field was appointed by President Abraham Lincoln.)

> The question presented is of the gravest importance...to the whole country. It is nothing less than the question of whether Amendments to the Constitution protect the citizens of the United States

against the deprivation of their common rights by state legislation. In my judgment the Fourteenth Amendment does afford such protection, and was so intended by the Congress which framed it and the States which adopted it.... The Amendment does not attempt to confer any new privileges or immunities upon citizens or to enumerate or define those already existing. It assumes there are such privileges and immunities which belong of right to citizens as such, and ordains they shall not be abridged by state legislation. If this inhibition has no reference to privileges and immunities of this character...it was a vain and idle enactment.

In the case of *Griswald v. Connecticut*, which was brought before the court in 1965, the appellants invoked the due process clause of the Fourteenth Amendment. They charged that the Constitution guarantees a right to privacy, and that this right had been violated without due process. This right to privacy, while not explicit in the Constitution or the Bill of Rights, was said to be implicit in the First, Fourth, Fifth, and Ninth Amendments.

The opinion of the Court was written by William O. Douglas. (Justice Douglas was appointed by President Franklin Roosevelt.) The following is excerpted from that opinion:

> Appellant Griswald is Executive Director of the Planned Parenthood League of Connecticut. Appellant Buxton is a licensed physician and a professor at the Yale Medical School who served as Medical Director for the League at its center in New Haven—a center open and operating from November 1 to November 10, 1961, when appellants were arrested....
>
> They gave information, instruction, and medical advice to married persons as to the means of preventing conception. They examined the wife and prescribed the best contraceptive device or material for her use. Fees were usually charged, although some couples were serviced free....

The Connecticut Law which was violated reads as follows:

> Any person who uses any drug, medicinal article or instrument for the purpose of preventing conception shall be fined not less than sixty days nor more than one year or be both fined and imprisoned. Any per-

This right to privacy, while not explicit in the Constitution or the Bill of Rights, was said to be implicit in the First, Fourth, Fifth, and Ninth Amendments.

anatomy of a supreme court decision

"**W**e do not sit as a

super-legislature to

determine the

wisdom, need, and

propriety of laws that

touch economic

problems, business

affairs, or social

conditions. This

law, however,

operates directly on

an intimate relation

of husband and

wife...."

son who assists, abets, counsels, causes, hires or commands another to commit any offense may be prosecuted and punished as if he were the principal offender.

The appellants (Griswald, et al.) were found guilty of violation of this law as accessories and fined $100 each. The appellants claim that the statute violates the Fourteenth Amendment, in that they were denied constitutional protection without due process of law.

Coming to the merits, we are met with a wide range of questions that implicate the due process clause of the Fourteenth Amendment....

(Justice Douglas here cites many cases as precedent that the due process clause cannot be used lightly to overturn state laws.)

We do not sit as a super-legislature to determine the wisdom, need, and propriety of laws that touch economic problems, business affairs, or social conditions. This law, however, operates directly on an intimate relation of husband and wife and their physician's role in one aspect of that relation.

The association of people is not mentioned in the Constitution nor in the Bill of Rights. The right to educate a child in a school of the parent's choice—whether public, private or parochial—is also not mentioned. Nor is the right to study any particular subject or foreign language. Yet the First Amendment has been construed to include certain of those rights.

By *Pierce v. Society of Sisters*, the right to educate one's children as one chooses is made applicable to the States by the force of the Fourteenth Amendment. By *Meyer v. State of Nebraska*, the same dignity is given the right to study the German language in a private school. In other words, the state may not, consistently with the spirit of the First Amendment, contract the spectrum of available knowledge. The right of freedom of speech and press includes not only the right to utter or to print, but the right to distribute, the right to receive, the right to read and the freedom of inquiry, freedom of thought, and freedom to teach—indeed the freedom of the entire university community.

torn by the issues

"In other words, the

First Amendment has

a penumbra where

privacy is protected

from governmental

intrusion."

(Justice Douglas here cites five previous rulings as precedent.)

Without those peripheral rights the specific rights would be less secure. In *NAACP v. State of Alabama,* we protected the freedom to associate and the privacy in one's associations, noting that freedom of association was a peripheral First Amendment right...In other words, the First Amendment has a penumbra where privacy is protected from governmental intrusion. In like contrast we have protected forms of association that are not political in the customary sense but pertain to social, legal, and economic benefit of the members.

(Several cases are cited here as precedent.)

These cases involved more than the right of assembly. The right of association is more than the right to attend a meeting. It includes the right to express one's attitudes or philosophies...and while it is not expressly included in the First Amendment its existence is necessary in making the express guarantees fully meaningful. The foregoing cases suggest that specific guarantees in the Bill of Rights have penumbras, formed by emanations from those guarantees that help give them life and substance.

Various guarantees create zones of privacy. The right of association contained in the penumbra of the First Amendment is one as we have seen. The Third Amendment in its prohibition against the quartering of soldiers "in any house" in time of peace without the consent of the owner is another facet of that privacy. The Fourth Amendment explicitly affirms the "right of the people to be secure in their persons, houses, papers, and effects, against unreasonable searches and seizures." The Fifth Amendment in its self-incrimination clause enables the citizen to create a zone of privacy which government may not force him to surrender to his detriment. The Ninth Amendment provides that "the enumeration in the Constitution, of certain rights, shall not be construed to deny or disparage others retained by the people." The Fourth and Fifth Amendments were described in *Boyd v. U.S.* as protection against all governmental invasions "of the sanctity of a man's home and the privacies of life." We have had many controversies over these penumbral rights of "privacy and repose...."

(Justice Douglas cites several cases as precedent here.)

These cases bear witness that the right of privacy which presses for recognition here is a legitimate one.

The present case, then, concerns a relationship (the marital relationship) lying within the zone of privacy created by several fundamental constitutional guarantees. And it concerns a law which, in forbidding the use of contraceptives rather than regulating their manufacture or sale, seeks to achieve its goals by means of having a maximum destructive impact on that relationship. Such a law cannot stand in light of the familiar principle, so often applied by this Court, that a governmental purpose to control or prevent activities constitutionally subject to state regulation may not be achieved by means which sweep unnecessarily broadly and thereby invade the area of protected freedoms. Would we allow the police to search the sacred precincts of marital bedrooms for telltale signs of the use of contraceptives? The very idea is repulsive to the notions of privacy surrounding the marriage relationship.

The dissenting opinion was written by Justice Hugo Black. (Justice Black was appointed by President Franklin Roosevelt.)

[I disagree with] the premise that this Court is vested with power to invalidate all state laws that it considers to be arbitrary, capricious, unreasonable or oppressive, or this court's belief that a particular state law under scrutiny has no "rational or justifying" purpose, or is offensive to a "sense of fairness and justice." If these formulas based on "natural justice" or others which mean the same thing, are to prevail, they require judges to determine what is or is not constitutional on the basis of their own appraisal of what laws are unwise or unnecessary. The power to make such decisions is of course that of a legislative body. Surely it has to be admitted that no provision of the Constitution specifically gives such blanket power to courts to exercise such supervisory veto over the wisdom and value of legislative policies and to hold unconstitutional those laws which they believe unwise or dangerous. I readily admit that no legislative body, state or national, should pass laws

torn by the issues

There are no firm

and unarguable

boundaries of the

due process clause

or the right to

privacy.

that can justly be given any of the invidious labels invoked as constitutional excuses to strike down state laws. But perhaps it is not too much to say that no legislative body ever does pass laws without believing that they will accomplish a sane, rational, wise, and justifiable purpose. While I completely subscribe to the holding of *Marbury v. Madison* (1803), and subsequent cases, that our Court has constitutional power to strike down statutes, state or federal, that violate commands of the Federal Constitution, I do not believe we are granted power by the due process clause or any other constitutional provision or provisions to measure constitutionality by our belief that legislation is arbitrary, capricious, or unreasonable, or accomplishes no justifiable purpose, or is offensive to our own notions of "civilized standards of conduct." Such an appraisal of the wisdom of legislation is an attribute of the power to make laws, not of the power to interpret them. The use by Federal Courts of such a formula or doctrine or what not to veto federal or state laws simply takes away from Congress and the States the power to make laws based on their own judgment of fairness and wisdom and transfers that power to this Court for ultimate determination—a power which was specifically denied to federal courts by the Convention that framed the Constitution....

I realize that many good and able men have eloquently spoken and written, sometimes in rhapsodical strains, about the duty of this Court to keep the Constitution in tune with the times. The idea is that the Constitution must be changed from time to time and that this Court is charged with the duty to make those changes. For myself, I must with all deference reject that philosphy. The Constitution makers knew the need for change and provided for it. Amendments suggested by the people's elected representatives can be submitted to the people or their selected agents for ratification. That method was good for our fathers, and being somewhat old-fashioned I must add it is good enough for me....

"Our task, of course,

is to resolve the issue

by constitutional

measurement, free of

emotion and of

predilection."

Roe v. Wade

As the excerpts above indicate, the interpretation of constitutional law is an inexact science. There are no firm and unarguable boundaries of the due process clause or the right to privacy. The framers of the Constitution intended the charter to be broad and elastic. The Supreme Court justices bring legal knowledge, experience and convictions to bear upon the thorny constitutional questions of the day. One of the most problematic issues facing the Court is abortion rights.

The case of *Roe v. Wade* was brought before the Court in 1973. Texas law made abortion a crime, except when necessary to save the life of the mother. A Texas woman, who wished to terminate her pregnancy through an abortion performed by a physician, sought a judgment against the Texas criminal abortion statutes. The Supreme Court agreed that the Texas law violated her "right of privacy" as implied in the Constitution, citing the precedent of the case of *Griswald v. Connecticut*.

Justice Harry A. Blackmun delivered the opinion of the Court, in which Chief Justice Burger and Justices Douglas, Brennan, Stuart, Marshall, and Powell joined. Chief Justice Burger and Justices Blackmun and Powell were appointed by President Richard Nixon. Justice Marshall was appointed by President Lyndon Johnson. Justices Brennan and Stuart were appointed by President Dwight Eisenhower. Justice Douglas was appointed by President Franklin Roosevelt.

Significant points from the majority opinion are quoted below.

> The statutes under attack here are typical of those that have been in effect in many states for approximately a century.... We forthwith acknowledge our awareness of the sensitive and emotional nature of the abortion controversy, of the vigorous opposing views, even among physicians, and of the deep and seemingly absolute convictions that the subject inspires. In addition, population growth, pollution, poverty, and racial overtones tend to complicate and not to simplify the problem....
>
> Our task, of course, is to resolve the issue by constitutional measurement, free of emotion and of predilection. We seek earnestly to do this, and, because we do, we have inquired into, and in this opinion place some emphasis on, medical and medical-legal history and what that history reveals about men's attitudes

370

"**T**he principal thrust
of Appellant's attack
on the Texas statutes
is that they improperly
invade a right, said to
be possessed by that
pregnant woman, to
choose to terminate
her pregnancy."

toward the abortion procedure over the centuries.
We bear in mind, too, Mr. Justice Holmes' admoni-
tion in his now-vindicated dissent in *Lochner v. N.Y.*
(1905):

> The Constitution is made for people of fun-
> damentally differing views, and the accident
> of our finding certain opinions natural and
> familiar or novel and even shocking ought
> not to conclude our judgment on the ques-
> tion whether statutes embodying them
> conflict with the Constitution of the United
> States.

Jane Roe, a single woman who was residing in Dallas
County, Texas, instituted this federal action in
March 1970 against the District Attorney of the
county. She sought a declaratory judgment that the
Texas abortion statutes were unconstitutional on
their face…[and] that they abridged her right of per-
sonal privacy, protected by the First, Fourth, Fifth,
Ninth, and Fourteenth Amendments.

The District Court declared the abortion statute
void…. The District Attorney filed his own appeal,
contending that the statute was constitutional.

The principal thrust of Appellant's attack on the
Texas statutes is that they improperly invade a right,
said to be possessed by that pregnant woman, to
choose to terminate her pregnancy. Appellant would
discover this right in the concept of personal "liberty" embodied in the Fourteenth Amendment's due
process clause; or in personal, marital, familial, and
sexual privacy said to be protected by the Bill of
Rights or its penumbras…or among those rights
reserved to the people by the Ninth Amendment.
(See *Griswald v. Connecticut.*) It perhaps is not generally appreciated that the restrictive criminal abortion laws in effect in a majority of states today are of
relatively recent vintage. Those laws, generally pro-
scribing abortion or its attempt at any time during
pregnancy except when necessary to preserve the
pregnant woman's life, are not of ancient or even of
common law origin. Instead they derive from the
statutory changes effected, for the most part, in the
latter half of the nineteenth century.

Ancient Attitudes: These are not capable of precise
determination. We are told that at the time of the
Persian Empire abortifacients were known and that
criminal abortions were severely punished. We are

371

also told, however, that abortion was practiced in Greek times as well as in the Roman era and that it was resorted to without scruple....

Greek and Roman law afforded little protection to the unborn. If abortion was prosecuted in some places, it seems to have been based on a concept of a violation of the father's right to his offspring. Ancient religion did not bar abortion. The Hippocratic Oath: "I will give no deadly medicine to anyone if asked, nor suggest any such counsel; and in like manner I will not give to a woman a pessary to produce abortion." Why did not the authority of Hippocrates dissuade abortion practice in his time and that of Rome? The oath was not uncontested even in Hippocrates' day; only the Pythagorean school (of which Hippocrates was a member) frowned on [abortion and] the related act of suicide. Most Greek thinkers, on the other hand commended abortion, at least prior to viability. See Plato, Republic, v.461, and Aristotle, Politics, VIII. For the Pythagoreans, however, it was a matter of dogma.

The Common Law: It is undisputed that at common law, abortion performed before quickening—the first recognizable movement of the fetus in utero...was not an indictable offense. The absence of a common-law crime for the pre-quickening abortion appears to have developed from a confluence of earlier philosophical, theological, and civil and canon law concepts of when life begins....

Although Christian theology and the canon law came to fix the point of animation at forty days for a male and eighty days for a female, a view that persisted until the nineteenth century, there was otherwise little agreement about the precise time of formation or animation.

There was agreement, however, that prior to this point the fetus was to be regarded as part of the mother, and its destruction, therefore, was not homicide....

The significance of quickening was echoed by later common-law scholars and found its way into the received common law in this country. Whether abortion of a quick fetus was a felony at common law, or even a lesser crime, is still disputed. Bracton, writing early in the thirteenth century, thought it homicide. But the later and predominant view, following the

372

great common-law scholars, has been that it was, at most, a lesser offense. In a frequently cited passage, Coke took the position that abortion of a woman "quick with child" is a great misprison, and no murder. (Misprison is a term translated as "misdemeanor.")

English Statutory Law: England's first criminal abortion statute...came in 1803. It made abortion of a quick fetus a capital crime, but provided lesser penalties for the felony of abortion before quickening and thus preserved the "quickening" distinction. This contrast was continued in the general revision of 1828.... It disappeared, however, together with the death penalty, in 1837...and did not reappear....

Recently, Parliament enacted a new abortion law. This is the Abortion Act of 1967.... The Act permits a licensed physician to perform an abortion where two other licensed physicians agree (a) "that the continuance of the pregnancy would involve risk to the life of the pregnant woman, or of injury to the physical and mental health of the pregnant woman or any existing children of her family, greater than if the pregnancy were terminated," or (b) "that there is a substantial risk that if the child were born it would suffer from such physical or mental abnormalities as to be seriously handicapped."

The American Law: In this country, the law until the mid-nineteenth century was the pre-existing English common law. Connecticut, the first state to enact abortion legislation, adopted in 1821 that part of [English common law] that related to a woman "quick with child." The death penalty was not imposed. Abortion before quickening was made a crime in that state only in 1860. It was not until after the War Between the States that legislation began generally to replace the common law. Most of these initial statutes dealt severely with abortion after quickening but were lenient with it before quickening. Gradually, in the middle and late nineteenth century the quickening distinction disappeared from the statutory law of most states and the degree of the offense and the penalties increased. By the end of the 1950s, a large majority of the jurisdictions banned abortion, however and whenever performed, unless done to save or preserve the life of the mother. The exceptions, Alabama and the District of Columbia, permitted abortion to save the mother's health....

> "**T**he Constitution does not explicitly mention any right of privacy. In a line of decisions, however, ...the Court has recognized that a right of personal privacy does exist under the Constitution."

anatomy of a supreme court decision

In the past several years, however, a trend toward liberalization of abortion statutes has resulted in adoption, by about one third of the states, of less stringent laws....

It is apparent that at common law, at the time of the adoption of our Constitution, and throughout the major portion of the nineteenth century, abortion was viewed with less disfavor than under most American statutes currently in effect....

The anti-abortion mood prevalent in this country in the late nineteenth century was shared by the medical profession. Indeed, the attitude of the profession may have played a significant role in the enactment of stringent criminal abortion legislation during that period.... [In 1859, the AMA issued a report that] observed that a committee had been appointed to investigate criminal abortion with a view to its general frequency...calling "attention of the clergy of all denominations to the perverted views of morality entertained by a large class of females—aye, and men also, on this important question."

In 1970, after the introduction of a variety of proposed resolutions. . . a reference committee noted "polarization of the medical profession on this controversial issue.... The best interests of the patient, sound clinical judgment, informed patient consent [were emphasized]...."

Three reasons have been advanced to explain historically the enactment of criminal abortion laws in the nineteenth century and to justify their continued existence.

It has been argued occasionally that these laws were the product of a Victorian social concern to discourage illicit sexual conduct. Texas, however, does not advance this justification in the present case, and it appears that no court or commentator has taken the argument seriously....

A second reason is concerned with abortion as a medical procedure. When most criminal abortion laws were first enacted, the procedure was a hazardous one for the woman. This was particularly true prior to the development of antisepsis.... Abortion mortality was high. Even after 1900, and perhaps until as late as the development of antibiotics in the 1940s, standard modern techniques such as dilation and curettage were not nearly so safe as they are

torn by the issues

"**T**he pregnant

woman cannot be

isolated in her

privacy. She carries

an embryo, and,

later, a fetus...."

today. Thus it has been argued that a state's real concern in enacting criminal abortion law was to protect the pregnant woman, that is to restrain her from submitting to a procedure that placed her life in serious jeopardy. Modern medical techniques have altered this situation....

The third reason is the state's interest—some phrase it in terms of duty—in protecting prenatal life. Some of the argument for this justification rests on the theory that a new human life is present from the moment of conception. The state's interest and general obligation to protect life then extends, it is argued, to prenatal life. Only when the life of the pregnant mother herself is at stake, balanced against the life she carries within her, should the interest of the embryo or the fetus not prevail. Logically, of course, a legitimate state interest in this area need not stand or fall on acceptance or belief that life begins at conception or at some other point prior to live birth. In assessing the state's interest, recognition may be given to the less rigid claim that as long as at least potential life is involved, the state may assert interests beyond the protection of the pregnant woman alone. . . . It is with these interests, and the weight to be attached to them, that this case is concerned. The Constitution does not explicitly mention any right of privacy. In a line of decisions, however, going back perhaps as far as...1891 (*Union Pacific R.R. Co. v. Botsford*), the Court has recognized that a right of personal privacy does exist under the Constitution.

(Several cases are cited here as precedent.)

These decisions make it clear that only personal rights that can be deemed "fundamental" or "implicit" in the concept of "ordered liberty" can be included in this guarantee of personal privacy. They also make it clear that the right has some extension to activities relating to marriage, procreation, contraception, family relationships and child rearing and education. This right of privacy, whether it be founded in the Fourteenth Amendment's concept of personal liberty and restrictions upon state action, as we feel it is, or, as the District Court determined, in the Ninth Amendment's reservation of rights to the people, is broad enough to encompass a woman's decision whether or not to terminate her pregnancy. The detriment that the state would impose upon the pregnant woman by denying this choice altogether is apparent.

On the basis of elements such as these, appellant argues that the woman's right is absolute and that she is entitled to terminate her pregnancy at whatever time, in whatever way, and for whatever reason she alone chooses. With this we do not agree.... The Court's decisions recognizing a right of privacy also acknowledge that some state regulation in areas protected by that right is appropriate. As noted above, a state may properly assert important interests in safeguarding health, in maintaining medical standards, and in protecting potential life. At some point in pregnancy, these respective interests become sufficiently compelling to sustain regulation of the factors that govern the abortion decision. The privacy right involved, therefore, cannot be said to be absolute. . . .

We therefore conclude that the right of personal privacy includes the abortion decision, but that this right is not unqualified and must be considered against important state interests in regulation.... That at some point the state interests as to protection of health, medical standards, and prenatal life become dominant....

Appellant (Roe), as has been indicated, claims an absolute right that bars any state imposition of criminal penalties in the area. Appellee (the Texas District Attorney) argues that the state's determination to recognize and protect prenatal life from and after conception constitutes a compelling state interest. As noted above, we do not fully agree with either determination.

The appellee...argues that the fetus is a "person" within the language and meaning of the Fourteenth Amendment. In support of this, they outline at length and in detail the well-known facts of fetal development. If this suggestion of personhood is established, the appellant's (Roe's) case, of course, collapses, for the fetus' right to life would then be guaranteed specifically by the Amendment. . . . The appellant (Roe) conceded as much on reargument. On the other hand, the appellee (the District Attorney) conceded on reargument that no case can be cited that holds that a fetus is a person within the

torn by the issues

*"**A**t the heart of the*

controversy in these

cases are those

recurring pregnancies

that pose no danger

to the life or health of

the mother but are,

nevertheless,

unwanted...."

meaning of the Fourteenth Amendment. The Constitution does not define "person" in so many words. . .

(Many cases are cited and discussed here regarding this question of how "person" has been defined.)

But in nearly all these instances, the use of the word is such that it has application only postnatally. None indicates, with any assurance, that it has any possible prenatal application.

All this, together with our observation that throughout the major portion of the nineteenth century prevailing legal practices were far freer than they are today, persuades us that the word "person" as used in the Fourteenth Amendment, does not include the unborn. This is in accord with the results reached in those few cases where the issue has been squarely presented.... This conclusion does not itself fully answer the contentions raised by Texas, as we pass on to other considerations.

The pregnant woman cannot be isolated in her privacy. She carries an embryo and, later, a fetus, if one accepts the medical definitions of the developing young in the human uterus.... The situation is therefore inherently different from marital intimacy, or bedroom possession of obscene material, or marriage or procreation or education.... As we have intimated above, it is reasonable and appropriate for a state to decide that at some point in time another interest, that of the health of the mother or that of potential human life, becomes significantly involved. The woman's privacy is no longer sole and any right of privacy she possesses must be measured accordingly.

Texas urges that apart from the Fourteenth Amendment, life begins at conception and is present throughout pregnancy, and that, therefore, the state has a compelling interest in protecting that life from and after conception. We need not resolve the difficult question of when life begins. When those trained in the respective disciplines of medicine, philosophy and theology are unable to arrive at any consensus, the judiciary, at this point in the development of man's knowledge, is not in a position to speculate as to the answer.

It should be sufficient to note briefly the wide divergence of thinking on this most sensitive and difficult question. There has always been strong support for the view that life does not begin until live birth. This was the belief of the Stoics. It appears to be the predominant, though not unanimous, attitude of the Jewish faith. It may be taken to represent also the position of the Protestant community, insofar as can be ascertained.... The Aristotelian theory of "mediate animation" that held sway through the Middle Ages and the Renaissance in Europe, continued to be official Roman Catholic dogma until the nineteenth century, despite opposition to this ensoulment theory from those who would recognize the existence of life from the moment of conception. The latter is now, of course, the official belief of the Catholic Church.... This is a view strongly held by many non-Catholics as well, and by many physicians. Substantial problems for precise definition of this view are posed by new embryological data that purport to indicate that conception is a process over time, rather than an event, and by new medical techniques such as menstrual extraction, the "morning after" pill, implantation of embryos, artificial insemination, and even artificial wombs. In areas other than criminal abortion, the law has been reluctant to endorse any theory that life, as we recognize it, begins before live birth or to accord legal rights to the unborn except in narrowly defined situations and except where rights are contingent upon live birth.... In view of all this, we do not agree that, by adopting one theory of life, Texas may override the rights of the pregnant woman that are at stake. We repeat, however, that the state does have an important and legitimate interest in preserving and protecting the health of the pregnant woman... and that it has still another important and legitimate interest in protecting the potentiality of human life. These interests are separate and distinct. Each grows in substantiality as the woman approaches term and, at a point during pregnancy, each becomes "compelling."

With respect to the state's important and legitimate interest in the health of the mother, the "compelling" point, in light of the present medical knowledge, is approximately the end of the first trimester. This is so because of the now-established medical fact... that until the end of the first trimester mortality in abortion may be less than mortality in normal

torn by the issues

childbirth. It follows that from and after this point, a state may regulate the abortion procedure to the extent that the regulation reasonably relates to the preservation and protection of maternal health....

This means, on the other hand, that, for the period of pregnancy prior to this "compelling" point, the attending physician, in consultation with his patient, is free to determine, without regulation by the state, that, in his medical judgment, the patient's pregnancy should be terminated. If that decision is reached, the judgment may be effectuated by an abortion free of interference by the state.

With respect to the state's important and legitimate interest in potential life, the "compelling" point is at viability. This is so because the fetus then presumably has the capability of meaningful life outside the mother's womb. State regulation protective of fetal life after viability thus has both logical and biological justifications. If the state is interested in protecting fetal life after viability, it may go so far as to proscribe abortion during that period, except when it is necessary to preserve the life or health of the mother.

Measured against these standards, Article 1196 of the Texas Penal Code, in restricting legal abortions to "those procured or attempted by medical advice for the purpose of saving the life of the mother," sweeps too broadly. The statute makes no distinction between abortions performed early in pregnancy and those performed later, and it limits to a single reason, "saving" the mother's life, the legal justification for the procedure. The statute, therefore, cannot survive the constitutional attack made upon it here.

This holding...is consistent with the relative weights of the respective interests involved, with the lessons and examples of medical and legal history, with the lenity of the common law, and with the demands of the profound problems of the present day. The decision leaves the state free to place increasing restrictions on abortion as the period of pregnancy lengthens, so long as those restrictions are tailored to the recognized state interests....

Our conclusion that Article 1196 is unconstitutional means, of course, that the Texas abortion statutes, as a unit, must fall....

It is so ordered.

"If the state is interested in protecting fetal life after viability, it may go so far as to proscribe abortion during that period, except when it is necessary to preserve the life or health of the mother."

"In my view its

judgment is an

improvident and

extravagant exercise

of the power of

judicial review that

the Constitution

extends to this

Court."

Two dissenting opinions were written in this case, by Justice Byron White, and by Justice William Rehnquist. Justice White was appointed by President John Kennedy. Justice Rehnquist was appointed by President Richard Nixon.

The dissenting opinion of Justice White:

> At the heart of the controversy in these cases are those recurring pregnancies that pose no danger to the life or health of the mother but are, nevertheless, unwanted for any one or more of a variety of reasons—convenience, family planning, economics, dislike of children, the embarrassment of illegitimacy, etc. The common claim before us is that for any one of such reasons, or for no reason at all, and without asserting or claiming any threat to life or health, any woman is entitled to an abortion at her request if she is able to find a medical advisor willing to undertake the procedure. The Court for the most part sustains this position....
>
> With all due respect, I dissent. I find nothing in the language or history of the Constitution to support the Court's judgment. The Court simply fashions and announces a new constitutional right for pregnant mothers, and with scarcely any reason or authority for its action, invests that right with sufficient substance to override most existing state abortion statutes. The upshot is that the peoples and the legislatures of the fifty states are constitutionally disentitled to weigh the relative importance of the continued existence and development of the fetus, on the one hand, against a spectrum of possible impacts on the mother, on the other hand. As an exercise of raw judicial power, the Court perhaps has authority to do what it does today; but in my view its judgment is an improvident and extravagant exercise of the power of judicial review that the Constitution extends to this Court.

The dissenting opinion of Justice Rehnquist:

> The Court's opinion brings to the decision of this troubling question both extensive historical fact and a wealth of legal scholarship. While the opinion thus commands my respect, I find myself in fundamental disagreement with those parts of it that invalidate the Texas statute in question, and therefore dissent....

I have difficulty in concluding, as the Court does, that the right of "privacy" is involved in this case. Texas, by the statute here challenged, bars the performance of a medical abortion by a licensed physician on a plaintiff such as Roe. A transaction resulting in an operation such as this is not "private" in the ordinary usage of that word, nor is the "privacy" that the Court finds here even a distant relative of the freedom from searches and seizures protected by the Fourth Amendment the Court has referred to as embodying a right to privacy....

If the Court means, by the term "privacy," no more than that the claim of a person to be free from unwanted state regulation of consensual transactions may be a form of "liberty" protected by the Fourteenth Amendment, there is no doubt that similar claims have been upheld in our earlier decisions on the basis of that liberty....

But that liberty is not guaranteed absolutely against deprivation, only against deprivation without due process of law....

The fact that the majority of the states reflecting, after all, the majority sentiment in those states, have had restrictions on abortions for at least a century is a strong indication, it seems to me, that the asserted right to an abortion is not "so rooted in the traditions of conscience of our people as to be ranked as fundamental." Even today, when society's views on abortion are changing, the very existence of the debate is evidence that the right to an abortion is not so universally accepted as the appellant would have us believe....

To reach its result, the Court necessarily has had to find within the scope of the Fourteenth Amendment a right that was apparently completely unknown to the drafters of the Amendment.

As the above majority and dissenting opinions show, abortion rights remain an unresolved question in the legal arena, as well as in the wider society. The composition of the Court has changed dramatically since *Roe v. Wade* was decided. As the issue of abortion rights comes before the Court again and again, the Constitution and its amendments will be scrutinized for applicability with the same care and concern the justices showed in *Roe v. Wade,* but the decision may not be the same.

Sources

Padover, Saul K., and Jacob W. Landynski. *The Living U.S. Constitution*, 2nd Revised Edition. New York: New American Library, 1983.

Plano, Jack C., and Milton Greenberg. *The American Political Dictionary*. Fort Worth, TX: Harcourt Brace Jovanovich, 1990.

Schambelan, J.D., ed. *Roe v. Wade*. Philadelphia: Running Press, 1992.

Van Geel, T.R. *Understanding Supreme Court Decisions*. New York: Longman, 1992.